HOW TO PASS THE UKCAT

Unbeatable practice for success in the
United Kingdom Clinical Aptitude Test

2009 edition

Mike Bryon and Jim Clayden

**KOGAN
PAGE**

London and Philadelphia

Publisher's note

Every possible effort has been made to ensure that the information contained in this book is accurate at the time of going to press, and the publishers and authors cannot accept responsibility for any errors or omissions, however caused. No responsibility for loss or damage occasioned to any person acting, or refraining from action, as a result of the material in this publication can be accepted by the editor, the publisher or any of the authors.

First published in Great Britain and the United States in 2009 by Kogan Page Limited

120 Pentonville Road
London N1 9JN
United Kingdom
www.koganpage.com

525 South 4th Street, #241
Philadelphia PA 19147
USA

© Mike Bryon and Jim Clayden, 2009

ISBN 978 0 7494 5333 6

British Library Cataloguing-in-Publication Data

A CIP record for this book is available from the British Library.

Library of Congress Cataloging-in-Publication Data

Bryon, Mike.
   How to pass the UKCAT : unbeatable practice for success in the United Kingdom clinical aptitude test / Mike Bryon and Jim Clayden.
      p. cm.
   ISBN 978-0-7494-5333-6
   1. UK Clinical Aptitude Test--Study guides. I. Clayden, Jim. II. Title.
   R838.5.B79 2009
   610.76--dc22

                              2008049565

Typeset by Saxon Graphics Ltd, Derby
Printed and bound in India by Replika Press Pvt Ltd

Contents

Use this book to maximize your UKCAT score

If you have been searching for a way to improve your UKCAT score then you have found it. This book provides practice to maximize your chances of getting into medical school with over 600 questions and signposts to thousands more. Use it to get down to some serious score-improving practice.

Our aim is simply to provide everything you need to ace the test. We will not spend time discussing why you want to be a doctor or how you might best prepare for medical school. Instead we will focus purely on giving you the practice you need to meet the challenge of the five sub-tests that make up the UKCAT.

You should have carefully studied the very important information provided at www.ukcat.ac.uk. You should be completely familiar with the details regarding the stated purpose of the test, what it attempts to predict and its key features. You should follow the online application process to the letter and regularly check your inbox for e-mails from UKCAT. You should have already downloaded the practice questions and tests. You will realize that the UKCAT is made up of sub-tests of verbal reasoning, decision making, quantitative reasoning, abstract reasoning and non-cognitive analysis. Note that some of the questions in each sub-test may be non-scoring as they are being trialled for inclusion as scoring items in future tests. You are not given any indication as to which are scoring, so treat every question with the same determination. You should also realize that, like all selection tests, the UKCAT is under almost constant development and so some things may change. You will find a great deal of interesting (soft) information about the UKCAT on forums, for example www.thestudentroom.co.uk. Take some of the views expressed on these sites with a largish pinch of salt.

The computer-administered test

Be sure to take the time to become entirely familiar with the way in which the UKCAT is administered onscreen. Pay attention to, for example, how to use the onscreen calculator in the qualitative sub-test. Be aware that diagrams on the computer screen can be misleading, especially in the case of geometric shapes, tables and graphs, as the screen can distort the image or the scale or both! The test author is aware of this and will have provided sufficient information to arrive at the answer. Take note what is said and avoid drawing unnecessary assumptions about the appearance of a diagram, table or graph on the screen. For example, if a shape is described as a cube but on the screen the sides do not all seem quite equal, ignore it and treat the shape as a cube. Equally, if a table or graph says that quality x is the largest but on the screen it looks like quality y is the same or in fact bigger, then take no notice and treat quantity x as the largest.

You need a good UKCAT score

Competition for places at medical (dental and veterinary) school and especially at the more prestigious schools is fierce. The score range for the UKCAT is 300–900, with 500–700 being the normal range and 600 being the average mark in each section (note that the non-cognitive paper is scored differently from the other four sub-tests). To ensure that your score supports your application you will generally need an above-average score in each sub-test. However, the averages are based on a very broad range. Some people will get into the school of their choice with lower scores than others. There will not be a minimum score that you have to achieve. The UKCAT is only one of the many assessments used to decide if an applicant is to be offered a place, but it is in your interests to try to maximize each element of your application.

You may also need a well-balanced score

Doing really well in, for example, the quantitative part of the UKCAT will compensate for a weaker performance in the verbal parts of the test, but this compensation needs to be within certain limits. Most schools will prefer candidates who do well across all five sub-tests. The need for a balanced score makes it really important that candidates identify and work to address areas of personal weakness. If you have always found maths difficult but until now have succeeded in spite of it, it is time to correct this. You will feel more confident and will recognize what is behind a question and the significance of the subtle differences in the suggested answers.

Most UKCAT candidates will have strengths and weaknesses, but if you believe that you have an imbalance that may be seen as too great, make sure you start work early to address it. Everyone can become proficient in the aptitudes examined; it is simply a matter of giving yourself enough time to practise. It takes some candidates longer to reach the required standard in any area of personal challenge, but given hard work and determination everyone can realize it. It can be boring, painful even, but if you have decided to follow a career that requires you to realize a good balanced pass in the

UKCAT then you have little alternative but to get down to some serious hard work. Once again, if you are not prepared to put in the hard work to maximize your scores on these tests, then it is likely that medical, dentistry or veterinary school and a related career are not for you.

Practice makes a big difference in UKCAT scores

It is important that you realize that most people who score well in the UKCAT will have worked hard preparing for the test. There is no secret. Studies show that those who put in the most hours do best, whether in sport, music or academic achievement. Above all else, this requires time and especially commitment. Without the latter it is unlikely that you will do very well.

In addition to plain hard slog, there are also some strategies to adopt so that you are not only working harder, but smarter too.

Adopt a 'no going back' philosophy

Treat every question as a passport to fulfilling your dreams. Adopt the mindset that each question counts, so be sure of every answer before moving on to the next. When practising, resist the temptation of going back and reviewing your answers. In the real test you will not have time to do this, so do not hit the submit button for each answer without a final, brief review.

Manage your time expertly

You need to work quickly through every sub-test. Sometimes you may find it difficult to attempt all the questions in the given time. You should practise answering the questions in this book in an average of 30 seconds per question, so that in the real test you will be able to concentrate on the questions and take your time management for granted. Resist wasting too much time on difficult questions.

Guess intelligently

If you do not know the answer you have little alternative but to guess. Straight guessing offers a 20 per cent chance of getting the right answer, but remember to look at the suggested answers to see if you can rule any out as definitely wrong. If you can, then you will improve your chances of guessing correctly. If the end of the test approaches and you have not attempted all the questions, then in the last 60 seconds or so, randomly guessing answers to the remaining questions may well secure a couple of extra percentiles.

Make a really good start

In the UKCAT every question counts, but try especially hard to get the first question right in each sub-test, then the first five questions and then all the rest! The opening questions in a computer-administered test are especially significant because these tests are often computer adaptive. This means that the first question will be of the level that the 'average' candidate should get right. The next question will be a bit harder and so on. But, and this is important, you have to get the question right before the program presents you with the harder questions. Keep getting the questions right and you will soon be following along branches into the upper percentiles, rapidly leading to the level that will win you a place at medical school.

Whatever you do, avoid a bad start

A bad start is something you should work hard to avoid in any test but especially in a computer-adaptive test like the UKCAT. Get the first few questions wrong and the computer-adaptive test will present you with easier questions and you will struggle to get back to the level expected by many institutions. This adaptive process continues through the test, so keep trying to get as many questions right as possible to maximize your chance of being awarded a winning score.

Key stages in preparing

We each have our preferred method of revising for exams and your study to date will have made you aware of what you have to do to meet the challenge of the UKCAT. However, if it is some years since you last sat an exam (and there are many mature applicants to medical schools), then the following advice should help you towards a successful UKCAT campaign.

Adopt a winning mindset

Doing well in the UKCAT is not simply a matter of intelligence. It is critical that you realize that to do well you have to try very hard indeed. Weeks before the test you will need to undertake extensive revision, then during the exam you will need to really 'go for it'. After the exam you should feel mentally fatigued. If you don't then you probably failed to apply yourself sufficiently and may not have fully done yourself justice. You may well have to dig deep towards the end of the test session and find the mental strength to keep going, otherwise you risk getting a disappointing score in the last paper because by this stage in the process you felt tired.

It is common to experience feelings of irritation or resentment about having to do a test like the UKCAT, as after all the institutions can see how good you are from, for example, your A level results, school references and so on. If you harbour these kinds of feelings then it is crucial that you put them aside. They can be very counterproductive. Try not to wonder about the validity of the test or how it is used by institutions. What you think of the UKCAT and its predictive value is entirely irrelevant. You need to do well in this test if you are to realize your goal of winning a place in medical/dental/veterinary school. Do well and an important opportunity will become possible. Focus on that goal and put all else aside for a few weeks. You really need to let your determination to do well in the UKCAT take over your life for a while.

Practise a successful exam technique

Some very clever and highly educated people do not do well at tests like the UKCAT. In some cases their training and inclination do not best serve them well under the rather artificial conditions and abstract questions of a tightly timed test. This happens when, for example, the candidate thinks too deeply about the question or reads the passages and questions too carefully. Some place too high an emphasis on accuracy at the expense of speed. The outcome is that their test result does not reflect their true ability or their achievements to date. If you are such a person then you may need to develop an approach that involves a slightly greater risk of getting a question wrong for the sake of speed, or you may need to accept the assertions and statements at face value and focus on the immediate task of answering the questions. Work hard on your exam technique and do not rest until you can demonstrate the necessary balance between speed and accuracy.

Equally, if you have not familiarized yourself with the challenge that each of the subtests presents before attending on the day, you may underachieve. Be completely sure that you understand each of the five styles of questions involved and what they demand of you. Practice is key to achieving this, so make sure you allow yourself lots of time to develop a winning approach.

Devise and implement an unbeatable study plan

The high-scoring candidate in every exam is confident of their abilities. They know what to expect and find that the exam contains few if any surprises. They turn up at the test centre looking forward to the opportunity to demonstrate how good they really are. To make sure you are such a candidate, begin by preparing a study plan well in advance of the test date.

Step 1   Understand each stage of the challenge

Make sure that you know exactly what to expect at each stage of the test. This should include the exact nature of each task and how long you are allowed.

Step 2   Make an honest assessment of your strengths and weaknesses

To prepare thoroughly for any test you should obviously try hard to improve the areas in which you are weakest. You probably already know which part of the UKCAT you would struggle with if you were to take the test tomorrow. You really need to try to go a step further than this and as objectively as possible assess the extent to which your area(s) of personal challenge will let you down. Only then can you ensure that you spend sufficient time addressing the challenge.

Step 3   Plan a programme of practice

Now you need to decide how much time you need to spend preparing for the challenge. A winning plan is likely to involve work over a minimum of two months, twice and preferably three times a week. If English is not your first language, if to date you have accomplished much despite never mastering maths or if you find the rules of English usage a complete enigma, then be prepared to set aside more time than this.

Step 4   Obtain enough practice material

Many candidates facing psychometric tests cannot find sufficient relevant practice material. The 600 practice questions this book contains will ensure you can get down to some serious practice. In the Kogan Page testing series the following titles also contain extra practice questions ideal for including in your UKCAT revision plan:

How to Pass Advance Numeracy Tests (over 400 questions)
How to Pass Advance Verbal Reasoning Tests (over 500 questions)
How to Pass Diagrammatic Reasoning Tests (over 300 questions)
How to Pass Graduate Psychometric Tests 3rd edition (over 500 questions)
Ultimate Psychometric Tests (1,000 questions)
The Graduate Psychometric Test Workbook (realistic practice tests)

If you need further advice on sources of practice then by all means e-mail us at help@mikebryon.com.

Step 5   Undertake two sorts of practice

First, to get the most from your practice, begin working in a relaxed situation without constraint of time, reviewing examples of questions and working out the answers in order to become familiar with the demands of typical questions. Feel free to review answers and explanations and to refer to textbooks and dictionaries or use a calculator. Each chapter of this book starts with questions for this sort of practice which we call 'warm up questions'.

Next, and once you are familiar with the challenge of each question type, you should start to practise under realistic test conditions. This involves putting aside the dictionary or calculator and working against the clock without help or interruption. The purpose is to develop a good exam technique and to improve your stamina and endurance. Learn not to spend too long on any one question and practise educated guessing. Each chapter contains a series of what we have called 'mini-tests' so that you can undertake this very important sort of practice. To get the most out of it, set yourself the personal challenge of trying to beat your last score each time you take a mini-test. You will need to try very hard and take the challenge seriously if you are to really succeed in beating your previous best score or getting all the questions right time after time, and sufficiently quickly. When you finish a mini-test you should feel satisfied that you are creating a realistic real-test feel.

Answers to, and explanation of, the practice questions are found in Chapter 7.

Things to remember on the day of the test

1. Read through the instructions sent with your invitation to the test centre regarding the conditions, procedures and regulations.
2. The most important thing to take with you when you attend the test centre is suitable ID. For reasons of test security the test administrator will want to be able to confirm that no one is impersonating you and completing the test on your behalf. The most usual forms of ID are a passport, a national ID card or a driving licence. Note that acceptable ID

should not have expired and should contain your name (spelt exactly the same as on your test appointment), a recognizable photograph and your signature.

You may also be required to sign a confidentiality statement and agree to follow the centre's regulations.

3. You will not be allowed to take very much into the test room. They provide you with everything you need or are allowed, including scrap paper for doing rough working. Once again, make sure you have thoroughly read all the information given in order to understand what you can and cannot take with you. You are not allowed any other sort of computer aid or mobile phone in the testing room. A stopwatch is provided on the computer screen.

It would be a big mistake to arrive late for your appointment, so locate the centre and make sure you can find it with time to spare. Aim to arrive at least 30 minutes before your appointment time.

If English is not your first language

The medical school of your choice may require you to pass the TOEF or IELTS as well as UKCAT. The school to which you apply will inform you of their policy.

Some parts of the UKCAT are likely to present a greater challenge to you, so you need to adjust your programme of revision accordingly. For a speaker of English as a second language the verbal reasoning, decision analysis and non-cognitive analysis questions are likely to prove the most challenging. The quantitative reasoning and abstract reasoning sections should be no more difficult for you than they would be for a native speaker.

Meet the challenge of the UKCAT by starting your programme of review at an early stage and spend time reading quality newspapers and journals, if possible daily. This will help build your vocabulary and improve your proficiency at assimilating the meanings of the complex sentences and sentence structures that occur in the UKCAT. Look up unfamiliar words. Practise writing 70-word reviews of articles found in these publications.

If you are planning to sit the UKCAT many years after studying

If it is some or many years since you studied, or more particularly since you sat a multiple-choice exam, then the UKCAT may well present a number of specific hurdles. The first thing to do is to review examples of each type of question and assignment that makes up the UKCAT and make an honest assessment of which of these components represents the greatest challenge. To demonstrate your full potential, well before sitting the test you will need to begin a programme of revision. Start with the aspects of the test that you feel you are least good at.

You may need to set aside a fairly considerable amount of time for revising the demands of the verbal and numerical sub-tests. Aim at 10 hours a week of practice, ideally over a number of months, in order to achieve a good, well-balanced score.

Making the necessary commitment will demand discipline and determination. The time spent practising will at times seem tedious and frustrating. For many people, revising for the UKCAT is not what they dream of doing in their spare time. But if you want to go to medical school and they insist on a good score, you have no real alternative.

Work to redevelop a good exam technique. We cannot emphasize enough that this demands a balance between speed and accuracy. Some very good candidates will need to unlearn a thoughtful, considered approach to issues. Practise answering realistic questions under the pressure of time and, where appropriate, refer to the suggested answers for clues. As it is likely that you will be pushed for time, practise informed guessing, where you can eliminate some of the suggested answers and then guess from those that remain.

On a positive note, practice should afford you a marked improvement in your performance in all tests, particularly perhaps the decision analysis and non-cognitive analysis sub-tests.

If you suffer a disability

If your ability to undertake the UKCAT could be adversely affected by a disability then speak to the school to which you are applying. Seek their advice at an early stage on how your requirements can best be accommodated. Provide full details of your condition and be clear about the special arrangements you require when you register online for the test so that the organizers have time to obtain formal proof if required. There is a version of the UKCAT designed especially for candidates with special needs and this longer version of the test may be more appropriate for you.

Verbal reasoning

For a sizable minority of candidates, tests of verbal reasoning are their worst nightmare. Often these individuals are accomplished in, for example, science or mathematics but they can do little better than realize the norm rating in these common verbal tests. If you are the sort of candidate who will shine in the quantitative reasoning and abstract reasoning tests but fear that you will struggle with the verbal reasoning paper of the UKCAT, now is the time to get down to some serious score-improving practice.

The verbal reasoning sub-test comprises a series of passages followed by questions. Each question is a statement and your task is to decide if, according to the passage, the statement is true or false or if you cannot tell if it is true or false. Typically these questions require you to comprehend meaning and significance, assess logical strength, identify valid inference, distinguish between a main idea and a subordinate one, recognize the writer's intention and identify a valid summary, interpretation or conclusion.

The subjects of the passages are drawn from a great many fields such as current affairs, business, science, the environment, economics, history, meteorology, health and education. In fact, expect almost any subject. If you know something of the area, take care not to use your own knowledge. Be especially careful if you know a great deal about the subject or if you believe the passage to be factually incorrect or controversial. You are expected to answer the questions using only the information the passage contains. It is not a test of your general knowledge, your knowledge of the latest findings in the discipline or your political views. So feel completely at ease about answering true to a statement which is true in the very limited context of the passage even if you know that it is false given what you have learnt at university or read in a newspaper that morning.

When a publisher of real tests develops an advanced verbal reasoning test they rely on fine distinctions between the suggested answers in order to distinguish between the scores of the large numbers of candidates. These distinctions are much finer than those we draw on a day-to-day basis. As a result, it is common for candidates to feel irritation and complain that these tests are to a large extent arbitrary. And in a way they are, for after all this is not how we use language at work or anywhere else but in the surreal world of tests. This is something you just have to accept and get used to and with practice you will get to recognize the subtle distinctions being drawn.

Take care not to err too much towards the 'cannot tell' suggested answer by making the mistake of applying too strict or too inflexible a test of proof. Be sure to read the questions as carefully as you read the passage and learn to pick up the many clues provided in the wording of it. For example, if the passage refers to 'a valid argument, inference or premise' or asks 'is it necessarily the case that…?', apply a strict criterion of proof. However, if the question asks 'is it reasonable…', 'on the balance of probability…', 'might the author…', then apply a less strict criterion. You will soon master these subtle differences and gain the necessary confidence to make the correct judgements.

If, when taking lots of time in the relaxed conditions of your home, you find these questions easy, take care that you do not slip into a false sense of security. In the real test you will be pressed for time and may well be suffering from some anxiety. You should aim at undertaking just one careful read of the passage before referring back to it in order to answer the question. Some people find it helps to read the questions before the passage.

There are 100 practice questions in this chapter. They are organized into 60 warm up questions and eight mini-tests. You will find hundreds more verbal reasoning questions and full-length verbal reasoning practice tests ideal for practice for the UKCAT verbal reasoning sub-test in *The Verbal Reasoning Test Workbook*, *How to Pass Advance Verbal Reasoning Tests*, *The Graduate Psychometric Test Workbook* and *How to Pass Graduate Psychometric Tests* (3rd edition), all published by Kogan Page.

Warm up questions

The aim of this practice is to realize the demands of verbal reasoning questions of the type found in the UKCAT so that you feel more confident when answering them. Practise these questions without a time limit and in an informal relaxed situation. Refer to the answers and explanations as often as you like and take time to check the precise meanings of the words you are unsure of in a dictionary or thesaurus.

Passage 1

Towns that have become commuter and second-home hotspots are valued for their housing stock, schools and unspoilt civic centres. It is now possible for working families to relocate away from cities without affecting their earning power. Commuting three days a week and working from home the rest has meant that many more people are willing to give up the city life and move to more rural areas to fulfil their dream of homes with gardens and cricket on the green. So many metropolitan dwellers have made the move that property prices in the more popular locations have become amongst the most expensive in the country.

Q1.   New technology is the reason why it is possible for working families to relocate
      without affecting their earning power.

      True ☐   False ☐   Cannot tell ☐

Q2.   The only reason for these locations becoming so popular is only due to commuting
      even if for just part of the week.

      True ☐   False ☐   Cannot tell ☐

Q3.   An idea of an unspoilt civic centre could include, along with cricket on the green,
      a traditional high street with local shops.

      True ☐   False ☐   Cannot tell ☐

Passage 2

Asparagus is a perennial and wild asparagus is found growing in light, well-drained soil
across Europe, northern Africa and central Asia. People from all over the world enjoy
eating it. The most sought-after domesticated varieties are from Canada and they prefer a
soil with a ph of around 6.5. The domesticated varieties grow best in a humus-rich
medium and will then each produce around half a kilo of crop. In the spring the plant
sends up the spears that if left will open to form new foliage but for the first six weeks of
each season these are cut when they are around 10 centimetres tall. After the cutting
season the spears are allowed to mature so that the plants can re-establish themselves.
The spears of the cultivated varieties are far thicker than those that grow in the wild and
the crown (the shallow root ball) much larger, but the flavour of wild asparagus is
superior. In the autumn the female plants fruit to produce small inedible berries.

Q4.   All asparagus plants like a soil with a ph of 6.5.

      True ☐   False ☐   Cannot tell ☐

Q5.   It can be inferred from the passage that when the author describes the fruit as
      inedible he means that humans can't eat it.

      True ☐   False ☐   Cannot tell ☐

Q6.   Asparagus only grows in Europe, northern Africa and central Asia.

True ☐   False ☐   Cannot tell ☐

Passage 3

When each year an average of 500,000 immigrants entered the country the Home Office calculated that the fiscal benefit of this level of inward migration was £2.5 billion a year. This calculation was used extensively by the government of the day to support their immigration policies. The findings of the Home Office stood out against the findings of other western nations which found the benefits of large-scale inward migration to be so small as to be close to zero. The difference in the findings arose because the Home Office figure was based only on the effect of inward migration on the country's total Gross Domestic Product (GDP), while the other studies measured the effect on GDP per head. However, the Home Office calculation was obviously flawed, and they have since stopped using it, because immigration manifestly increases both the total GDP and the population. While the overall effect of inward migration may be negligible nationally in fiscal terms, the indigenous low paid and low skilled stand to lose out because as a consequence of the inward migration they face greater competition for work. Some employers have much to gain from the improved supply of labour and savings made from not having to train young people.

Q7.   It is no longer the case that half a million immigrants enter the country.

True ☐   False ☐   Cannot tell ☐

Q8.   The author's intended meaning when he wrote 'However, the Home Office calcu-
       lation was obviously flawed, and they have since stopped using it, because immi-
       gration manifestly increases both the total GDP and the population' would be
       better served if instead of immigration he wrote inward migration.

True ☐   False ☐   Cannot tell ☐

Q9.   There are no clear winners in an economy experiencing large-scale inward migration.

True ☐   False ☐   Cannot tell ☐

Passage 4

Jupiter orbits the sun every 12 years and is five times the distance of Earth from the sun. It is a huge gaseous planet with a rocky core twice the size of Earth and has four principal moons, Io, Europa, Ganymede and Callisto. These moons were first recorded by Galileo in 1609. The outer reaches of our solar system contain three giant gaseous planets, the others being Uranus and Neptune which both lie beyond Jupiter. Uranus takes 84 years to orbit while Neptune takes 165 years. These planets were visited by Voyager space probes between 1979 and 1989 and all were found to have distinctive rings, satellites (or moons) and experience enormous storms in their upper atmospheres identifiable as large white or coloured rotating spots, some of which last for months or even years.

Q10. The huge gaseous planets of the outer reaches of our solar system have rocky cores.

True ☐   False ☐   Cannot tell ☐

Q11. In the passage we can conclude that the words 'huge, giant' and 'moon, satellite' are treated as synonyms.

True ☐   False ☐   Cannot tell ☐

Q12. Of the three gaseous planets Neptune is the furthest from the sun.

True ☐   False ☐   Cannot tell ☐

Passage 5

If anyone was surprised when it eventually weakened it was only because it did not happen sooner. People can live beyond their means for quite some time before they run out of credit and must start to address the accumulated debt. An enormous economy like that of the United States can live beyond its means for years and accumulate an enormous amount of debt before the inevitable happens. The correction occurred when too many of the dollars held by America's creditors were sold. The American central bank responded to the crisis by lowering interest rates which triggered further selling as investors sought higher returns in alternative currencies. The emergent Chinese and Indian economies have also contributed to the weakness of the dollar. Rising living standards in those countries have led to their currencies strengthening. The dollar is trading against the currencies of these fast-developing nations at a much lower historic rate and this is a trend that is bound to continue.

Q13. Even if the US economy was free of debt the dollar would have weakened and remained trading at below the historic rate at least against some of the world's currencies.

True ☐   False ☐   Cannot tell ☐

Q14. What the author meant by the term 'inevitable' is that the US economy would go into recession.

True ☐   False ☐   Cannot tell ☐

Q15. For years people had predicted that the dollar would weaken.

True ☐   False ☐   Cannot tell ☐

Passage 6

The giant wind turbines on the nearby hill supply the community with 8 million kilowatt hours of electricity each year. Several hundred homeowners have erected solar panels on their roofs to provide most of their summer-time hot water needs. Bio-waste is collected for fermentation to produce methane gas which drives a local generator to augment the town's electricity needs when there is insufficient wind to fully power the turbines. Better insulation has cut the fuel requirements of many homes. Local generation in this isolated, rural community has led to saving on the investment cost of additional transmission lines in the national network. Further efficiencies are gained because the local production of power avoids losses to electrical resistance in the long-distance transmission of power.

Q16. The motives for this community's investment in the local generation of its energy needs are rising fuel costs and climate worries.

True ☐   False ☐   Cannot tell ☐

Q17. When the wind is blowing and the sun is shining, locally generated power accounts for most of this community's energy needs.

True ☐   False ☐   Cannot tell ☐

Q18. This isolated rural community is located in a part of the world where the national power network is practically non-existent.

True ☐   False ☐   Cannot tell ☐

Passage 7

The outsourcing of jobs to India from Europe and America has evolved from giving them relatively low-skilled work to passing on highly skilled roles. Multinationals have decreased the number of employees in Europe and America that undertake engineering design, science and software writing and instead now employ tens of thousands of skilled Indian workers in these challenging roles. Some are establishing second headquarters in the country because they have so many senior executives working on key projects there. The shift is in part due to it being easier in India to fill highly skilled, English-speaking positions and because, for the time being anyway, the wages for these roles are notably lower than wages in Europe and America. But it is also because companies want to position their businesses where they believe the future lies. India is one of the world's three biggest pools of highly skilled English-speaking labour and some commentators believe that as many as 30 million European and American skilled jobs are at risk of being moved.

Q19. The case that many more skilled jobs will be moved to India would be strengthened if even more than 30 million European and American jobs were at risk of moving.

True ☐   False ☐   Cannot tell ☐

Q20. Three rationales for the outsourcing to India are portrayed.

True ☐   False ☐   Cannot tell ☐

Q21. The claim that American and European jobs are being lost to India because Indian workers are prepared to work harder than their American and European counterparts can be rebutted.

True ☐   False ☐   Cannot tell ☐

Passage 8

Annually the average household spends on running electrical appliances: £82 on washing and drying, £49 on lighting, £38 on refrigeration of food, a rather wasteful £95 on the wide-screen TV, £17 powering computers, wireless networks and charging phones and, not surprising for the British, £23 on boiling the kettle for all those endless cups of tea. If families were more attentive and for example did not leave unnecessary lights on then they could save a considerable sum of money. Just appliances left unnecessarily on standby are guesstimated to waste £25 a year per household. The typical family's electricity bill could be quite significantly cut if we learnt to use electricity more frugally and became a little more attentive in order to reduce the waste. A trial showed an average saving of £75 a year on electricity bills which should prove a big incentive for most families.

Q22.   You can infer that the average household's annual electricity bill (net of taxes etc) is a little over £300 (the sum of all the individual items listed).

True ☐   False ☐   Cannot tell ☐

Q23.   The main point of the passage is an account of the saving that could be made if we were more frugal with our use of electrical appliances.

True ☐   False ☐   Cannot tell ☐

Q24.   Were we to learn to use electricity more frugally and become a little more attentive in order to reduce the waste, we would hardly notice the difference in terms of the impact on our daily lives.

True ☐   False ☐   Cannot tell ☐

Passage 9

A thing of beauty can completely lack physical form. We find some experiences beautiful despite their lack of physical appearance and we find some theories beautiful despite them being ideas that lack any physical structure. Perfume is the only beauty product that just plays on the emotions. We cannot see a scent and despite its complete lack of visual structure it can have an immediate and intimate effect. We can love or hate a smell for the image it elicits. A smell can evoke memories of an unhappy episode while someone else will identify it as warm and pleasing. We can be moved to describe a scent as beautiful because of the delicate impression or because of its zesty, exciting chemistry. Interestingly a scent can smell different on different people. We can love a scent for the way it smells on others but hate the way it smells on us. The perfume we are provoked into calling beautiful is not something we can objectively decide. Freewill and personal choice play no part in the process.

Q25. Beauty is in the eye of the beholder.

True ☐   False ☐   Cannot tell ☐

Q26. In the opening sentence of the passage when it is said that a thing of beauty can completely lack physical form it means that it lacks physical structure.

True ☐   False ☐   Cannot tell ☐

Q27. The passage would be improved if the author wrote 'we can love or hate a smell for the reminiscence it elicits' rather than 'we can love or hate a smell for the image it elicits'.

True ☐   False ☐   Cannot tell ☐

Passage 10

Over $50 billion was spent shopping online last year and it is hardly surprising that criminals want a share of the action. No businessman or woman in his or her right mind would leave a shop unattended, unlocked and without an alarm and most take precautions to protect their virtual shops too but not to the same degree of security. Many businesses do little more than install a firewall and antivirus and anti-spyware software and they believe this is all the security that is required. But the more recent developments in online threats are no longer guaranteed to be excluded by the most commonly available security software. Retailers should take professional advice on the system and consider redirecting all of their inbound and outbound traffic to web security specialists who scan all traffic and block threats. Extra special care needs to be taken with the management of systems involved in the handling of payments by credit cards.

Q28. Online shopping offers the criminal the promise of rich pickings.

True ☐   False ☐   Cannot tell ☐

Q29. Firewalls and antivirus and anti-spyware software are the virtual equivalents of shop assistants, locks and alarms.

True ☐   False ☐   Cannot tell ☐

Q30. The antivirus and anti-spyware software usually updates automatically and so the business owner is led to believe that their security will remain up to date too.

True ☐   False ☐   Cannot tell ☐

Passage 11

As an institution the British public house, usually called a pub, has a very long tradition of selling alcoholic drinks, in particular beer, which people consume on the premises. In recent years, however, profits of British pubs have fallen by 20 per cent and many have reported a further worsening of their financial state since the introduction of a new law and a series of tax increases. The new law involved the banning of smoking in public places and this has led to a marked decrease in pub custom. The increase in taxes involves a series of above-inflation rises in the duty charged on alcohol sold both in pubs and off-licences (the name of licensed premises allowed to sell alcohol for home consumption) that has markedly increased the cost of drinking alcohol. The combined effect of the smoking ban and increase in the alcohol duty are reported to have led to the loss of many jobs in the pub trade.

Q31. The author is opposed to the new laws and the effects they are having on the pub trade and this is evidenced by the last sentence of the passage and the loss of jobs in the pub trade.

True ☐   False ☐   Cannot tell ☐

Q32. It is reasonable to infer that some pubs are operating at a loss or at no profit.

True ☐   False ☐   Cannot tell ☐

Q33. The smoking ban has encouraged traditional pub customers to drink and smoke less.

True ☐   False ☐   Cannot tell ☐

Passage 12

Taking recreational drugs in the privacy of your own home should be no one else's business but your own and yet the government has made it illegal. Millions of law-abiding citizens have used recreational drugs. Studies suggest that some 10 million people have used recreational drugs at some stage of their lives and 2 million use them on a regular and long-term basis. The studies suggest that it's not just young people who are recreational drug users either; most studies find that close to half the long-term users are aged over 24 years of age. Recreational drugs are classified into three categories according to the level of harm they cause. Penalties for possession of class C drugs, the lowest classification, include imprisonment for up to two years and an unlimited fine. Dealing in these drugs can result in imprisonment for up to 14 years. Possession of class A drugs can result in seven years' imprisonment. Cannabis, perhaps the most commonly used recreational drug, is soon to be reclassified as class B from its current classification of class C.

Q34. It is not true to say that people who use recreational drugs are law-abiding citizens.

True ☐   False ☐   Cannot tell ☐

Q35. The author of the passage does not agree that it should be illegal to use recreational drugs in the privacy of your own home.

True ☐   False ☐   Cannot tell ☐

Q36. Dealing in all classes of these drugs can result in imprisonment for up to 14 years.

True ☐   False ☐   Cannot tell ☐

Passage 13

In 1997 a previously long-dormant volcano on the Caribbean island of Montserrat erupted. In just a few minutes a fast-moving lava flow surged down the mountain covering a great swathe including the capital Plymouth. The lava was followed by mud slides and almost the whole of the south of the island was buried in a choking layer of ash. The residents of the capital and the affected parts of the island had been evacuated prior to the eruption. A great many lives were undoubtedly saved but 19 lives were still lost and everyone knew that life there would never be the same again. Twenty years after the eruption only 4,000 of the original population of 12,000 remain.

Q37. Twenty years after the eruption only 4,000 people lived on the island.

True ☐   False ☐   Cannot tell ☐

Q38. The evacuation prior to the eruption averted a disaster.

True ☐   False ☐   Cannot tell ☐

Q39. There must be a mistake in the claim that the eruption occurred in 1997 because
      this book was published in 2009. Twenty years could not have passed since it was
      found that 4,000 of the original 12,000 population remain.

      True    False   Cannot tell

Passage 14

The early manned missions visited lowlands and plains while the later missions explored
highlands. Selecting a suitable site was never going to be easy as even the apparently
flattest of locations were found to be on closer inspection potholed from meteorite strikes
and plastered with small boulders. The moon is rugged and very mountainous and in the
1960s a number of lunar probes had photographed the moon's surface during close orbit
passes and even performed soft landings in the search for suitable sites for the manned
missions that were to follow. In 1969 Neil Armstrong and Edwin Aldrin in Apollo 11
made the first ever manned lunar landing. The last manned landing was made in 1972
with Apollo 17.

Q40. The first lunar landing was made in the 1960s.

      True   False   Cannot tell

Q41. Apollo 17 visited a mountainous region of the moon.

      True   False   Cannot tell

Q42. When referring to a 'suitable site' in the second sentence it means suitable sites for
      the landing of manned missions.

      True   False   Cannot tell

Passage 15

We suffer a suspension of judgement when we hand over a card to purchase something and
spend funds that we intended to use for something essential or unintentionally create an
unauthorized overdraft. These spur-of-the-moment lapses are more likely to occur when
we pay for something electronically or with credit than with hard cash. This is because of
a widely held perception that electronic money and credit are somehow not as real or
valuable as notes and coins. Retailers play on this emotional weakness with offers of in-
store cards and 'buy now play later' deals. But, nowhere is our Achilles' heel exploited
more than on the internet where it is impossible to pay with ready money and perhaps the

sites that have perfected this form of exploitation are those that offer gambling. The sites regulated by the Gaming Commission have safeguards but the unregulated sites set out to encourage people to stake more to recover their losses and do not provide facilities to allow the gambler to set limits on how much they will fritter.

Q43. We suffer a suspension of judgement when we hand over a card to purchase something.

True ☐   False ☐   Cannot tell ☐

Q44. Electronic money and credit have a lower psychological value than cash in your hand.

True ☐   False ☐   Cannot tell ☐

Q45. Sites unregulated by the Gaming Commission are unlicensed.

True ☐   False ☐   Cannot tell ☐

Passage 16

Poor farmers and poor food-exporting countries have for years suffered the disincentive of low food prices but recently they have seen their returns improve by an average of 20 per cent and this has brought real benefits to communities that rank amongst the poorest in the world. On the other hand, many, many millions of the world's poor are landless and live on a $1 a day or less and these people already living in absolute poverty now face famine. Most governments of the poorest food-importing countries are counterbalancing the rapid rises in staple food prices with improved food subsidy programmes. Those that have not are facing domestic food price protests. Already modest educational and health programmes are being squeezed in order to fund these plans.

Q46. Rising food prices weigh more heavily in some places than others.

True ☐   False ☐   Cannot tell ☐

Q47. The main issue in the passage is rising food prices and how they create winners and losers.

True ☐   False ☐   Cannot tell ☐

Q48. Food subsidy programmes are intended to ease the pain of the effect rather than stop the development.

True ☐   False ☐   Cannot tell ☐

Passage 17

The estimated cost to widen both sides of 240 miles of the world's busiest motorway has been priced at a figure higher than the annual gross domestic product (GDP) of one quarter of the world's nations. It is a major construction project but with the same sum of money many of the world's nations fund their entire annual government expenditure, including road building. The rate of inflation for raw materials and therefore for construction is running many times higher than general inflation and given this and the fact that such projects have a record of overrunning their estimates there must exist a real possibility that the scheme will cost even more than the estimate. Construction work has not yet started but the pre-construction phase has begun even if the decision to proceed with the project has still to be made.

Q49. An estimate is not a commitment to spend.

True ☐   False ☐   Cannot tell ☐

Q50. The sum of one quarter of the world's nations' GDP is less than the estimated cost to widen both sides of a length of the world's busiest motorway.

True ☐   False ☐   Cannot tell ☐

Q51. The project involves 480 miles of road building.

True ☐   False ☐   Cannot tell ☐

Passage 18

Due to Private Finance Initiatives (PFIs), schools and hospitals are being built that the government would otherwise not be able to afford. PFIs are currently preferred by government over traditional public procurement for the building of schools, hospitals, social housing and prisons. Straight public procurement is notorious for cost overruns and delays while PFI projects rarely suffer either. Another advantage and the most important for the government is that PFIs are what are called off-balance-sheet expenditure. The cost of building is not funded by the government upfront. Instead the private sector pays for the building and the government lease the building from the private owner and guarantee an annual rent. This allows the government to spread out the cost and so PFIs help the Treasury to balance the books.

Q52. Given the advantages of PFI over public procurement it is hard to imagine that public procurement will again be used to fund the building of public buildings.

True ☐   False ☐   Cannot tell ☐

Q53. Even if all initiatives, both PFI and public procurement, suffered the same delay and overspend, government may still prefer the PFI route.

True ☐   False ☐   Cannot tell ☐

Q54. The last sentence would be less open to misinterpretation if it was rewritten to read 'This allows the government to spread out the cost of building and so PFIs help the Treasury to balance the books'.

True ☐   False ☐   Cannot tell ☐

Passage 19

All too often organizations jump onto the real food bandwagon to cynically exploit the public's appetite to know more about where their food comes from and by whom and how it is grown. An example might be a pack of processed meat with a picture on the packaging of a farmhouse, a kind-looking farmer and country scene and yet its content is processed in a factory from meat grown on countless farms and transported from all over the world. The same is sadly true with respect to the rise of responsible tourism. Tourists want a guilt-free holiday and so they prefer to use the services of a tour operator who is contributing to the local community and contributes to rather than distracts from the ecosystem they visit. An example might be a holiday resort that provides the land and building for a school and employs local people in the resort. Visitors to the resort are encouraged to contribute to the running costs of the school and to fund the provision of a meal each day for the children.

Q55. The owners of the holiday resort that provides the land and building for a school for local children is portrayed in the passage as an example of a tour operator who is cynically exploiting our appetite for responsible tourism.

True ☐   False ☐   Cannot tell ☐

Q56. To say that 'organizations jump on the real food bandwagon' is to offer a metaphor.

True ☐   False ☐   Cannot tell ☐

Q57. Tourists do not want to use the services of a tour operator who is contributing to the local community and ecosystem only because they want a guilt-free holiday.

True ☐   False ☐   Cannot tell ☐

Passage 20

The jet stream is a two-mile-high column of wind and in this part of the world it determines the boundary between the Arctic and Atlantic air. When it moves south, much of northern Europe and North America is subjected to cold air and when it moves north, northern Europe and North America enjoy warmer air. In the spring and autumn the jet stream moves much more than at other times of the year and this largely explains why spring and autumn weather in the northern hemisphere can be so changeable. In a matter of a few days the position of the jet stream can fluctuate and warm and possibly wet spring or autumn weather can suddenly be replaced by cold air and dry, clear skies.

Q58. It can be inferred from the information provided that in relative terms Arctic air is cold and Atlantic air is warm.

True ☐   False ☐   Cannot tell ☐

Q59. By 'this part of the world' it implies northern Europe.

True ☐   False ☐   Cannot tell ☐

Q60. If it were in fact untrue that the jet stream was a two-mile-high column of wind then the explanation of why spring and autumn weather in the northern hemisphere is so changeable would be compromised.

True ☐   False ☐   Cannot tell ☐

Eight mini-tests for the UKCAT verbal reasoning paper

The remaining 40 questions of this chapter are organized as eight mini-tests. It is far better to practise little and often when preparing for a test and most people can find a few minutes without distraction to undertake one of these mini-tests. Each contains five multiple-choice questions and you are allowed four minutes in which to attempt them. The first question is of average difficulty and they become progressively harder. This is what you can expect to happen in the real UKCAT. Use these questions to get down to some really serious score-improving practice and be sure of the very best start in your real UKCAT verbal reasoning paper.

Read the first passage and answer the questions that relate to it and, when you have very briefly rechecked your choice, enter your answer in the answer box and move on to the next question. Try to avoid going back to reconsider a previous answer because you will risk wasting precious time, so practise getting the answer right first time and move confidently on to the next question. You will find that each mini-test comprises two passages and each is followed by either two or three questions (always making a total of five).

Put away the dictionary and thesaurus and treat these mini-tests like a real test. Get the most out of this practice by setting yourself the personal challenge of trying to beat or, if you get all five right, match your last score each time you take a mini-test. That way you will create a realistic, real-test feel. You will need to try very hard and take the challenge seriously if you are to really succeed in beating your previous best score or getting five out of five every time. Time management will be critical, so be sure to stick to the four-minute time limit and not spend too long on any one question, and practise making one careful detailed read of the passage to save on time going back to check detail. Keep practising until you consistently get all five questions right. Achieve this and you can take strength from the fact that you are likely to make a very good start in your real UKCAT verbal reasoning paper. The only thing then left to do is to keep up that rate of success through to the end of the real test!

Mini-test 1

Passage 1

The world's population is expected to increase to more than 10 billion by 2050. Having a child in the developed world has a greater environmental impact than having a child in the developing world. Likewise having a large family in the developed world has a far greater environmental impact than having a large family in the developing world. This is because a child born into the developed world is much more likely to go on to have a high carbon dioxide emission lifestyle given that they are more likely to take regular flights, drive cars, live in a large energy-hungry home and so on. This has led some campaigners to argue that families in the developed world should think far more seriously about the environmental consequences of having children and should elect or be encouraged to have fewer.

Q1. If it were the case that all of the world's future population growth was projected to occur in the developing world and that the population of most developed countries would have fallen if it wasn't for immigration, then the case made for smaller families in the developed world would be weakened.

True ☐   False ☐   Cannot tell ☐

Q2. If families living in the developing world were to have fewer children then they too would make a major cut in their families' future carbon dioxide output.

True ☐   False ☐   Cannot tell ☐

Passage 2

To enjoy a comfortable retirement, many retired people recommend retiring on two-thirds of final salary and around 4 million workers have paid into pension schemes for the bulk of their working lives in order to realize this goal. Those who have contributed to a final salary pension scheme will reach that standard and in fact exceed it when the person's state pension is added to the equation. Those workers who have contributed to a pension scheme that lacks the final salary guarantee and instead depend on the investment value of their total contributions to purchase their pension on retirement are less fortunate. Even when their state pension is included the bulk of these people will retire on an income of around 40 per cent of their final salary. As for the remaining 11 million workers who have made little or no contribution to any other pension scheme than the compulsory state scheme, it is feared that they will find themselves dependent on means-tested benefits.

Q3.   Four million workers will reach or exceed the standard where they retire on two-thirds of the final salary.

True ☐   False ☐   Cannot tell ☐

Q4.   Workers with pension schemes without the final salary guarantee will have to manage on a lot less than the amount thought to be needed for a secure retirement.

True ☐   False ☐   Cannot tell ☐

Q5.   The country to which the passage refers has a total population of 15 million.

True ☐   False ☐   Cannot tell ☐

End of test

Mini-test 2

Passage 1

Twice as many people live till they are 100 in France as in Britain. Yet the two countries have similar sized populations and have diets with similar amounts of fat. In fact life expectancy is considerably better in France from the age of 65 onwards and it seems that lifestyle and diet may have a lot to do with it. Leaving aside the fact that the French probably have the best national health service in the world, statistics suggest that the French remain active longer and consume more units of fruit and vegetables. They also enjoy considerably more glasses of red wine and it seems these differences give rise to far lower levels of death caused by heart disease and this allows significant numbers of people to live until their centenary.

Q1.   Four differences are attributed to the reason the French have a far lower level of death caused by heart disease: the best national health service, remaining active, consuming more fruit and vegetables and enjoying more red wine.

True ☐   False ☐   Cannot tell ☐

Q2.   Even if twice as many people in France see their centenary it may be that very few people live to see their 100th birthday in either country.

True ☐   False ☐   Cannot tell ☐

Passage 2

Last year's summer was noteworthy for being very wet and very windy and yet neither of these qualities featured in the meteorological service's long-term forecast. We were advised that we could expect a typical summer with above-average temperatures and average or slightly above-average levels of rainfall. There was no mention whatsoever of the widespread flooding that occurred. This raises the question of whether the forecast was wrong and they in principle could have but did not forecast the exceptional weather or whether it is in principle impossible to forecast specific long-term exceptional events. Long-term forecasts are based on baseline averages over an extended period and trends in that baseline are used to build the forecast and predict, for example, if that trend is to continue. If extreme weather is occurring more frequently then it is feasible that the forecast might include the prediction that the frequency of these events will continue to be higher than the historic average.

Q3.   It is a mistake to believe that the exceptional can be forecast over the long term.

True ☐   False ☐   Cannot tell ☐

Q4.   The summer of 2007 was noteworthy for being very wet and windy.

True ☐   False ☐   Cannot tell ☐

Q5.   It is not possible to predict long-term specific weather events such as the flooding last summer.

True ☐   False ☐   Cannot tell ☐

End of test

Mini-test 3

Passage 1

In almost zero gravity and no wind very large droplets of water can form. In normal atmospheric conditions and no wind droplets of around 2 millimetres diameter commonly occur. In normal conditions with wind smaller droplets form and the diameter of those found in a typical summer gale might measure less than one millimetre. In every situation droplets do collide and these combine to form larger droplets that may well survive but air resistance and the relatively weak surface tension of water mean that droplets with a diameter larger than 5 millimetres very quickly break up.

Q1. The claim that giant globules of water cannot form is rebutted by the passage.

True ☐   False ☐   Cannot tell ☐

Q2. Droplets of between 2–5mm only occur in windless conditions.

True ☐   False ☐   Cannot tell ☐

Passage 2

So what is it that decides if a language is to endure or to be threatened with extinction? The number of languages spoken in the world is expected to continue to decrease dramatically but what decides the winners and the losers? Surprisingly some commentators argue that along with languages spoken by very small communities the really 'big' languages like English also face extinction. The case against the small linguistic community is obvious; if there is no one left to speak a language then that language dies. The case against a dominant, apparently all-conquering, language like English is less apparent and is therefore so much more interesting. As more and more of the world speaks English it is inevitable, the argument runs, that it will break up first into dialects and then distinct languages linked only by their common linguistic heritage. This is a controversial point because it goes against the view that dialects need isolation before they can form (without isolation, speech is standardized by the dominant language promulgated through international science, engineering, medicine and business and worldwide printed and digital media and this squeezes out dialects).

Q3. The case made for the extinction of English derives from its worldwide dominance.

True ☐   False ☐   Cannot tell ☐

Q4. The passage does not answer the question asking what decides if a language is to endure or become extinct.

True ☐   False ☐   Cannot tell ☐

Q5. The passage is ambivalent in respect to whether or not English will become extinct.

True ☐   False ☐   Cannot tell ☐

End of test

Mini-test 4

Passage 1

At a university campus in 1971, 23 male volunteers spent two weeks role playing prisoners and guards. The volunteers were upright ordinary 'good' students. The exercise sought to explore the extent to which the external environment influences human behaviour and in particular our potential for evil. Early on in the experiment the guards started subjecting the prisoners to psychological and physical punishments. As the experiment proceeded the punishments got worse. Philip Zimbardo, the originator of the experiment, identified that conformity and anonymity were two of a number of factors that can bring about callous behaviour in otherwise caring people. Anonymity was important because it led the perpetrators to believe that they would not have to answer for their actions. Conformity was significant because it pressurized the more humane guards to adopt the behaviour of their less humane peers. Another of Zimbardo's factors was boredom.

Q1. In this experiment in social psychology there were more prisoners than guards.

True ☐   False ☐   Cannot tell ☐

Q2. It would be wrong to deduce from the passage that women volunteers in the same circumstances would not act callously.

True ☐   False ☐   Cannot tell ☐

Q3. Two of Philip Zimbardo's factors that can bring about callous behaviour in otherwise caring people are identified.

True ☐   False ☐   Cannot tell ☐

Passage 2

Japan's population is projected to fall from the current almost 130 million to around 90 million by the middle of the next century and this smaller population will be faced with the added challenge that it will be disproportionately elderly. By then Japan's total GDP will be half that of India's and one-fifth the size of China's and Japan will have slipped to being the fifth largest super power in terms of the size of its GDP. Japan's answer to the challenge to its competitiveness is to seek out even greater innovation. It is currently very innovative if you measure it in terms of the number of patents registered and the amount spent on research and development. But in other measures of innovation it does not score so well. When compared to the European Union and the United States of America (currently the economic zones with the largest GDPs) its working practices are considered inflexible and it shuns foreign investment and cultural influences. The latter two are considered important because unless Japan engages in new ways of thinking and changes in worldwide values it is hard to see how it will remain the pioneer of bestselling products to future generations.

Q4. The big question for Japan is how it is to remain competitive.

True ☐   False ☐   Cannot tell ☐

Q5. The tone of the passage suggests that the ability to engage in new ways of thinking can be attributed to India and China.

True ☐   False ☐   Cannot tell ☐

End of test

Mini-test 5

Passage 1

English is spoken as a first language by 400 million people and one in four of the world's population claims to speak elementary English. In an English dictionary the C section contains the second largest number of entries and is the second longest. The S section contains the largest number and the P section is the third largest in terms of entries. One of the shortest sections lists the words beginning with Q but the section with the fewest entries is the W. Italian is spoken by around 60 million people and in an Italian dictionary the sections J, K, Y and W are very short and contain only foreign words used in Italian while the U and Q sections contain the least number of Italian entries. The longest section in the Italian dictionary and the section that contains the most entries is the S section and the next longest is the C section.

Q1. The S section of the Italian and English dictionaries both contain the largest number of entries.

True ☐   False ☐   Cannot tell ☐

Q2. In the English dictionary the S section is the longest.

True ☐   False ☐   Cannot tell ☐

Q3. The Q sections of both English and Italian dictionaries contain close to the fewest number of entries.

True ☐   False ☐   Cannot tell ☐

Passage 2

Andy, Betty, Charles, Diana, Edward, Fay, George, Hope. In an average hurricane season meteorologists in the Atlantic expect to name nine tropical storms. The christening of storms began when weather forecasts were broadcast over shortwave radio and naming them helped mariners to keep track of the weather system. The tradition evolved so that each successive storm was given a name beginning with successive letters of the alphabet. Initially only girls' names were used but later this was changed so that the names alternated from boy to girl names. If a named storm turns out to be particularly savage then the name may be dropped and not used in future years. The same system of naming storms is adopted in the north and south Pacific forecast regions.

Q4. The list of names at the beginning of the passage could be the list of names used in a year that experienced an average hurricane season.

True ☐   False ☐   Cannot tell ☐

Q5. When weather forecasts were broadcast over shortwave radio the storms were only given girls' names.

True ☐   False ☐   Cannot tell ☐

End of test

Mini-test 6

Passage 1

Except for Nepal's, which is the shape of two connected triangles, all modern national flags are rectangular and their colours hark back to the days when flags were extensively used for identification and communication. Nowadays the colour red is intimately associated with nations born from left-wing political movements but at the time of the French revolution the tri-colour (blue, white and red) was the symbol of the fight for freedom and inspired the design of many national flags including, for example, those of the United States of America and the Republic of Ireland. In many instances green stands for Islam (along with the crescent moon) while the cross shape usually signifies a Christian nation. The pan-African movement adopted the colours of the Ethiopian flag (green, yellow and red), the oldest independent African nation, and many African states when they emerged from colonialism adopted these colours.

Q1. The reason given for most flags being rectangular is that in the past they were extensively used for identification and communication.

True ☐   False ☐   Cannot tell ☐

Q2. Despite the fact that it is not, you can infer from the passage that the flag of the Republic of Ireland should be blue, white and red.

True ☐   False ☐   Cannot tell ☐

Q3. Today symbolic designs as well as colours are used to convey meaning and identity on national flags.

True ☐   False ☐   Cannot tell ☐

Passage 2

You can find out so much about people on the internet these days that civil liberty campaigners are arguing for new laws so that people can get back some vestige of control over their personal data. The 1998 Data Protection Act gives us the right to know the personal information companies are holding. But the new threat to personal liberty is quite the opposite – it is the threat of complete strangers finding out our personal details. Undertake an internet search on someone you know with any of the main search engines and you are likely to obtain thousands of results which if trawled through can provide particulars of employment, a work phone number and e-mail address. Find a CV belonging to that person and you will get hold of their home address, date of birth, home telephone number, personal e-mail address and a listing of their educational history and interests. If the person for whom you are searching is active on a social network site or an internet specialist interest forum then you may well be able to identify a database of friends and contacts and by reading recent postings obtain a flavour of their views and preferences. Search the database of a genealogy site and you may well be able to identify generations of family members.

Q4. The threat to personal liberty is no longer one of secrecy and finding out what organizations know about us.

True ☐   False ☐   Cannot tell ☐

Q5. The penultimate sentence of the passage illustrates the sort of things that people post on the internet.

True ☐   False ☐   Cannot tell ☐

End of test

Mini-test 7

Passage 1

Do scientific investigations of our past add to our understanding or do they whittle away at the mystery? Archaeology, carbon dating and DNA analysis have been used to 'disprove' popular explanations of historic events and to claim that supposed historic events could never have taken place.

Q1. An example of the scientific debunking of popular belief is the use of satellite images to locate a fabled, lost city.

True ☐   False ☐   Cannot tell ☐

Q2. Science can play a positive role and rather than be seen to discredit popular belief instead enrich it.

True ☐   False ☐   Cannot tell ☐

Passage 2

In terms of territory Russia is the world's largest country and Canada the second. Between them these huge nations occupy most of the northern part of the northern hemisphere. Both countries include a sizable extent of frozen wilderness. Canada covers the northern part of the North American continent while the Russian federation sits astride the northern parts of Europe and Asia. The two nations both have vast areas of forest and their forestry industries produce a large part of the world's softwood and wood pulp. Both countries hold extensive mineral deposits and the mining of zinc, uranium and nickel in Canada and iron ore, tungsten, gold, silver and diamonds in Russia rank these countries among the world's key producers. Five per cent of Canadian land is suitable for the growing of crops while 10 per cent of Russian land is arable. The majority of Russians live in the temperate, European part of the country while the bulk of Canadians have settled in the clement conditions found within 400 km of the border with their southern neighbour the United States.

Q3 You can infer that Russian arable production is greater than that of Canada.

True ☐   False ☐   Cannot tell ☐

Q4. The second sentence may have been more correct if it read '… the Russian federation covers the northern part of both Europe and Asia' rather than 'sits astride the northern part of Europe and Asia'.

True ☐   False ☐   Cannot tell ☐

Q5. The author of the passage would agree that the polar regions of both countries are relatively sparsely populated.

True ☐   False ☐   Cannot tell ☐

End of test

Mini-test 8

Passage 1
Waves become swell when they leave the area of wind in which they were generated. Long after the wind that created it has stopped blowing, swell can continue to travel for thousands of miles and have a life span dependent on its wave length and the extent of ocean. The longer the wave the faster it travels and given sufficient sea room the longer it continues to travel. Wind can generate waves that travel faster than the wind itself and after a few hours of blowing the wave can be a long way ahead of the wind. At sea the arrival of a swell can be an indication of bad weather to come. If a long low swell arrives and it steadily increases in height then you should prepare for an approaching gale. If the swell remains long and low then it is likely that the wind that generated it is a long way away and you will escape it. Sometimes a swell generated far away crosses the waves generated by another wind. This can lead to a confused and in the extreme a dangerous sea state.

Q1. The views expressed in the passage are a statement of the findings of experimental investigations.

True ☐   False ☐   Cannot tell ☐

Q2. The sentence 'wind can generate waves that travel faster than the wind itself and after a few hours of blowing the wave can be a long way ahead of the wind' would be more correct if it read 'Wind can generate waves that travel faster than the wind itself and after a few hours of blowing the swell can be a long way ahead of the wind.'

True ☐   False ☐   Cannot tell ☐

Passage 2

The world's major religions are Islam, Christianity, Hinduism, Buddhism, Judaism and Sikhism. The oldest is Hinduism which is believed to have been worshipped for at least 5,000 years. Religion provides a sense of community, a shared set of values that shape daily life, a definition of the meaning of life and a set of beliefs as to how the world began and what happens after death. Except for Buddhism the major religions all identify a supreme god and define the way in which followers commune with that god. Religions have sacred texts, for example in Sikhism the text is called the Adi Granth, and religions have revered places for communal worship. In Judaism the synagogue is the place for communal prayer and religious learning. All religion involves ceremony and festivals and observances at points in a religious calendar and at significant stages in the life of its prophet or prophets and the lives of its followers. For example, followers of the Christian faith celebrate baptism, the rite of a person's entry into the faith, and Muslims celebrate important events in the life of the Prophet, including his birthday.

Q3. Providing an explanation of what happens after death is attributed to all major religions except for Buddhism.

True ☐   False ☐   Cannot tell ☐

Q4. The passage is illustrated with specific details from five of the six major religions of the world.

True ☐   False ☐   Cannot tell ☐

Q5. The main theme of the passage is an examination of the ceremonies, festivals and observances of the world's major religions and the lives of the prophet or prophets and the followers.

True ☐   False ☐   Cannot tell ☐

End of test

Decision analysis

These tests are about making good judgements in less than ideal circumstances – as is often the case in real life. The information provided is deliberately incomplete and the rules being followed are deliberately ambiguous. It is your task to decipher the code and then despite the fact that the information is incomplete and that there is uncertainty, decide which of the suggested answers are best. You have to do this within a tight time frame.

This chapter comprises 100 practice questions for the UKCAT decision analysis sub-test. You are provided with a short description of a situation – this is the context – and a list of codes and their corresponding meanings. The situation and codes are followed by questions and each question involves a sequence of code and a series of suggested answers. In some instances more than one suggested answer is correct. It is your task to identify which of the suggested answers are the best interpretation of the code given the context and the given meaning of the codes. Note that in these practice questions, and this is important, the sequence of codes can be used in a different order from that in which they are presented in the question. So, for example, the code xx (meaning rock) and yy (meaning paper) can be used to correctly construct the interpretation rock, paper or paper, rock. Also note that other words (not covered by the code and not contradicted by the context) can be added to the suggested answer and it can still be correct. For example, it would be correct to translate the code xx, yy as rock and paper, paper or rock and so on. Pay particular attention to the commas in the questions. If two codes are *not* separated by a comma then they relate to each other and only each other. If the codes are separated by commas then they may relate to any of the other codes in the given sequence. You are expected to answer the questions using only the information provided, so be especially careful to stick to the content of the situation. In the real decision analysis sub-test, some suggested answers to the questions can be rejected because they are not consistent with the information provided in the situation. In many of the questions below, you can select the answer or reject suggested answers depending on the information provided in the context.

Warm up questions

This section comprises a total of 80 questions. It starts with 20 that involve no situation and require you simply to identify synonyms, antonyms, expanded or contracted terms and correctly identify terms that are similar. Feel free to refer to a thesaurus to check synonyms and antonyms as you work. These are followed by four situations and 60 practice decision analysis questions. The practice starts with easy questions which get progressively more difficult, so practise not spending too long on any one question and educated guessing. In the real test you may be presented with further information in the form of table text or graphs and you may have to click a separate button to obtain this extra information (as a general rule, always read extra information). Note that these practice questions do *not* include additional information. Some of the codes used below may involve more items than occur in the real sub-test. This is intentional and will help you build up your speed and accuracy at interpreting codes.

At least to begin with, practise without a time limit and in an informal relaxed situation. Refer to the answers and explanations as often as you like and take the time to check the precise meanings of words about which you are unsure. Later you may prefer to practise under the constraint of time. When you are ready, allow yourself 1 minute 30 seconds per question. If you wish to construct a full-length practice test then select 26 questions starting with one of the situations and allow yourself 30 minutes in which to complete them. The chapter concludes with four timed mini-tests.

Synonyms, antonyms, expanded or contracted terms and terms that are similar

One of the skills tested in the UKCAT decision analysis sub-test involves the identification of synonyms and antonyms and words that are related in some way. Use the following 20 questions to become confident in this important ability. Identify which of the suggested answers is correct and enter it in the answer box.

Q1.   Turn around the word humble

    A. Modest
    B. Ordinary
    C. Belittle
    D. Self-important
    E. Unpretentious

Answer ☐

Q2.   Enlarge deepen

    A. Lessen
    B. Dig
    C. Excavate
    D. Hollow

Answer ☐

Q3.   Decrease poisonous

    A. Venomous
    B. Corrupting
    C. Fatal
    D. Cleansing

Answer ☐

Q4.   Find the equivalent to social

    A. Friendly
    B. Personal
    C. Cool
    D. Private

Answer ☐

Q5.   Find the term least similar to block

    A. Lump
    B. Fool
    C. Obstruction
    D. Building

Answer ☐

Q6.   Turn around request

    A.   Demand
    B.   Appeal
    C.   Offer
    D.   Seek

Answer ☐

Q7.   Decrease unsurpassed

    A.   Best
    B.   Worst
    C.   Very good
    D.   Even better

Answer ☐

Q8.   Past of copy

    A.   Scanned
    B.   Fake
    C.   Forgery
    D.   Reproduction

Answer ☐

Q9.   Find the word that is not the equivalent to necessity

    A.   Requirement
    B.   Superfluous
    C.   Obligation
    D.   Essential

Answer ☐

Q10. Find the term least similar to display

    A. Show
    B. Reveal
    C. Extend
    D. Mask

Answer [   ]

Q11. Find the term corresponding to enigma

    A. Paradox
    B. Axiom
    C. Platitude
    D. Message

Answer [   ]

Q12. Find the contradictory of resemble

    A. Like
    B. Like chalk and cheese
    C. Comparable
    D. Kindred

Answer [   ]

Q13. Extend carve

    A. Cut
    B. Etch
    C. Chop
    D. Engrave

Answer [   ]

Q14. Find the term most akin to margin

    A. Perimeter
    B. Small
    C. Middle
    D. Major

Answer ☐

Q15. Shrink slap

    A. Whack
    B. Knock
    C. Punch
    D. Stroke

Answer ☐

Q16. Find the term analogous to assort

    A. Mixed
    B. Group
    C. Miscellaneous
    D. Sundry

Answer ☐

Q17. Make bigger peel

    A. Thunder
    B. Boom
    C. Unwrap
    D. Dissect

Answer ☐

Q18. Diminish unwise

    A. Sensible
    B. Shrewd
    C. Ill-advised
    D. Imprudent

Answer ☐

Q19. Find the converse of might

    A. May
    B. Weakness
    C. Strength
    D. Force

Answer ☐

Q20. Find the term most analogous to thing

    A. Slender
    B. Belongings
    C. Article
    D. Journal

Answer ☐

Sixty warm up decision analysis questions

Read each situation and answer the 15 questions that follow it, deciding which in your opinion is the best suggested answer or answers. Note that the first 10 examples have one best answer and the last 5 more than one best answer. Be sure to consider that your answer both applies the code sequence correctly and is consistent with the situation.

Situation 1

The official inflation rate is announced annually and determines monetary policy. Investors try to anticipate the rate and for this reason the government statisticians codify their internal communications. The rate is derived from monitoring the prices of a basket of goods and services sold. Each year items are deleted or new items added depending on consumer trends and these changes are especially confidential because the inclusion of items that traditionally suffer inflation will inflate the official rate while the inclusion of deflationary items will deflate the official rate. A criminal investor has intercepted the following communications between statisticians working on the calculation of the official rate. Use your judgement to identify which of the suggested answers best explains the meaning of the coded messages.

Codes

Modifiers

321. Parallel
322. Append
323. Reverse

324. Lessen
325. Akin

Features and instructions

601. Elevated
602. Temperate
603. Tiny
604. Popular
605. Unfashionable

606. Add
607. Delete
608. Inflation
609. Deflation

Lexis

930. Service
931. Commodity
932. Wide screen TV
933. Milk
934. Cigarettes
935. Banking
936. Landscaped gardening

937. Pasta
938. Mobile phone contract
939. Refrigerator
940. Wooden flooring
941. Gasoline
942. Soft furnishings
943. The basket of goods and services

The first 10 questions have only one correct answer.

Q1.   323 607, 940

    A.   Delete wooden flooring.
    B.   Add wooden flooring.
    C.   Should we add or delete wooden flooring?
    D.   Reverse the decision to delete wooden flooring.

Answer ☐

Q2.   606 937, 934 321 607

    A.   Delete cigarettes and add pasta.
    B.   Add cigarettes and delete pasta.
    C.   Add pasta and delete cigarettes.
    D.   Remove cigarettes and add pasta.

                                                    Answer

Q3.   941, 325 606, 321 943

    A.   Gasoline is on the list.
    B.   Add gasoline to the inventory.
    C.   Put gasoline in the basket of goods and services.
    D.   Put gasoline in the basket.

                                                    Answer

Q4.   322 604, 321 601, 937

    A.   Fashionable pasta is all the rage.
    B.   Promote pasta; it has become all the rage.
    C.   Pasta has become very popular.
    D.   Popular, eminent, pasta.

                                                    Answer

Q5.   323 931, 938, 936

    A.   Landscape gardening and mobile phone contracts are services.
    B.   Remove from the basket of goods and services landscape gardening and mobile phone contracts.
    C.   Mobile phone contracts and landscape gardening are not commodities.
    D.   Mobile phone contracts and landscape gardening are not goods.

                                                    Answer

Q6.   935, 322 930, 325 602, 608

    A.   Banking facilities are experiencing soaring inflation.
    B.   Pleasant inflation is occurring in banking provision.
    C.   Inflation is rising in the banking sector.
    D.   Banking services are experiencing moderate inflation.

Answer [   ]

Q7.   933, 325 606, 608, 321 324

    A.   The inclusion of milk will cut inflation.
    B.   Remove milk and you will add to inflation.
    C.   Decrease inflation by cutting out milk.
    D.   Increase inflation by promoting milk.

Answer [   ]

Q8.   605, 938, 937, 323

    A.   Reverse the decision not to include mobile phone contracts and pasta.
    B.   Pasta and mobile phone contracts are popular.
    C.   Mobile phone contracts and pasta are out of favour.
    D.   Pasta and mobile phone contracts are out of date.

Answer [   ]

Q9.   323 607, 324 932, 322 605

    A.   Add TVs because they are hated.
    B.   Small screen TVs are very unpopular but don't delete them.
    C.   Add TVs; they are very unfashionable.
    D.   Add small screen TVs; they are very unpopular.

Answer [   ]

Q10. 942, 324 607, 604, 321 601, 608

    A. Soft furnishings are popular but they experience high inflation.

    B. Soft furnishings are very popular but consider deleting them as they suffer very high inflation.

    C. Think about deleting soft furnishings; while popular, they have high inflation.

    D. Don't delete soft furnishings; though they experience inflation they remain very popular.

Answer ☐

The next five questions have more than one correct answer. Enter your choice of correct answers in the answer box.

Q11. 321, 606, 941

    A. Include gasoline.

    B. Put petrol on the list.

    C. Put gasoline on the list.

    D. Add petrol.

    E. Add gasoline.

Answer ☐

Q12. 942, 607, 939

    A. Delete soft furnishings and refrigerator.

    B. Delete both soft furnishings and refrigerator.

    C. Delete refrigerator or soft furnishings.

    D. Delete soft furnishings not refrigerator.

    E. Delete refrigerator not soft furnishings.

Answer ☐

Q13. 321 607, 322 935

    A. Remove banking and all other similar services.

    B. Erase all financial services.

    C. Cut out banking and financial services.

    D. Eliminate banking and its related services.

    E. Cancel everything involved with the entry banking.

Answer ☐

Q14. 607, 941, 321 602, 604, 606, 934

    A. Add gasoline as it has become moderately popular and delete cigarettes.

    B. Delete cigarettes and add gasoline as it is quite popular.

    C. Add gasoline because it is reasonably popular but delete cigarettes.

    D. Delete moderate strength cigarettes and add popular gasoline.

    E. Delete gasoline even though mildly popular and add cigarettes.

Answer ☐

Q15. 325 933, 943, 606, 323 603

    A. Add butter to the basket of goods and services.

    B. Sales of white paint are vast so add it to the basket of goods and services.

    C. Sales of yogurt are minute but still add it to the basket of goods and services.

    D. Trade in dairy products is immense so add them to the basket of goods and services.

    E. Cows are big so why are they not in the basket of goods and services?

Answer ☐

Situation 2

Gasoline and diesel generate large amounts of the pollutant carbon-dioxide and the race is on to find green bio-fuel alternatives that do not require large-scale investment in new infrastructure. The returns on this research could be enormous because it would allow a whole-scale switch from polluting crude oil to green bio-fuels. Petro-corporations jealously guard the findings of this research but some environmental activists hacked into one of the corporations' network and posted the following encrypted messages on the internet in the hope that someone would be able to decipher them. Some mathematicians from Bangalore have proposed the following matrix – use it to identify in your judgement the best interpretation of the messages.

Codes

Language

101. Vegetable	108. Alternative
102. Oil	109. Investment
103. Octane	110. Bio
104. Alcohol	111. Fuel
105. Ethanol	112. Tell
106. Gasoline	113. Know
107. Diesel	

Transformers

311. Equivalent	314. Decrease
312. Enlarge	315. Similar
313. Turn around	316. Join

Features and values

521. New	524. Green
522. High	525. Gain
523. Few	526. More

Possibilities

731. Can	733. May
732. Could	734. Contradiction

Q16.   101, 102, 107, 108, 524

A. Vegetable oil is a green alternative to diesel.

B. Vegetable oil is an alternative to green diesel.

C. Vegetable oil is a green form of diesel.

D. The alternative to diesel is vegetable oil.

Answer [   ]

Q17.   103, 104, 106, 521, 522

A. The new green fuel is high-octane alcohol.

B. Interest in high-octane alcohol has long surpassed gasoline and reached a new high.

C. High-octane alcohol is the new gasoline.

D. It's high time industry switched from gasoline to high-octane alcohol.

Answer [   ]

Q18. 525, 313 734, 733

    A. They may deny it but try to gain permission.
    B. You may gain agreement.
    C. This may mean we gain some opposition.
    D. Gain their trust and you may just beat the challenge.

Answer ☐

Q19. 107, 524, 312 108, 315 521, 526

    A. Today we have greener choices than just diesel.
    B. This innovative alternative to diesel is more green.
    C. There are innovative green alternatives to diesel.
    D. Recent alternatives to diesel are more green.

Answer ☐

Q20. 109, 521, 110, 315 113, 111

    A. No new investment in bio-fuel is needed.
    B. He knows that new investment in bio-fuel is high risk.
    C. I know someone who might invest in a new bio-fuel.
    D. Investment in new bio-fuels is now risky.

Answer ☐

Q21. 107, 102, 101, 108, 312 521

    A. The most recent alternative to oil is made from vegetables.
    B. Diesel and vegetable oil are not new and not alternatives.
    C. Vegetable oil is the latest alternative to diesel.
    D. Diesel oil is the hottest alternative to vegetable oil.

Answer ☐

Q22. 112, 313 732

    A. We couldn't tell the difference from the results.
    B. This might possibly tell between the options.
    C. The test ought to tell them apart.
    D. Tell the project manager that we can do it.

Answer ☐

Q23. 524, 313 733, 105

    A. Maybe ethanol is not all that green.
    B. Might it be the case that ethanol is not all that green?
    C. Ethanol may not be all that green.
    D. Ethanol may well be the greenest of them all.

Answer ☐

Q24. 312 108, 312 526, 109, 526

    A. Additional alternatives require more investment.
    B. Most alternatives need more investment.
    C. More investment is required if alternatives are to be found.
    D. Extra investment in alternatives is needed most.

Answer ☐

Q25. 525, 315 522, 313 731, 112, 521, 102

    A. The price will soar so gain as much new oil as you can.
    B. Gain as high a price as possible for the new oil product.
    C. You could sell the new oil product but better to wait for the forecast price gains.
    D. We can't tell if oil will gain new highs.

Answer ☐

The following five questions have more than one correct answer. Enter the corresponding letter of each correct answer in the answer box.

Q26. 524, 108, 105, 107

    A. Ethanol is green and an ecological alternative to diesel.
    B. As an alternative to diesel ethanol is rated as on the whole green.
    C. Ethanol is green in colour and in environmental terms a better alternative to diesel.
    D. Diesel is green and an ecological alternative to ethanol.
    E. Ethanol is a green alternative to gasoline not diesel.

Answer ☐

Q27. 315 734, 315 109, 110, 111

    A. The take-up of bio-fuel by the big consumer nations has been inconsistent.
    B. Disagreement exists over how good a venture bio-fuel represents.
    C. There is conflicting evidence as to how safe a speculation bio-fuel is.
    D. The production of this bio-fuel is far less capital intensive.

Answer ☐

Q28. 315 523, 105, 109, 108

    A. The minority think ethanol a good alternative investment.
    B. As an alternative investment hardly any think ethanol a good choice.
    C. Only a small amount of investment is required in the alternative ethanol.
    D. As the best investment in the alternative market ethanol is backed by many.

Answer ☐

Q29. 313 525, 107, 111, 106, 313 521

    A. Supplies of gasoline and diesel will dwindle as deliveries of substitute fuel increase.
    B. Production of bio-fuel will increase as production of gasoline and diesel falls.
    C. The decline in traditional gasoline and diesel markets will be sudden and novel.
    D. Sales of all conventional fuel like diesel and gasoline will decrease.

Answer ☐

Q30. 105, 106, 111, 103, 522

    A. Ordinary fuel when blended with ethanol makes it high-octane.
    B. An ethanol and gasoline mix is a high-octane fuel.
    C. Cars can run on a high-octane ethanol gasoline mix.
    D. Gasoline and ethanol are both classed as high-octane fuel.

Answer ☐

Situation 3

The consequences that follow from the theft of valuable data cannot be over-estimated. Most people perceive the threat to be an external one, and we are all aware of the threat posed by, for example, viruses, worms and spyware unintentionally downloaded from the internet. But the threat is just as likely to come from within an organization. A malicious employee is perfectly placed to know what information is the most valuable and to steal it. If that information includes details of bank accounts and personal information then criminal gangs are willing to pay large sums of money for it. You work in the security department of a large corporation and must decode the following messages, which all refer to an employee stealing the personal details of a large number of his colleagues, before a departmental meeting to review the progress in uncovering the identity of the thief. The risk is very serious as all but the most secure of the organization's networks are known to be compromised. The letter S is used to signify the thief.

Codes

Modifiers

201. Past	204. Reverse
202. Similar to	205. Contract
203. Same as	206. Expand

Vocabulary

310. He or S	321. Prefers
311. We	322. High
312. Know	323. Seems
313. Online	324. Looks
314. Try	325. Proves
315. Steal	326. No
316. Information	327. Only
317. Staff	328. If
318. Believe	329. Works
319. All	330. Week
320. Ready	

Select *one* of the following answers as in your judgement the best interpretation of the sequence of code.

Q31. 310, 311, 312, 329

    A. We know he works for a competitor.
    B. We know he works in one of our US offices.
    C. S works online and knows his way around our systems.
    D. He knows a lot about how our organization works.

Answer ☐

Q32. 316, 206 314, 310, 313

    A. S never tries to take information before 10 am.
    B. The information he takes is always decrypted before it is copied.
    C. We believe he simply e-mails the information to an outside contact.
    D. Look he is online now trying to access information.

Answer ☐

Q33. 310, 202 316, 321, 322

    A. Somewhere in all this data are the clues to stop this man and this has to be our high priority.
    B. The inside story is that he prefers to damage the corporation's reputation than to sell the details to the highest bidder.
    C. He prefers the details of high earners.
    D. The data S holds will fetch a high price and kill this small business when it falls into the wrong hands.

Answer ☐

Q34. 329, 310, 323, 204 330

    A. It seems S works at the weekend.
    B. Some days he works later than others.
    C. Weekly he seems to work from one particular terminal.
    D. My hunch is that he works as a casual on an hourly contract.

Answer ☐

Q35. 204 310, 312, 310, 311

    A. We know that he may in fact be a she.
    B. We know he is not a she.
    C. We know S uses the contact name 'revenge'.
    D. For all we know he may have accomplices.

Answer ☐

Q36. 311, 204 318, 206 312, 310

    A. We think we will recognize him when we meet him.
    B. I doubt if he knows we are so close.
    C. S must be on very familiar terms with our security systems.
    D. I don't think he realizes that it's worthless and no one will want to buy it.

Answer ☐

Q37. 311, 203 320, 313, 310

    A. If news goes online that all this personal detail has been stolen we can expect a lot of negative publicity.
    B. We are online and standing by.
    C. We are all set for when he next goes online.
    D. Until S is caught nothing online is safe and we have one major security headache.

Answer ☐

Q38. 201 202 317, 324, 310

    A. S looks to target employers with over 1,000 employees.
    B. It looks as if S must be a disgruntled ex-employee.
    C. S looks for the records of personnel who have left the organization too.
    D. S must have once worked for the organization and it looks as if he left on very bad terms.

Answer ☐

Q39. 317, 202 326, 316, 206 320, 310, 318, 311

    A. We believe S already has information on over 1,000 staff.

    B. He believes we do not have enough information or staff to catch him.

    C. No, we don't believe he will stop until he has a lot more information.

    D. The personal information of no member of staff is safe until we have caught this individual.

Answer ☐

Q40. 205 319, 327, 312, 317

    A. Not only staff networks but every single one of our networks is compromised so for all we know he is reading this.

    B. The entire staff must know the risk of financial loss they face from fraud.

    C. Not only does he hold the staff details but he knows how to decipher them too.

    D. Only a few staff know the scale of the problem.

Answer ☐

The following questions have more than one correct answer.

Q41. 310, 325, 329

    A. This proves he operates from the eastern seaboard.

    B. S works from a US office and this proves it again.

    C. That proves he works alone.

    D. He works late many evenings but never when the New York Giants are playing.

Answer ☐

Q42. 311, 326, 202 310

    A. They are sure we will get our man in the end.

    B. She thinks we must wait until he makes a mistake.

    C. He's so careful not to give away his identity.

    D. We are nowhere near catching him.

Answer ☐

Q43.   329, 311, 312, 328, 310

    A.   If it works we will know who he is.
    B.   It will be a major breakthrough and we will know if he works for us or a
        competitor.
    C.   We will know which office S works from if this is opened.
    D.   If this is accessed we will have established his workstation.

                Answer [   ]

Q44.   310, 311, 312

    A.   We know nothing about S.
    B.   We know he is out to destroy us.
    C.   We know he is very careful.
    D.   He may very well know that we are on to him.

                Answer [   ]

Q45.   205 311, 203 318, 325, 206 326

    A.   I expect it proves nothing.
    B.   I think it proves that none of the current theories are correct.
    C.   In my best judgement it proves we have our man.
    D.   I trust no one until they prove themselves.

                Answer [   ]

Situation 4

A courageous group of citizens at great personal risk formed a secret order, the aim of which is to campaign by peaceful means for reform of the great divide between the rich and poor in their society. They champion the poor and the disenfranchised and highlight the inadequate public infrastructure such as the bad schools to which the poor must send their children and the polluting industries in which they work. They argued for the introduction of welfare programmes and the modernization of industry. They propose the redistribution of wealth by taxing the rich and thus raising the funds needed to fund their reforms. Most of their members are imprisoned and continue their work using coded messages passed to the outside world by sympathetic prison staff. You work for an international human rights group which decodes their messages and publishes them on the internet. Use the matrix to identify in your judgement the best interpretations of the code sequences.

Codes

Converters

81. Equivalent	84. Decrease
82. Enlarge	85. Similar
83. Turn around	

Key terms

221. Wrong	229. Public
222. Reform	230. Better
223. Industry	231. Must
224. Children	232. Pollution
225. Rich	233. Education
226. High	234. Vote
227. Result	235. Accept
228. Poverty	236. Merit

Select only one best answer to the next 10 questions.

Q46. 234, 231, 83 225, 83 221

    A. The poor must never be given the right to vote.
    B. The rich must give the poor the right to vote.
    C. The poor must struggle for the right to vote.
    D. How can it be right that the poor cannot vote?

Answer ☐

Q47. 81 236, 224, 230, 233

    A. Our children deserve a better education.
    B. The children of the disadvantaged crave to be educated.
    C. All children irrespective of their background value a good education.
    D. Education should only be for the children of the better off.

Answer ☐

Q48. 231, 226, 235, 225

    A. There is no reason why the rich must accept such high levels of taxation.

    B. We must accept that the rich will not accept our proposals.

    C. The rich must be forced to accept our proposal for high taxation.

    D. We must convince the rich to accept that high taxation is in their interest too.

Answer ☐

Q49. 223, 231, 232, 85 222, 85 83 226

    A. Pollution is the unavoidable consequence of the drive for greater productivity in industry.

    B. Pollution must be stopped through the transformation of industry.

    C. Industry must be modernized to lower pollution.

    D. Dirty industries must be closed to counter pollution.

Answer ☐

Q50. 221, 85 228, 229, 85 225

    A. Wealth alongside public squalor is wrong.

    B. Public displays of affluence are wrong when there are shortages.

    C. It is naive to say that public affluence is wrong when there is squalor.

    D. If I were poor I would feel wronged by public displays of wealth.

Answer ☐

Q51. 82 222, 84 230, 231

    A. Revolution would be OK but it must be peaceful.

    B. Change by any reasonable means is acceptable.

    C. Change by any means possible must be more tolerable to the status quo.

    D. Civil disobedience as a means to an end must be all right.

Answer ☐

Q52. 228, 232, 83 227

    A. Pollution is the foundation of poverty.

    B. Inequality is the cause of poverty and pollution.

    C. Poverty is the basis of pollution.

    D. Poverty and pollution are unconnected.

Answer

Q53. 233, 224, 83 221, 85 230

    A. It is mistaken to believe that all children benefit from education.

    B. A good education is the right of every child.

    C. A good education for a few gifted children is superior to a poor schooling for every child.

    D. All children have a right to a good education.

Answer

Q54. 225, 232, 81 230, 85 83 226

    A. The rich suffer from the effects of high pollution as well.

    B. Improve pollution and the rich benefit too.

    C. Lower pollution is healthier for the rich too.

    D. The rich are worse placed to avoid the consequences of pollution.

Answer

Q55. 225, 83 225, 231, 230

    A. Rich and poor must work for the better.

    B. For the better of society the rich must stay rich.

    C. We can only achieve our goals if the rich and the poor work much better together.

    D. The rich must always be regarded as better than the poor.

Answer

The next five question have more than one 'best' answer.

Q56. 85 231, 228, 235

    A. We should accept the necessity of poverty.

    B. We ought not to accept that people have to live in poverty.

    C. In such a rich country we are not obliged to accept that people must live in poverty.

    D. It is a fact that poverty can be abolished and we should work to achieve it.

    Answer ☐

Q57. 224, 221, 233, 83 225

    A. It's wrong that some children receive a poor education.

    B. It's wrong that underprivileged children receive a poor education.

    C. Deprived children should at least receive a good education.

    D. It's wrong that poor children are deprived of a good education.

    Answer ☐

Q58. 226, 85 229, 222

    A. Unrestricted taxation is necessary if we are to reform our community.

    B. The planned reform of the civic sphere necessitates high taxation.

    C. High taxation is needed if we are to reform our community.

    D. The reform of the system of taxation will fund the proposed welfare programmes.

    Answer ☐

Q59. 81 236, 222, 223

    A. Many plus points will result from the reform of industry.

    B. The reform of industry will bring many advantages.

    C. Industry badly needs reform and it will bring great value.

    D. There is great worth in the wish to reform industry.

    Answer ☐

Q60. 222, 223, 235, 232, 85 234

    A. Mark your ballot for reform and stop pollution from industry.

    B. The choice is reform industry or accept pollution.

    C. Accept only change vote for the reform of industry and the abolition of pollution.

    D. Don't accept pollution and reform industry by putting your cross on the ballot paper.

Answer ☐

Four decision analysis mini-tests

Working quickly is especially important in the decision analysis sub-test. We can all get most of these questions right if we take lots of time over them but in the real test you are pressed for time and may well be suffering from some anxiety. Be sure to practise decoding the question quickly and correctly and making a fast, accurate decision. That way you will correctly complete more questions in the time allowed and consequently achieve a higher score.

The remaining 20 questions of this chapter are organized as four mini-tests. Each contains five multiple-choice decision analysis questions and you are allowed five minutes in which to attempt all five. As you can expect to happen in the real UKCAT, the first question is of average difficulty and they become progressively harder. Use these questions to be sure of the very best start in your real UKCAT decision analysis paper. You are told in every instance when you are required to identify more than one best answer. If there is no instruction to identify more than one best answer, identify one of the suggested answers as best.

Put away the dictionary and thesaurus and treat these mini-tests like a real test. Get the most out of this practice by setting yourself the personal challenge of trying to beat or, if you get all five right, match your last score each time you take a mini-test. That way you will create a realistic, real-test feel. You will need to try very hard and take the challenge seriously if you are to really succeed in beating your previous best score or getting five out of five every time. Time management will be critical, so be sure to stick to the four-minute time limit and not spend too long on any one question, and practise making one careful, detailed read of the passage to save on time going back to check detail. Keep practising until you consistently get all five questions right. Achieve this and you can take strength from the fact that you are likely to make a very good start in your real UKCAT decision analysis paper. The only thing then left to do is to keep up that rate of success through to the end of the real test!

Mini-test 1

Situation

Philately attracts both collectors and investors and has performed well, beating the return on most of the rest of the economy. Some of the best returns have been realized on examples of otherwise everyday stamps that carry even very small differences. Investors dominate this part of the market and compete fiercely to acquire examples of some of the world's most rare and valuable stamps. The market makers are constantly alert to the infrequent occasions when examples come up for sale.

You work for a leading dealer and are preparing for the auction of a unique British stamp dating from the 1920s on which the king's head appears upside down. You must decide which of the suggested answers are, in your best judgement, the correct interpretation of the following five sequences of code.

Note: unless otherwise stated, each question has only one best answer.

Codes

Modifiers

99. Expand	101. Reverse
100. Reduce	102. Similar to

Terms

222. Makes	231. Smith
223. Unique	232. Million
224. Buy	233. Stamp
225. Small	234. Sold
226. Feature	235. Jones
227. Price	236. Investment
228. Twenty	237. Any
229. Cheap at	238. Bid
230. Collectors	239. Years

Q1. 224, 237, 102 227

    A. It is worth any price.
    B. Buy at any cost.
    C. Buy no matter the consequences.
    D. Buy any of them no matter the outlay.

Answer ☐

Q2. 232, 228, 231, 238

    A. Smith will bid to 20 million.
    B. We already have an offer of 20 million from Smith.
    C. Expect the bids to go way beyond 20 million.
    D. Smith bid 20 million.

Answer ☐

Q3. 102 224, 236, 233. Identify more than one of the suggested answers as 'best'.

    A. An investor will most likely buy the stamp.
    B. The stamp will be acquired for a collection.
    C. The stamp will be bought as an investment.
    D. He plans to purchase the stamp as an investment.

Answer ☐

Q4. 228, 239, 99 232, 234, 233

    A. Twenty years ago an identical stamp sold for millions.
    B. Countless collectors would give 20 years of their life to own such a stamp.
    C. Twenty millions are too much for a stamp so it will not be sold for years.
    D. This stamp is the most exciting thing for 20 years and will be sold for millions.

Answer ☐

Q5. 226, 233, 229, 223, 101 102 225, 227

    A. The unique upside-down head is an eye-catching feature and makes this stamp worth every cent of its anticipated high price.
    B. The unique feature of the stamp is striking and makes it cheap at any price.
    C. This stamp is titanic and its unique feature makes it cheap at the price.
    D. The unique, conspicuous feature of this stamp makes it cheap whatever the price.

Answer ☐

End of test

Mini-test 2

Situation
Home-completed assignments contribute between 20 and 60 per cent of the marks to many national examinations. Most students believe such assignments are a fairer method of assessment compared with 'all or nothing' exams. Many educationalists are opposed to home-completed assignments because they are so difficult to invigilate. A confidential survey found that cheating was widespread and that the situation had become much worse due to plagiarizing from the internet. Use the matrix to identify the best interpretations of the findings and conclusions of the survey.

Codes

Transformers

01. Like	03. Inflate
02. Nothing like	04. Trim down

Dictionary

101. Help	110. Model
102. Easy	111. Siblings
103. Admit	112. All
104. Children	113. Do
105. Cheat	114. Offer
106. Grade	115. Students
107. Websites	116. Increase
108. Parents	117. Big
109. Assignments	

Q1. 103, 104, 108, 109. Note: more than one of the suggested answers is 'best'.

A. Parents admit to doing assignments for their children.
B. Assignments are often completed by the parents and not the children.
C. Children admit that parents sometimes do the assignments for them.
D. Children admit that their parents help with the assignments.

Answer ☐

Q2. 02 117, 107, 110, 114

    A. For a fee websites offer full-length model essays.
    B. For a small fee websites offer model answers to assignments.
    C. Perfect 'A Star' grade assignments can be bought off the internet.
    D. Examples of faultless assignments can be bought for a modest fee from a whole host of websites.

Answer ☐

Q3. 115, 01 103, 102, 105

    A. Students declare that it does not matter if it is easy to cheat because no one does.
    B. Students who cheat are encouraged to come clean and admit what they have done.
    C. Students like to say that they cheat but most do not because they are too afraid of the consequences if they are caught.
    D. Students confess that it is all too easy to cheat.

Answer ☐

Q4. 02 115, 115, 101

    A. Students complain that teachers help them too much.
    B. Some learners receive so much help that it is not possible to say that the work is entirely theirs.
    C. Teachers have been caught giving students too much help.
    D. In some cases it is not entirely their own work because learners have received too much help.

Answer ☐

Q5. 111, 101, 106, 108, 01 116

    A. Inappropriate help from parents and siblings has led to grade inflation.
    B. Parents and siblings have helped boost the grade awarded.
    C. Parents and siblings help students get a higher grade than they otherwise would.
    D. Cases of enlarged grades have resulted from the help provided by parents and siblings.

Answer ☐

End of test

Mini-test 3

Situation

To make his lazy relatives work for their inheritance an agoraphobic and severely moral billionaire buried a horde of precious jewels and metals in a secret location. He confided in no one and left the following coded clues and a set of street maps of most of the world's capital cities as directions to the treasure. The family have been looking ever since and have assembled the following suggested answers to the encoded clues. Use your best judgement to decide which of the suggested answers is the most likely best interpretation.

Codes

Modifiers

55. Join
56. Similar to
57. Turn around

58. Equivalent to
59. Type of

Lexis

30. Circle
29. Wood
28. Stop
27. Treasure
26. Fish
25. Cow
24. Me
23. Look
22. Flat

21. Card game
20. Mountain
19. City
18. Broken
17. Dig
16. Rock
15. Three
14. Under
13. Primitive plant

Q1. 27, 55 29 16, 56 24

    A.   I buried the treasure in a rocky outcrop above the tree line.

    B.   You'll find the treasure in a wooden box covered with rock.

    C.   The treasure is in an abandoned coal mine.

    D.   Dig for my treasure where the rocks stand as tall as trees.

Answer ☐

Q2.   28, 15, 59 21

    A.   Stop at the town with three casinos.
    B.   Stop by the three men playing a game of cards.
    C.   Play three hands of poker and then stop.
    D.   Stop by the bridge with three spans.

Answer ☐

Q3.   16, 23, 58 22. Note that more than one of the suggested answers should be judged as best.

    A.   From the top of the jagged rock look west.
    B.   Look for a place where the rock is smooth.
    C.   Find the flat rock and look carefully.
    D.   Look in the apartment for a piece of rock.

Answer ☐

Q4.   56 29, 56 30, 58 18 16

    A.   You will find it in the wooden hold of the sunken wreck on the reef.
    B.   Lift the planks and find the ring of stones.
    C.   You will find it in the tree that has grown around the rock.
    D.   Find the old pump in the timber yard and slowly move the handle up and down.

Answer ☐

Q5.   57 20, 55 13 25, 19

    A.   Take a plane to Moscow.
    B.   You can see the city from the hill top.
    C.   It's a frighteningly steep valley where dense rainforest covers the ancient city.
    D.   It was placed in the ground near a flat patch where the animals graze.

Answer ☐

End of test

Mini-test 4

Situation

The secret of the ultimate paper plane made from a single sheet of A4 paper and not involving any cuts or the addition of anything such as sticky tape, glue or weights is a closely guarded secret. The indoor world flight record for such a plane when launched at a height of 2 metres is in excess of 20 seconds over a distance of 60 metres. The keys to the ultimate design are a snub nose and delta wings. To discover more of the secrets to how to build a record-beating paper plane of your own, decipher the following codes and identify the suggested answer that represents the best interpretation of them.

Codes

Transformers

999. Akin to   997. Equivalent of
998. Expand

Vocabulary

100. Tape   91. Nose
99. Increase   90. Folds
98. Design   89. Slant
97. Stable   88. Choice
96. Minimize   87. Wing or wings
95. Important   86. Lift
94. Flight   85. Construct
93. Drag   84. Strength
92. Upwards

Q1. 94, 91, 97

    A. A pointed nose is superior to a blunt one because it ensures more stable flight.
    B. A blunt nose ensures a more stable flight than a sharp one.
    C. A pointed nose ensures the flight is more stable than a snub one.
    D. A blunt nose is better than a pointed one because it ensures more stable flight.

Answer [ ]

Q2. 98, 85, 999 88. Note that more than one of the suggested answers are 'best'.

A. The best designs are uncomplicated to construct.
B. Choose a design that is straightforward to construct.
C. Design a plane that is easy to construct.
D. Select a delta wing design that is simple to construct.

Answer [ ]

Q3. 90, 100, 84, 96, 93

A. Folds are used to give strength and if you tape over them you minimize drag.
B. Maximize the strength of your design by using folds and tape to impart strength and minimize drag.
C. Minimize drag and use folds but not tape to impart strength.
D. While folds give strength minimize the number so as to reduce drag.

Answer [ ]

Q4. 999 89, 86, 99, 87, 92. Note that more than one answer is the 'best'.

A. Incline the wings upwards to increase lift.
B. Increase the wing size to produce more upwards lift.
C. Lift the wings upwards to increase the camber.
D. Adjust the wing to increase the lift.

Answer [ ]

Q5. 998 95, 98, 87, 91

A. Fundamental to the design is the choice of the nose and wing.
B. The design of the nose and wings is vital.
C. Significant features of the design are the nose and wings.
D. The wings are more central to the design than the nose.

Answer [ ]

End of test

Quantitative reasoning

Objectives

At the end of this chapter you will be able to answer questions of the type used in the UKCAT quantitative reasoning sub-test principally on the following subjects:

A. Addition, subtraction, multiplication and division
B. Proportion and ratios, including conversions
C. Powers and roots
D. Statistics, including mean, median, mode and range of both grouped and non-grouped data
E. Fractions, decimals and percentages
F. Formulae and equations

The intention of this chapter is to give you skills necessary to maximize your score by practising the type of questions you will meet in the quantitative reasoning sub-test.

The test

The test consists of 40 multiple-choice questions divided up into 10 blocks of 4 questions for which you will have 21 minutes, ie 2 minutes per block, or 30 seconds per question. As there are no penalties for incorrect answers, you have nothing to lose by guessing answers if you are short of time towards the end.

Format

Each block of questions starts with a brief description of the scenario and then some information, often in the form of a table. There are then four multiple-choice questions with five possible answers, A, B, C, D, E, of which only one is correct. This is the format used here for the examples.

The test is described by Pearson VUE as being more about testing your problem-solving ability than your numerical faculty. It is the intention of this chapter to develop not only your problem-solving ability, but also your numerical ability. Time is of the essence! The more familiar you are with number and mathematical concepts the quicker you will be in all numerical questions.

The questions in this chapter start easily and rapidly become more difficult at a level equivalent to an A level standard, not simply the 'good GCSE' as described by Pearson. You are aiming to get into a competitive field in a numerical subject; you need this ability with numbers.

There are a total of 152 questions, including some which are in the form of timed mini sub-tests. Good luck.

Questions 1 to 4 concern the population of a certain town which can be divided into the following age groups:

Age group	Population
0–4	6,450
5–9	7,600
10–14	8,450
15–19	7,400
20–24	5,550
25–29	6,150
30–34	8,100
35–39	8,750
40–44	8,450
45–49	8,400
50–54	10,150
55–59	9,600
60–64	7,950
65–69	7,450
70–74	7,100
75–79	6,450
80–84	4,500
85–89	2,750

1.   How many people are younger than 20?

    A. 5,550
    B. 7,400
    C. 29,000
    D. 29,900
    E. 30,000

Answer ☐

2.   If the total population is 131,250, approximately what percentage are under 25?

    A. 10%
    B. 15%
    C. 20%
    D. 25%
    E. 30%

Answer ☐

3.   If everyone retires at 65, what fraction of the population is within 10 years of retirement?

    A. 1/4
    B. 1/5
    C. 1/7
    D. 1/10
    E. 1/20

Answer ☐

4.   What is the ratio of schoolchildren (5–19) to retired people (65+)?

    A. 4 : 5
    B. 4 : 3
    C. 1 : 1
    D. 2 : 1
    E. 1 : 2

Answer ☐

Questions 5 to 8 concern the television viewing of children in a town in the east of the country and a town in the west:

East		West	
Child	Minutes	Child	Minutes
A	95	K	145
B	78	L	70
C	91	M	102
D	87	N	121
E	65	O	109
F	71	P	89
G	92	Q	96
H	69	R	113
I	82	S	121
J	80	T	98

5. What is the average viewing time for a child in the east?

    A. 82.3
    B. 91.0
    C. 79.9
    D. 81.5
    E. 81.0

    Answer ☐

6. What is the median viewing time for a child in the east?

    A. 80
    B. 81
    C. 82
    D. 80.4
    E. 81.7

    Answer ☐

7.   How does the range of the viewing times for the west compare with the east?

A. The mode is greater.
B. The median is greater.
C. It is smaller.
D. It is twice as big.
E. It is two and a half times greater.

Answer ☐

8.   What is the mode of the viewing times in the west?

A. 75
B. 106.4
C. 121
D. 105.5
E. 145

Answer ☐

Questions 9 to 12 concern the cost of calling abroad. A student has two possible phone companies' cards she can use to call her home country:

	Green		Black	
	£10 card	£20 card	£10 card	£20 card
Connection cost (p)	10	10	8	6
Cost per minute (p)	0.4	0.35	0.5	0.4

9.   If she intends to call home 10 minutes every day for a month (30 days), which card would be the cheapest?

A. Green £10
B. Green £20
C. Black £10
D. Black £20
E. Black £20 or Green £20, the same price

Answer ☐

10.   If she chooses the Black £10 card, but it is only valid for a month, what percentage of the cost will she have wasted, to the nearest 5%?

   A.   40%
   B.   60%
   C.   45%
   D.   55%
   E.   50%

Answer ☐

11.   She recorded her phone calls for a year in the table below. What was the average length of call in minutes?

Month	No. of calls	Total duration
January	20	226
February	25	320
March	40	330
April	32	450
May	33	290
June	29	237
July	23	211
August	5	37
September	26	233
October	26	256
November	30	338
December	36	315

   A.   270.1
   B.   10.0
   C.   27.0
   D.   10.1
   E.   9.9

Answer ☐

12.   If the Black company increases its prices per minute by 70%, which card would now be the cheapest for the calls described in question 9?

A. Green £10
B. Green £20
C. Black £10
D. Black £20
E. Black £20 or Green £20, the same price

Answer ▢

Questions 13 to 16 concern the type of employment in a particular region in thousands of people:

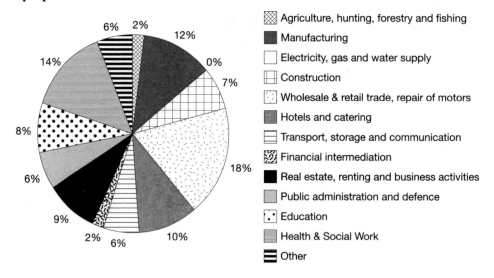

13.   If the total population is 200,000, how many sectors employ more than 19,000 people?

A. 3
B. 4
C. 5
D. 6
E. 7

Answer ▢

14.   If those working in manufacturing generate a third more revenue per person than those in agriculture, fishing etc, how much more total revenue do they generate?

   A.   8 times
   B.   7 times
   C.   6 times
   D.   7.2 times
   E.   6.75 times

   Answer ☐

15.   Half of the agricultural produce is sold to continental Europe. If the total revenue for the sector is £100m, calculate the revenue generated from these European sales in euros (1 pound = 1.25 euros).

   A.   12.5m
   B.   75m
   C.   125m
   D.   60m
   E.   62.5m

   Answer ☐

16.   The average number of people employed per employer in hotels and catering is 20. How many employers are there?

   A.   1,000
   B.   4,000
   C.   10,000
   D.   400
   E.   2,000

   Answer ☐

Questions 17 to 20 concern the salt content in grams of some supermarket pre-prepared foods per 100 g:

Budget's Best Chicken Tikka with Pilau Rice	2.0
Charlie's Champion Chilli	1.2
Red Dragon Lo-salt Vegetable Chow Mein	0.3
Luigi Lambretta's Pasta Carbonara	1.8
Thai Me Up Prawn Curry	1.1
Barry's Bargain Range Paella	1.9
Cheap As Chips Shepherd Pie	1.6
Luigi Lambretta's Spaghetti Bolognese	1.5
Sadek's Fish Curry	1.2
Mo's Cushy Couscous	1.7
John Bull's British Classics Toad In The Hole	1.8

17. Expressed as a decimal, what fraction of the above products are high in salt, ie greater than or equal to 1.5%?

   A. 0.55
   B. 0.54
   C. 0.45
   D. 0.44
   E. 0.32

Answer

18. If the maximum recommended daily intake of salt is 6 g, what percentage does a 350 g portion of Chicken Tikka with Pilau Rice represent?

   A. 35%
   B. 117%
   C. 86%
   D. 111%
   E. 33%

Answer

19. The Fish Curry is twice as expensive as the Paella, which itself is 10% more expensive than the Shepherd's Pie. If the pie costs £1.50, how much does the curry cost?

A. £3.00
B. £1.65
C. £3.60
D. £3.30
E. Cannot tell

Answer

20. The Toad in the Hole is also sold in continental Europe. The price in Britain is £2.65 and the exchange rate used to print the prices is £1 = €1.50. If the actual exchange rate is £1 = €1.25, how much more is the rest of Europe paying for it than it should?

A. 25 cents
B. 44.50 cents
C. 66.25 cents
D. 58.75 cents
E. 31.45 cents

Answer

Questions 21 to 24 concern the number of people in different groups. One hundred and six (106) people were stopped in the street and the following information obtained: 62 were born in this country, 50 were taller than 1.6 m and 14 were left-handed.

21. What percentage were 1.6 m or under?

A. 36%
B. 64%
C. 60%
D. 53%
E. 34%

Answer

22. If three people were taller than 1.6 m, born in this country and left-handed, how many people were only one of these things?

A. 62
B. 76
C. 103
D. 89
E. Cannot tell

Answer ☐

23. What percentage of those born in this country were left-handed?

A. 13%
B. 60%
C. 20%
D. 25%
E. Cannot tell

Answer ☐

24. There are three people who are left-handed, born in England and taller than 1.6 m, two people who are left-handed and taller than 1.6 m. There are twice as many people who are just left-handed as are left-handed and born in London. How many are just left-handed?

A. 6
B. 14
C. 9
D. 5
E. Cannot tell

Answer ☐

Questions 25 to 28 concern the prices of different foods:

25.   If an order of three cod and two portions of chips costs a total of £12.85 and two cod with three chips costs £10.40, what would be the formulae for determining the different prices?

A. $2C + 3F = 12.85, 3C + 2Y = 10.40$
B. $C + F = 7.85, F = 1.3$
C. $X + Y = £5.00, 2X + 2Y = £10$
D. $F = £3.50, C = £1.05$
E. $3X + 2Y = 1285, 2X + 3Y = 1040$

Answer [ ]

26.   If the price of cod increases by 20% and the price of chips by 10%, what would be the new cost of a portion of cod and chips to the nearest penny?

A.   £4.57
B.   £5.47
C.   £4.65
D.   £4.10
E.   £5.37

Answer [ ]

27.   What is the ratio of the old price to the new price?

A. $1 : 1.17$
B. $1.55 : 1$
C. $1.17 : 1$
D. $1 : 1.18$
E. $1.2 : 1$

Answer [ ]

28.   If the shop accepts euros at an exchange rate of 1.20 euros = 1 pound, how much would a tourist pay at the original prices for three cod and three chips?

    A. €13.95
    B. €16.74
    C. €20.91
    D. €15.24
    E. €11.26

Answer ☐

Questions 29 to 32 concern the results of an exam for schoolchildren:

29.   A particular exam board requires schools to mark the work internally and send a sample of the work. The number of scripts required is given by the square root of the number of children sitting the exam rounded up to the nearest one. If 26 children sit the exam, how many scripts should be sent?

    A. 21
    B. 5
    C. 6
    D. 10
    E. 13

Answer ☐

30. The student scores are shown below. If all those below the average mark fail, how many will do so?

Student no.	Score
1.	26
2.	91
3.	35
4.	55
5.	57
6.	59
7.	46
8.	63
9.	28
10.	34
11.	88
12.	62
13.	67
14.	29
15.	32
16.	51
17.	54
18.	56
19.	79
20.	75
21.	66
22.	63
23.	36
24.	51
25.	62
26.	60

A. 11
B. 13
C. 9
D. 10
E. 15

Answer ☐

31.   If the system is set up so that 85–90% pass, what should the pass mark be?

    A. 36
    B. 35
    C. 30
    D. 33
    E. 31

Answer ☐

32.   If the pass mark is set at the lowest score plus 10% of the range, how many will fail?

    A. 6
    B. 5
    C. 2
    D. 3
    E. 4

Answer ☐

Questions 33 to 36 concern fuel prices in Europe:

Country	Fuel price (p)
Austria	75
Belgium	95
Czech Rep	71.5
Denmark	92.2
Eire	74.5
Finland	89.4
France	85.2
Germany	90
Greece	65.7
Netherlands	100.3
Hungary	83.5
Italy	87.5
Luxembourg	76.5
Norway	94.8
Poland	79.5
Portugal	85.8
Spain	66.4
Sweden	82.1
Switzerland	72.1
United Kingdom (Av)	96.5

33.   What would be the cost of driving a car which does 30 miles per gallon a distance
of 95 miles in Italy if one gallon is 4.75 litres?

    A. (95 / 30) × (87.5 / 4.75)
    B. (95 × 30) / (87.5 × 4.75)
    C. (95 × 30 × 4.75) / 87.5
    D. (87.5 × 4.75) / (95 / 30)
    E. (95 × 87.5 × 4.75) / 30

Answer ☐

34.   The bar chart below shows the increase in price in one month. Which countries have seen the greatest increases?

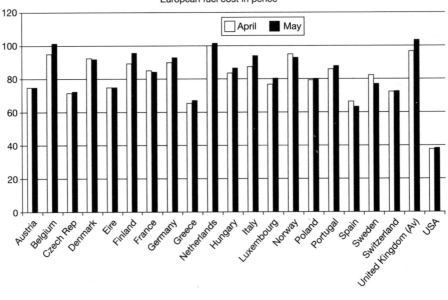

European fuel cost in pence

A. Hungary, Luxembourg, Germany
B. Sweden, Spain
C. Belgium, Finland, United Kingdom, Italy
D. Luxembourg, Germany, United Kingdom, Italy
E. Belgium, Finland, Germany

Answer ☐

35.   If the price of fuel continues to rise at 7% per month in the UK, what would be the percentage increase to drive 100 miles with the car in question 33 after three months?

A. 14.0%
B. 21.0%
C. 21.7%
D. 22.5%
E. 28.0%

Answer ☐

36. If the driver is planning to drive 210 miles in the Netherlands starting at the German border, how much cheaper would it be to buy the fuel in Germany using the car and prices in question 33?

   A. 297p
   B. 342.5p
   C. 333.275p
   D. 10.3p
   E. Cannot tell

   Answer ☐

Questions 37 to 40 concern aircraft flight:

37. The power required to keep an aeroplane in flight is given by $P = Av^3$, where A is a constant and v the velocity. If the velocity increases by 25%, how much more power is required?

   A. Nearly twice as much
   B. Around 50% more
   C. 25% more
   D. About a third more
   E. About the same

   Answer ☐

38. If the pilot increases the thrust by 50%, how much faster will the plane fly?

   A. 10%
   B. 15%
   C. 20%
   D. 25%
   E. 30%

   Answer ☐

39. If a full fuel tank represents 60% of the total weight of the plane and the speed is proportional to the square root of the weight, how much slower can the plane fly when nearly empty of fuel?

   A. $\sqrt{0.4}$
   B. $\sqrt{0.6}$
   C. 0.4^2
   D. 0.6^2
   E. Cannot tell

   Answer ☐

40. How much more power is required on take-off (full) than on landing (empty)?

   A. 0.6^3
   B. $(0.6 / 0.4)^3$
   C. 2.5
   D. $2.5^{1.5}$
   E. Cannot tell

   Answer ☐

Questions 41 to 44 concern two tests to detect the presence of a certain substance:

SUBSTANCE PRESENT	Yes	Allcheck = 95% Truespot = 92%	Allcheck = 10% Truespot = 2%
	No	Allcheck = 5% Truespot = 8%	Allcheck = 90% Truespot = 98%
		Positive result	Negative result
TRIAL RESULTS		RESULTS OF TRIAL	

41. A trial was carried out on 780 samples using Allcheck. How many would be identified as having the substance present?

   A. 702
   B. 741
   C. 78
   D. 62
   E. Cannot tell

   Answer ☐

42. If 500 of the 780 have the substance present, how many samples would be expected to be incorrect?

A. About 43
B. 40
C. About 46
D. 10
E. Cannot tell

Answer

43. If half the 780 samples had the substance present, what would be the difference in the number of wrong results for Allcheck compared to Truespot?

A. About 10 more
B. About 5 less
C. About 8 less
D. About 20 more
E. Cannot tell

Answer

44. In another trial of 800 samples, Allcheck identifies 475 with the substance. How many are likely to have the substance present?

A. About 488
B. About 465
C. About 475
D. About 325
E. Cannot tell

Answer

Questions 45 to 48 concern the video game-playing habits of students:

Time playing video games per week	
Hours	Number of students
10–14	2
15–19	12
20–24	23
25–29	60
30–34	77
35–39	38
40–44	8

45.   What is the approximate average time spent playing games per week?

   A. 30
   B. 27
   C. 26
   D. 25
   E. 24

Answer ☐

46.   How many play less than 20 hours a week?

   A. 35
   B. 37
   C. 14
   D. 206
   E. 24

Answer ☐

47.   What fraction plays more than the average?

   A. 3/7
   B. 5/7
   C. 3/4
   D. 1/2
   E. 5/9

Answer ☐

48.   If, during exam term, the three heaviest users reduce their playing by 10%, the three least-heavy user groups by 20% and the middle group remains unchanged, what would be the approximate average number of hours spent playing?

   A. 24
   B. 25
   C. 26
   D. 27
   E. 28

Answer ☐

Questions 49 to 52 concern the measure of appropriate weight, the Body Mass Index (BMI):

49.   BMI is defined as being the mass of a person (in kg) divided by the square of the height (in metres). Which of the following has the greatest BMI?

Person	Height (m)	Weight (kg)
A	1.45	45
B	1.50	50
C	1.55	55
D	1.70	60
E	1.80	70

   A. A
   B. B
   C. C
   D. D
   E. E

Answer ☐

50.   If an adolescent's height increases by 10% and their mass by 10%, by how much will their BMI change?

    A. Plus 11%
    B. Plus 10%
    C. Minus 9%
    D. Minus 10%
    E. Unchanged

Answer ☐

51.   Person A has a BMI index of 28, but would like to be in the 'normal' range, 18.5–24.9. If person A weighs 80 kg, how much do they need to lose?

    A. 9 kg
    B. 8 kg
    C. 7 kg
    D. 6 kg
    E. 5 kg

Answer ☐

52.   A 1.8 m person has a BMI of 24.9, at the top end of the 'normal' range. By what fraction will their weight have to increase to be in the 'obese' range?

    A. 1/3
    B. 1/4
    C. 1/5
    D. 1/6
    E. 1/7

Answer ☐

Questions 53 to 56 concern house prices in two different regions:

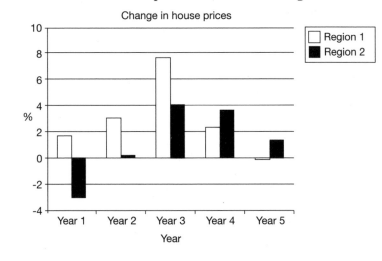

Change in house prices

53.   Where and when did prices fall most?

    A. Region 1, year 3
    B. Region 2, year 3
    C. Region 2, year 2
    D. Region 1, year 5
    E. Region 2, year 1

                                            Answer [   ]

54.   Which year had the greatest difference in price changes between the two regions?

    A. Year 1
    B. Year 2
    C. Year 3
    D. Year 4
    E. Year 5

                                            Answer [   ]

55.   If a region 1 house and a region 2 house are both worth £200,000 at the start of year 3, what will be the difference in value at the end?

    A. £15,000
    B. £7,000
    C. £8,000
    D. £7,500
    E. Cannot tell

Answer ☐

56.   What is the total price change over the five years for region 1?

    A. $1.5 + 3 + 7.5 + 2.3 - 0.1$
    B. $1.05 \times 1.03 \times 1.075 \times 1.023 \times -1.01$
    C. $1.05 \times 1.03 \times 1.075 \times 1.023 \times 0.99$
    D. $1.05 + 1.03 + 1.075 + 1.023 + -1.01$
    E. Cannot tell

Answer ☐

Questions 57 to 60 concern the habits of a group of people surveyed in the street:

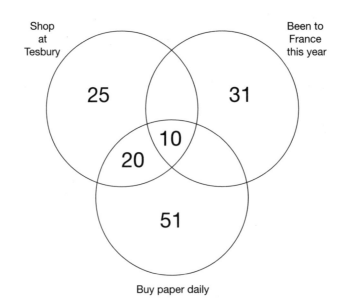

57.   How many people were surveyed?

    A. 51
    B. 108
    C. 98
    D. 118
    E. Cannot tell

Answer ☐

58.   What is the largest number that could be in the group having 'been to France this year' and 'buy paper daily'?

    A. 21
    B. 41
    C. 51
    D. 32
    E. 25

Answer ☐

59.   How many 'buy paper daily' and 'shop at Tesbury'?

    A. 20
    B. 30
    C. 51
    D. 25
    E. Cannot tell

Answer ☐

60.   If the two blank spaces both contain the number 20, how many people answer yes to two questions?

    A. 20
    B. 30
    C. 50
    D. 60
    E. Cannot tell

Answer ☐

Questions 61 to 64 concern the results of two political parties, the Direct Union for Democracy and the People's Union for Power, in monthly polls showing voting intentions. People expressed a preference for one or other party or the intention not to vote:

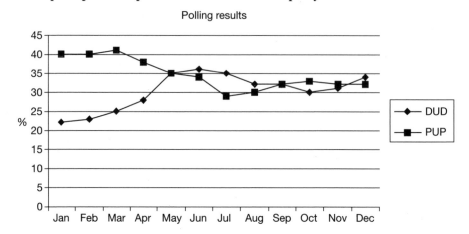

Polling results

61.   What fraction of those intending to vote would have chosen the Direct Union for Democracy party in September?

A.   1/3
B.   1/4
C.   1/5
D.   1/2
E.   2/3

Answer [   ]

62.   Which month would have seen the greatest number of abstentions?

A.   August
B.   September
C.   October
D.   November
E.   December

Answer [   ]

63.   If 10% of the people abstaining now decide to vote following the pattern of the other voters, what would be the expected results for the parties in January? From 40% and 22% to:

A.   44.0% and 24.2% respectively
B.   42.5% and 23.5% respectively
C.   44.0% and 22.0% respectively
D.   36.0% and 19.8% respectively
E.   41.5% and 20.5% respectively

Answer ☐

64.   Which month saw the biggest relative gain for any party?

A.   September to October
B.   June to July
C.   July to August
D.   March to April
E.   April to May

Answer ☐

Questions 65 to 68 concern the exchange rates at different bureaux de change:

Financial institution	Exchange rate (£1 buys…)
Happy Holidays	€1.20 + £1.20 fee and 3% commission
Better Bank	€1.18 + no fee and no commission
X-change	€1.22 + £2.50 fee and 2% commission
Four Eyes Currency	€1.22 + no fee and 3% commission
Concurrency	€1.20 + £2.00 fee and no commission

65.   Which of the following equations gives the number of euros for £200 with Happy Holidays?

A. $(200 \times 1.20) - (0.03 \times 200)$
B. $0.03 \times 200 \times 1.20 - 1.20$
C. $0.97 \times 200 \times 1.20 + 1.20$
D. $(200 - 1.20) \times 0.97 \times 1.20$
E. $(200 - 0.03) \times 1.20 - 1.20$

Answer ☐

66.   Which would be the most worthwhile for converting a large sum?

    A. Happy Holidays
    B. Better Bank
    C. X-change
    D. Four Eyes Currency
    E. Concurrency

Answer ☐

The table below shows the number of euros for different sterling transactions:

£	Bureau de change				
	HH	BB	XC	FEC	CON
10	10.24	11.80	8.97	11.64	9.60
20	21.88	23.60	20.92	23.28	21.60
30	33.52	35.40	32.88	34.92	33.60
40	45.16	47.20	44.84	46.56	45.60
50	56.80	59.00	56.79	58.20	57.60
60	68.44	70.80	68.75	69.84	69.60
70	80.08	82.60	80.70	81.48	81.60
80	91.72	94.40	92.66	93.12	93.60
90	103.36	106.20	104.62	104.76	105.60
100	115.00	118.00	116.57	116.40	117.60
110	126.64	129.80	128.53	128.04	129.60
120	138.28	141.60	140.48	139.68	141.60
130	149.92	153.40	152.44	151.32	153.60
140	161.56	165.20	164.40	162.96	165.60
150	173.20	177.00	176.35	174.60	177.60
160	184.84	188.80	188.31	186.24	189.60
170	196.48	200.60	200.26	197.88	201.60
180	208.12	212.40	212.22	209.52	213.60
190	219.76	224.20	224.18	221.16	225.60
200	231.40	236.00	236.13	232.80	237.60
210	243.04	247.80	248.09	244.44	249.60
220	254.68	259.60	260.04	256.08	261.60
230	266.32	271.40	272.00	267.72	273.60
240	277.96	283.20	283.96	279.36	285.60
250	289.60	295.00	295.91	291.00	297.60

67. What is the biggest difference between the different bureaux for changing £150?

   A. 3%
   B. 4.4%
   C. 2.5%
   D. 3.5%
   E. 2%

   Answer [   ]

68. If the exchange rate is €1.22 to the pound, what fraction is lost changing £10 with Concurrency?

   A. 1/10
   B. 1/5
   C. 1/4
   D. 1/7
   E. 1/3

   Answer [   ]

Questions 69 to 72 concern the market share of different soft drinks:

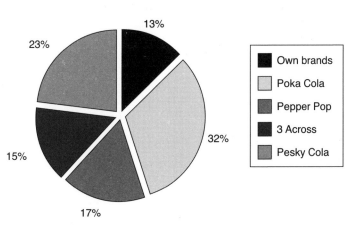

Soft drink market share

Own brands	
Poka Cola	
Pepper Pop	
3 Across	
Pesky Cola	

69.   Approximately what fraction of the market do the colas represent?

   A. 1/3
   B. 1/2
   C. 3/4
   D. 1/5
   E. 5/9

   Answer [ ]

70.   If Pepper Pop increases its market share by 3% at the expense of 3 Across, what would be the new ratio of Pepper Pop to 3 Across?

   A. 4 : 3
   B. 1.67 : 1
   C. 3 : 5
   D. 20 : 15
   E. 17 : 15

   Answer [ ]

71.   A new brand is launched which succeeds in capturing 5% of the market within a year. If the ratio of Pesky Cola to Pepper Pop to 3 Across to Poker Cola remains the same, what is the maximum market share of the own brands?

   A. 8%
   B. 15%
   C. 20%
   D. 25%
   E. 95%

   Answer [ ]

72.   If 3 Across increases its sales by 15%, what would be its new market share, if the sales of the others remain static?

   A. 15%
   B. 16%
   C. 17%
   D. 20%
   E. 30%

   Answer [ ]

Questions 73 to 76 concern the dosage of a particular treatment:

Dosage in millilitres, $D = 0.5 \times H^{0.5} \times W^{0.75}$, where W is the weight in kilograms and H the height in metres. (1 in = 2.54 cm, 1 kg = 2.2 lbs and 1 stone = 14 lbs)

73.   If a patient's weight increases by 10% during the treatment, by what factor will the dose increase?

   A.   1.1
   B. $1.1^{0.75}$
   C. $10^{0.75}$
   D.   1.01
   E.   Cannot tell

   Answer ☐

74.   A 1.80 m patient has a brother who is 5 cm taller and 3 kg heavier. How much larger will the brother's dose be?

   A. $\sqrt{(1.85/1.80)} \times (1.03)^{0.75}$
   B. $(1.85/1.80)^{0.5} \times ((1.03)^{0.25})^{3}$
   C. $(1.85/1.80)^{0.5} \times ((1.03)^{3})^{0.25}$
   D. $(1.85/1.80)^{0.5} \times (1.03)^{0.75}$
   E.   Cannot tell

   Answer ☐

75.   If the average height of a particular population is 5' 10" and the average weight 10 stone, what would be the average dose?

   A.   110 ml
   B.   120 ml
   C.   130 ml
   D.   140 ml
   E.   150 ml

   Answer ☐

76.   If the weight of a particular population is 20% higher than here and the cost of the
       drug 15% more, how much more will it cost to treat people?

   A. 20%
   B. 32%
   C. 38%
   D. 30%
   E. 35%

Answer [   ]

**Questions 77 to 80 concern the time taken from receiving a call to the ambulance
arriving at the destination:**

Time in minutes	0–4.9	5–9.9	10–14.9	15–19.9	20–24.9	25–29.9
Number	15	157	154	92	51	4

77.   In which group is the median time?

   A. 0–4.9
   B. 5–9.9
   C. 10–14.9
   D. 15–19.9
   E. 20–24.9

Answer [   ]

78.   Estimate the average response time.

   A. 12.5 mins
   B. 10 mins
   C. 15 mins
   D. 11.5 mins
   E. 15.5 mins

Answer [   ]

79.   What percentage were above 12.5 minutes?

    A.   50%
    B.   35%
    C.   40%
    D.   45%
    E.   Cannot tell

Answer ☐

80.   If the ambulance consumes 0.1 litres per minute, roughly how much fuel was consumed getting to these destinations?

    A.   900 litres
    B.   9,000 litres
    C.   6,000 litres
    D.   600 litres
    E.   90 litres

Answer ☐

Questions 81 to 84 concern the distance travelled by a falling object, where velocity is the rate of change of distance with time and acceleration is the rate of change of velocity with time:

Time (s)	Distance (m)
1	5
2	20
3	45
4	80
5	125
6	180
7	245
8	320
9	405

81.   Estimate the speed at 6 seconds in metres per second.

   A. 30
   B. 60
   C. 40
   D. 20
   E. 180

                                                        Answer [   ]

82.   Estimate the acceleration.

   A. 10
   B. 30
   C. 20
   D. 40
   E. 50

                                                        Answer [   ]

83.   A second object is dropped which produces the following set of results. If the first object is dropped 3 seconds after the second object, how long will it take to overtake the second?

Time (s)	Distance (m)
1	8.0
2	11.8
3	16.1
4	20.7
5	25.4
6	30.2
7	35.2
8	40.1
9	45.1

   A. Between 0 and 1 seconds
   B. Between 1 and 2 seconds
   C. Between 2 and 3 seconds
   D. Between 3 and 4 seconds
   E. Cannot tell

                                                        Answer [   ]

84.   What is the time at which this second object has greatest acceleration?

    A. 1 second
    B. 2 seconds
    C. 3 seconds
    D. 4 seconds
    E. None of the above

Answer ☐

Questions 85 to 88 concern the prices of petrol observed at various garages in a certain city:

Price in pence
96.5
99.9
97.5
98.3
99.6
99.6
100.3
100.1
100.5
99.9
99.9
98.7

85.   How much bigger is the mode than the average, 99.2?

    A. 0.55
    B. 0.70
    C. 0.75
    D. 0.65
    E. 0.45

Answer ☐

86.   The program used to calculate the average was only designed to accept prices up to 99.9p. If it reads 101.3 as 01.3, what will be the difference between the actual numerical mean and that calculated by the program?

A.   12
B.   4
C.   12.5
D.   25
E.   9.5

Answer ☐

87.   If the prices all increase by 2%, what fraction will be above 100p?

A.   1/4
B.   9/12
C.   5/6
D.   2/3
E.   All of them

Answer ☐

88.   If, as a result of price increases, all the prices are between 100 and 200 and the same program is used to determine the average, which of the following could be used to give the correct answer?

A.   Answer + 100
B.   Answer x (number of samples) × 100 / (number of samples)
C.   Answer + ((number of samples) × 100)
D.   Answer + 200
E.   Answer + number of samples

Answer ☐

Questions 89 to 92 concern the reliability of various brands based on the number of warranty claims of various brands of car:

Brand	Claims per 100	Average claim cost (£)
Bonza	9.9	325
Havanaisday	16.2	135
Frort	36.4	223
Perja	30.8	228
MT	37.7	433

89.   Which brand has the lowest cost per 100?

    A. Bonza
    B. Havanaisday
    C. Frort
    D. Perja
    E. MT

Answer ☐

90.   If the cost of the claims has not been factored in, how much will MT have to add to the price of a car to take this into account?

    A. £143
    B. £149
    C. £155
    D. £160
    E. £163

Answer ☐

91.   Through improved quality and better working practices, Frort is able to reduce the number of claims per hundred to 25 and the cost per claim to £200. What is the fractional saving?

    A. 2/5
    B. 1/4
    C. 3/10
    D. 1/3
    E. 4/9

Answer ☐

92.   Perja decides to offer an additional insurance policy beyond the warranty period. If the probability of a breakdown with an average repair cost of £250 is 1 in 12 per year, what price should the premium be to make a 20% return?

    A. £25
    B. £20.74
    C. £30.92
    D. £20.10
    E. £27

Answer ☐

Questions 93 to 96 concern exchange rates:

Dollally	Kroni	Pounze	Robbers	Yangs	Barts
1	5.91	1.97	23.69	104.93	33.15

93.   What is the exchange rate from Robbers to Yangs?

    A. 0.226
    B. 4.429
    C. 0.262
    D. 23.69
    E. 4.492

Answer ☐

94.   If the exchange rate from Dollally to Pounze drops by 20% and the rate from Dollally to Yangs increases by 25%, by how much will the Pounze–Yangs rate change?

A. 56%
B. 45%
C. 5%
D. 20%
E. 25%

Answer ☐

95.   A virtual currency is defined as the value of Dollally times Robbers divided by Pounze times Kroni. If the value of the Pounze drops 20% against the Dollally, by how much will this virtual currency change?

A. Up ¼
B. Up 1/5
C. Down 1/5
D. Down 1/4
E. Down 1/3

Answer ☐

96.   A tourist changes 100 Dollally to Barts. If the tourist then returns home and changes the remaining 100 Barts back to Dollally, how much would they have lost in total if the commission is 3% in both directions?

A. 6.00 Dollally
B. 3.00 Dollally
C. 3.09 Dollally
D. 6.33 Dollally
E. 4.27 Dollally

Answer ☐

Mini-tests

Mini-test 1

You have four minutes to answer eight questions in the two sections below.

Questions 97 to 100 concern the sales of ice cream:

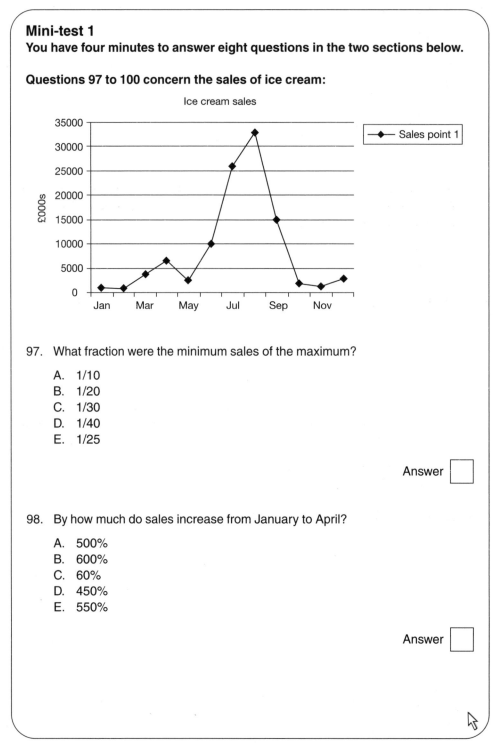

Ice cream sales

97. What fraction were the minimum sales of the maximum?

    A. 1/10
    B. 1/20
    C. 1/30
    D. 1/40
    E. 1/25

Answer ☐

98. By how much do sales increase from January to April?

    A. 500%
    B. 600%
    C. 60%
    D. 450%
    E. 550%

Answer ☐

99. If the company needs £5m sales per month to break even, how much profit do they make in the year?

   A.   £0.5m
   B.   £400m
   C.   £500,000
   D.   £5m
   E.   £45m

   Answer ☐

100. If inflation rises at 0.1% per month, what is the increase in cost at the end of the year?

   A. 1.001^{12}
   B. 12×0.1
   C. 1.1^{12}
   D. 0.1^{12}
   E. $(1 + (12 \times 0.001))$

   Answer ☐

Questions 101 to 104 concern the recovery rates of trials of different drugs, based on number of days for substance X in blood to drop to certain level:

Number of days				
Drug A	Drug B	Drug C	Drug D	Drug E
20	11	5	11	25
21	20	6	16	26
27	16	30	12	24
19	15	25	13	23
28	19	9	15	25
25	15	24	17	25
23	14	11	14	26
21	13	15	16	23
20	12	27	13	21
21	12	9	15	29
22	12	8	15	27
21	11	25	15	25
19	15	13	11	26
26	16	25	12	26
23	18	8	13	24
21	20	24	11	23
20	16	15	13	21
17	17	21	16	20

101. Which drug has the best average?

    A. Drug A
    B. Drug B
    C. Drug C
    D. Drug D
    E. Drug E

                                                    Answer ☐

102. Which drug has the lowest median value?

    A. Drug A
    B. Drug B
    C. Drug C
    D. Drug D
    E. Drug E

                                                    Answer ☐

103. If each of the values in the drug C trials were 10% nearer the average, how would this affect the average?

    A. 10% larger
    B. 10% smaller
    C. 20% larger
    D. Cannot tell
    E. Unchanged

                                                    Answer ☐

104. If the range of values in the drug C trials changed by 10%, how would this affect the average?

    A. 10% larger
    B. 10% smaller
    C. 20% larger
    D. Cannot tell
    E. Unchanged

                                                    Answer ☐

End of test

Mini-test 2
You have four minutes to answer eight questions in the two sections below.

Questions 105 to 108 compares the time taken for various journeys:

Journey	Distance (miles)	Time (hours and mins)
A	115	1h 55m
B	97	2h 6m
C	65	1h 11m
D	88	1h 45m
E	95	1h 35m

105. Which journey has the fastest average speed?

   A.   A
   B.   A and E
   C.   E and C
   D.   C
   E.   E

   Answer [   ]

106. Which formula gives the average speed for journey C in miles per hour?

   A. $s = 65 / 1.11$
   B. $s = 65 / 1 + (11/60)$
   C. $s = 65 / (1 + (11/60))$
   D. $s = 65 \times 1.11$
   E. $s = 65 / (1 \times (11/60))$

   Answer [   ]

107. The time taken for journey C can vary by as much as plus or minus 20%. By how much will the corresponding average speed change?

   A.   + 20%, −20%
   B.   +25%, −25%
   C.   +25%, −17%
   D.   +17%, −20%
   E.   Cannot tell

   Answer [   ]

108. If there are 1.609 km to a mile, what is the average speed for journey E in metres per second?

    A. 26.82 m/s
    B. 1609 m/s
    C. 96552 m/s
    D. 25.66 m/s
    E. 95562 m/s

Answer ☐

Questions 109 to 112 concern traffic on the internet through a particular server during the day (1 TeraByte = 1,000 GigaBytes):

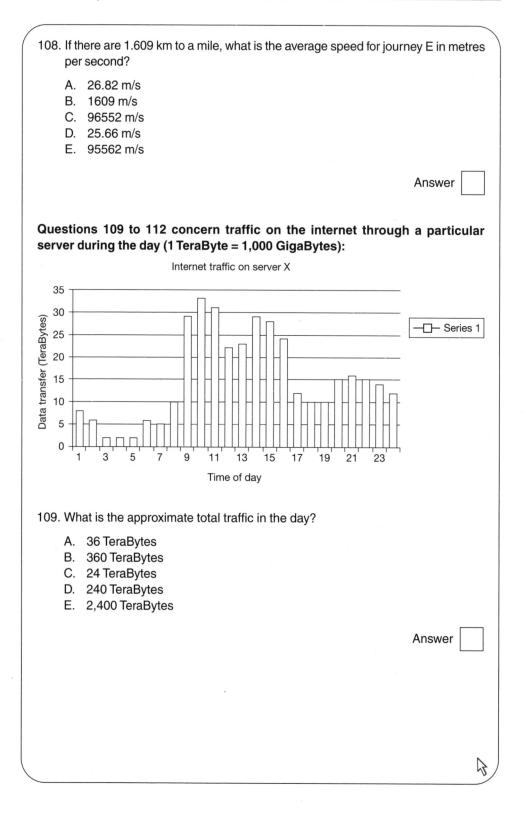

Internet traffic on server X

109. What is the approximate total traffic in the day?

    A. 36 TeraBytes
    B. 360 TeraBytes
    C. 24 TeraBytes
    D. 240 TeraBytes
    E. 2,400 TeraBytes

Answer ☐

110. What fraction of the day exceeded 15 TeraBytes?

    A. 5/6
    B. 1/2
    C. 1/ 4
    D. 11 /24
    E. 9/24

Answer ☐

111. Between which times did the traffic increase the most?

    A. 8 and 9
    B. 5 and 6 or 8 and 9
    C. 5 and 6
    D. 16 and 17
    E. 30%

Answer ☐

112. In order to cope with demand a second server is activated when the data transfer rate exceeds 3 GigaBytes per second. Approximately how many hours a day will this occur?

    A. 14
    B. 10
    C. 3
    D. 2
    E. 0

Answer ☐

End of test

Mini-test 3
You have four minutes to answer eight questions in the two sections below.

Questions 113 to 116 concern Boyle's law relating pressures and volumes of a gas, PV = constant:

113. If the pressure changes by a factor of 3/4, by how much does the volume change?

    A. 3/4
    B. 4/3
    C. 1.5
    D. 2
    E. 1.25

Answer ☐

114. If the volume changes to 5/6 the original volume, by how much must the pressure change?

    A. −1/ 6
    B. +1/6
    C. +1/ 5
    D. +5/6
    E. −5/6

Answer ☐

115. The following results were taken during an experiment. It appears that the experimenter has made a mistake. Where?

Pressure (kPa)	Volume (m³)
100	0.020
95	0.021
90	0.022
65	0.031
150	0.133

    A. The volume 0.020 should read 0.200.
    B. The pressure 100 should read 10.
    C. The volume 0.022 should read 0.220.
    D. The volume 0.133 should read 0.013.
    E. Cannot tell.

Answer ☐

116. The pressure in the above experiment is increased to 900 KPa. If the experimenter only reads to three decimal places, what percentage error will this introduce?

    A.   10%
    B.   15%
    C.   5%
    D.   2%
    E.   3%

Answer

Questions 117 to 120 concern the results of a comparison test between two populations and two types of orange juice. The percentages give the number who preferred the particular juice:

	Population X	Population Y
Juice A	85%	55%
Juice B	10%	30%

117. What fraction of population Y was undecided?

    A.   85/100
    B.   25/100
    C.   1/5
    D.   3/20
    E.   15/50

Answer

118. If the population Y were twice as big as population X, what would be the average preference percentage for Juice A for the entire population of X and Y together?

    A.   83%
    B.   79%
    C.   65%
    D.   70%
    E.   67%

Answer

119. The polling company then carried out a later test where juice A was identified
as being 10% more expensive than juice B and the question asked as to which
juice people would buy. Which section has shown the greatest points change?

	Population X	Population Y
Juice A	65%	62%
Juice B	29%	32%

A. Population X for juice A
B. Population X for juice B
C. Population Y for juice B
D. Population Y for juice A
E. Cannot tell

Answer ☐

120. Given that the same quantity of juice is sold and the populations remained as
in question 118, by how much would it benefit the makers of juice A to sell it at
the higher price?

A. Around 10% more
B. Around 10% less
C. Around 7% more
D. Around 5% more
E. Cannot tell

Answer ☐

End of test

Mini-test 4
You have four minutes to answer eight questions in the two sections below.

Questions 121 to 124 concern the results of a particular competition:

Team	Won	Drawn	Lost	Points
A	2	2	0	26
B	1	3	1	18
C	0	3	3	18
D	1	2	1	19
E	2	1	0	21

121. How many points for a draw?

    A. 1
    B. 2
    C. 3
    D. 4
    E. 5

Answer ☐

122. How many matches are left to play if each team plays the others twice?

    A. 9
    B. 8
    C. 7
    D. 6
    E. 5

Answer ☐

123. What is the maximum total number of points?

    A. 175
    B. 192
    C. 183
    D. 157
    E. 162

Answer ☐

124. If all the remaining matches are drawn, what fraction of the teams will have less than 30 points?

A. 1/5
B. 2/5
C. 3/5
D. 4/5
E. Cannot tell

Answer

Questions 125 to 128 concern mathematical functions:

Mathematical functions y = f(x)

125. Which function does the line A represent?

A. $y = \sqrt{x}$
B. $y = 5x + 2$
C. $y = 0.58x$
D. 81.5
E. 81.0

Answer

126. Which has the highest average value between 0 and 3?

    A.   A
    B.   B and C
    C.   D
    D.   C
    E.   Cannot tell

                                                    Answer [   ]

127. What is the value of y when line D has an x value of 10?

    A.   12
    B.   10
    C.   5
    D.   6
    E.   7

                                                    Answer [   ]

128. If all the y values of line C were reduced by a factor of 3, at what value of x would it cross line C?

    A.   3
    B.   4
    C.   5
    D.   6
    E.   7

                                                    Answer [   ]

End of test

Mini-test 5
You have four minutes to answer eight questions in the two sections below.

Questions 129 to 132 concern a set of exam results:

Student	Result (%)
A	44
B	46
C	55
D	91
E	88
F	66
G	57
H	80
I	72
J	55
K	36
L	38
M	48
N	57
O	87
P	83
Q	55
R	61
S	59
T	54

129. If the exam board intends that only 10% of students should receive the maximum grade, what mark should be the minimum to achieve this grade?

    A. 80
    B. 87.5
    C. 88
    D. 87
    E. 82.5

    Answer ☐

130. If 10% also fail, what is the largest range between the mark separating the top group and the mark separating the bottom group?

   A.   49
   B.   45
   C.   47.5
   D.   48.5
   E.   50

   Answer ☐

131. A second set of results was obtained as follows. By how much has the mode improved?

Result (%)
37
39
45
47
49
55
56
56
56
58
58
60
62
67
73
82
85
89
90
93

   A.   1
   B.   2
   C.   3
   D.   4
   E.   5

   Answer ☐

132. If all the scores in the first set improved by 3%, how many would now achieve the top grade if the dividing mark remained unchanged?

    A. 2
    B. 3
    C. 4
    D. 5
    E. Cannot tell

    Answer ☐

Questions 133 to 136 concern the speeds of different types of transport:

Transport	Speed
Running	10 m/s
Horse	23 m/s
Bicycle	16 m/s
Electric car	32 m/s
Car	50 m/s

133. If the electric car starts ahead of the car, what is the car's closing speed?

    A. 18 m/s
    B. 32 m/s
    C. 50 m/s
    D. 82 m/s
    E. 9 m/s

    Answer ☐

134. If all the forms of transport pass the start together at their given speeds, how much further will the car have gone compared to the horse after one minute?

    A. 3,000 m
    B. 1,380 m
    C. 1,620 m
    D. 960 m
    E. 1,220 m

    Answer ☐

135. How many metres' head start should the horse give the bicycle if they are to finish the 100 m together?

    A.   7 m
    B.   70 m
    C.   39 m
    D.   25.25 m
    E.   30.43 m

Answer

136. If the runner has a 100 m head start over the horse, what will the distance, s, between them be at time, t?

    A. $s = 100 + 23t - 10t$
    B. $s = 100 - 13t$
    C. $s = (100 + 10)t - 23$
    D. $s = (10 - 23)t - 100$
    E. $s = 33t - 100$

Answer

End of test

Mini-test 6
You have four minutes to answer eight questions in the two sections below.

Questions 137 to 140 concern rates of interest:

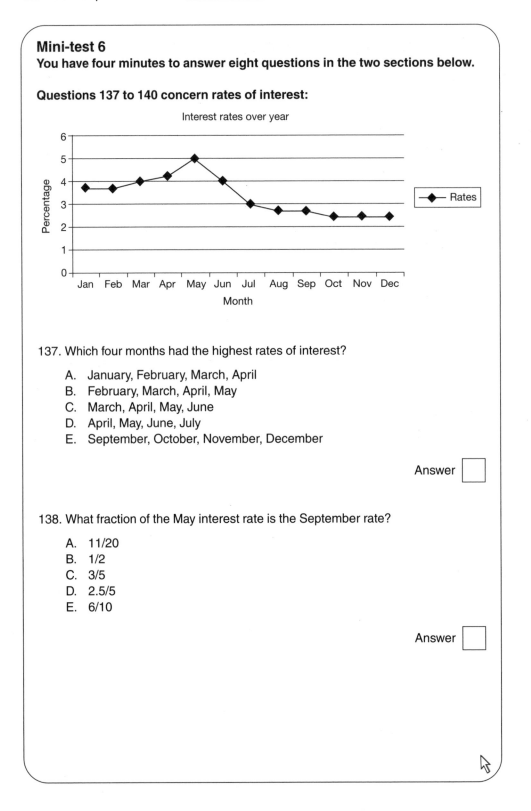

Interest rates over year

137. Which four months had the highest rates of interest?

    A.   January, February, March, April
    B.   February, March, April, May
    C.   March, April, May, June
    D.   April, May, June, July
    E.   September, October, November, December

    Answer ☐

138. What fraction of the May interest rate is the September rate?

    A.   11/20
    B.   1/2
    C.   3/5
    D.   2.5/5
    E.   6/10

    Answer ☐

139. If the average interest rate over the year can be used to determine the interest paid on borrowings, how much will be paid on a £250,000 loan?

    A. £102,000
    B. £10,200
    C. £840
    D. £8,500
    E. £9,600

Answer ☐

140. If £50,000 is borrowed for the month of May, how much will it cost?

    A. $C = 50{,}000 \times 5^{(1/12)}$
    B. $C = 50{,}000 \times 1.05^{(1/12)}$
    C. $C = 50{,}000 \times 5 / 12$
    D. $C = 50{,}000 \times 1.05 / 12$
    E. Cannot tell

Answer ☐

Questions 141 to 144 concern the activity of a typical student during a college day:

Student working day

141. How much more time is spent on leisure than on travelling?

    A. 300%
    B. 400%
    C. 40%
    D. 200%
    E. 25%

    Answer ☐

142. If the travelling time is double at the expense of leisure time, what is now the ratio of leisure to travel?

    A. 4 : 1
    B. 3 : 2
    C. 2 : 1
    D. 2 : 3
    E. 1 : 4

    Answer ☐

143. During the holidays the study time is replaced by working at £6.50 per hour. If the travel costs are £1.20 to get to work, how long does the student have to work to pay the travel costs?

    A. 10.5 minutes
    B. 20 minutes
    C. 18.5 minutes
    D. 11 minutes
    E. 15.5 minutes

    Answer ☐

144. If the student can work six hours a day and they find a job which is more lucrative, but further away, travel costs are now £3.00. How much more will they have to earn to make the new job worthwhile?

    A. 10p/hour
    B. 15p/hour
    C. 20p/hour
    D. 25p/hour
    E. 30p/hour

    Answer ☐

End of test

Mini-test 7

You have four minutes to answer eight questions in the two sections below.

Questions 145 to 148 concern the equations associated with the increase of a certain value, V, with time in seconds, t:

Equation 1: $V_1 = 3t + 5$
Equation 2: $V_2 = t^2$
Equation 3: $V_3 = 4t + 1$
Equation 4: $V_4 = 10(1 - e^{-0.2t})$
Equation 5: $V_5 = 5\sqrt{t}$

145. If t is very large, which equation would give the highest =t value of V?

    A.   Equation 1
    B.   Equation 2
    C.   Equation 3
    D.   Equation 4
    E.   Equation 5

Answer

146. How much larger is the V_2 than V_1 at 5 seconds?

    A.   10%
    B.   15%
    C.   20%
    D.   25%
    E.   30%

Answer

147. If V_2 and V_5 are started together, when will they have the same value?

    A. $t^3 = 25$
    B. $t = 1$
    C. $t = \sqrt{25}$
    D. $25t = t^2$
    E.   30%

Answer

148. Which equation has the highest average value between 0 and 1?

    A. Equation 1
    B. Equation 2
    C. Equation 3
    D. Equation 4
    E. Equation 5

Answer ☐

Questions 149 to 152 concern the student satisfaction levels in various faculties of a university:

Faculty satisfaction levels

149. Which year had the greatest difference in points between the best performing and the worst?

    A. 2001
    B. 2003
    C. 2005
    D. 2007
    E. 2004

Answer ☐

150. The graph shows that...

   A.   Teaching is consistently better in the Philosophy faculty than in Maths.
   B.   Teaching is consistently better in the Maths faculty than in English, but not as good as in Philosophy.
   C.   Teaching is consistently better in the Physics faculty than in English, but not as good as in Philosophy.
   D.   All the above.
   E.   None of the above.

Answer ☐

151. The respondents had three choices for most questions, A 'not good', B 'good' and C 'very good'. If the number of people polled was n, the score, S, was calculated as $S = 100 \times (B + 2C) / 2n$. What would the score be if everyone replied 'good'?

   A.   100
   B.   75
   C.   50
   D.   25
   E.   60

Answer ☐

152. If the English results continue to improve and the Philosophy results continue to decline as in the year 2007–2008, how long will it take for the English faculty to overtake the Philosophy faculty?

   A.   2
   B.   3
   C.   4
   D.   5
   E.   6

Answer ☐

End of test

Abstract reasoning

The abstract reasoning sub-test is described as being intended to assess an ability to identify patterns amongst abstract shapes. The way the UKCAT sub-test does this is by asking the candidate to identify to which group a particular shape, or set of shapes, belongs as illustrated below:

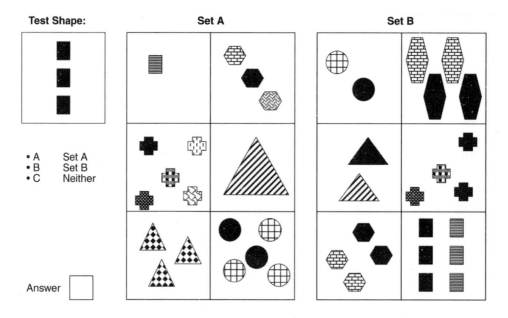

For each SET A and SET B there will be five items (screens) and you will have to click on one of the buttons, A, B or C, to indicate whether you think the test shape belongs to the set A, set B or to neither.

What you have to do, therefore, is to try to identify a particular rule, or set of rules, that governs the contents of the cells in each set. For example, set A may have an odd number of shapes and set B an even number. It is unlikely to be quite as simple, however, as this particular example would preclude the possibility of belonging to neither set. What is more likely is that there will be more than one rule, ie there is an odd number of shapes, triangles are shaded and other shapes may or may not have shading, and possibly even certain conditions – when there is triangle present the rectangles are shaded, for example. Some of these rules will be readily apparent, but others, equally crucial for determining whether or not a particular test shape belongs, will be more obscure and will require careful scrutiny of *all* the cells in the set.

The kinds of things you should be looking for include:

- number;
- size;
- shape;
- number of sides;
- enclosed or not;
- type of shading or colour;
- patterns;
- position in the cell;
- direction (up or down, left or right, etc);
- rotation;
- reflection;
- intersection.

This particular sub-test will allow you one minute to read the instructions and 15 minutes to determine the appurtenance, or otherwise, of 65 test shapes divided into 13 groups. As before, the test screen will show the time remaining at the top right and the item number, out of 65, at the bottom right.

Simply dividing the time available by the number of test shapes to consider would give about 13 seconds for each shape. What you should do, however, is to spend a little time trying to establish the rules for each set and then more quickly determine the appropriate response (Set A, Set B or Neither) for each of the related five shapes. You should, therefore, aim to spend about one minute on each of the 13 groups of five test shapes.

This chapter provides 150 practice questions with answers, divided up into 100 'introductory' questions and 50 questions in the form of five mini-tests lasting two minutes, each containing 10 questions in two groups of five test shapes. Neither these examples nor the real test is intended to be easy. Good luck.

Introductory questions

Q1.

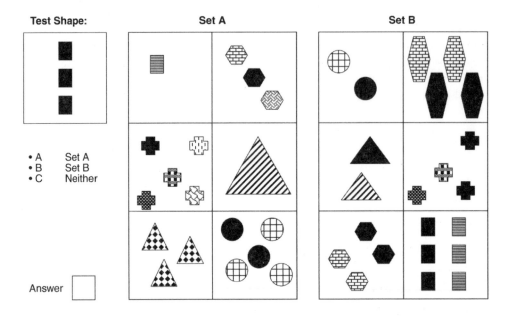

Q2.

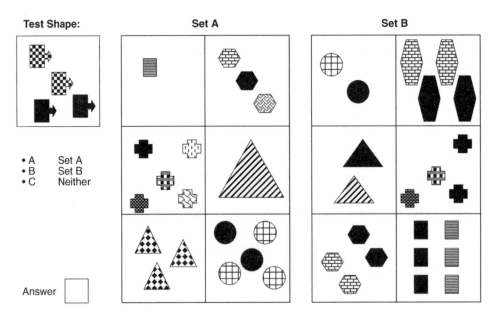

Q3.

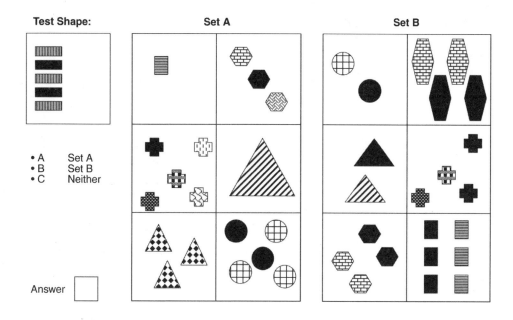

Q4.

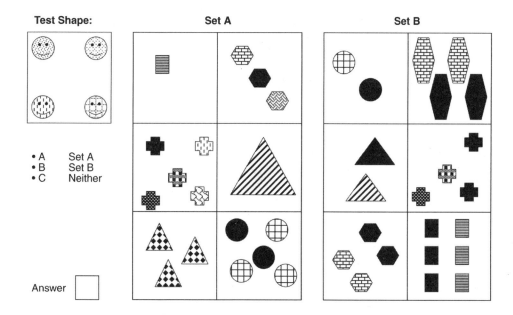

Q5.

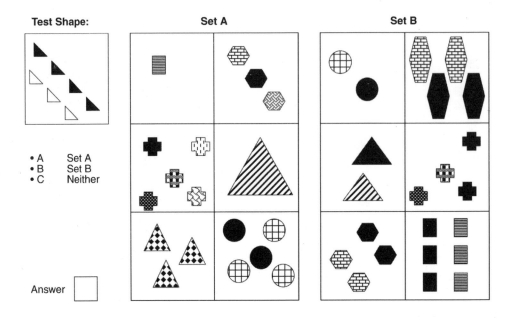

Q6.

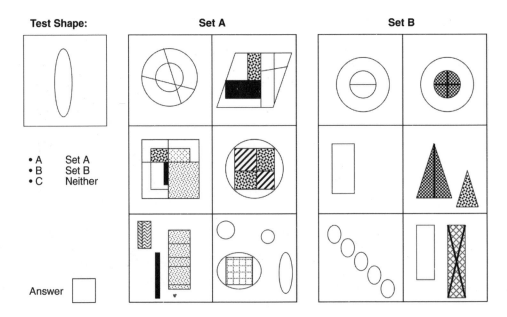

Q7.

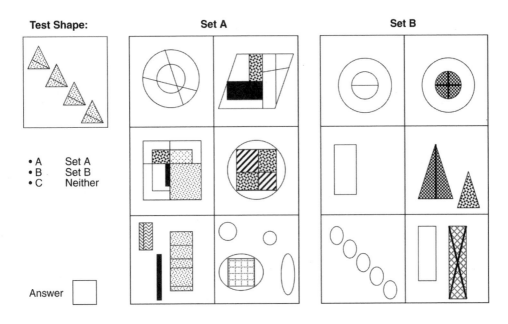

Test Shape:

- A   Set A
- B   Set B
- C   Neither

Answer

Q8.

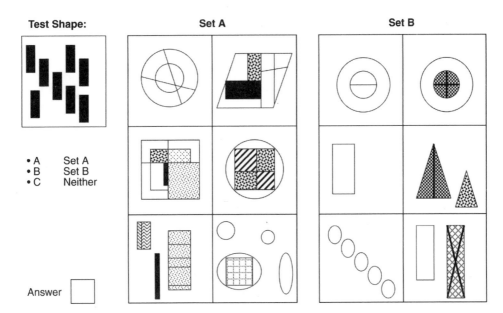

Test Shape:

- A   Set A
- B   Set B
- C   Neither

Answer

Q9.

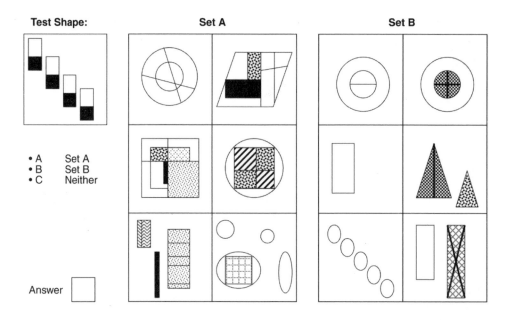

Q10.

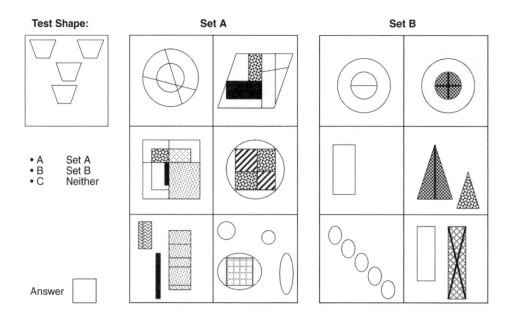

Q11.

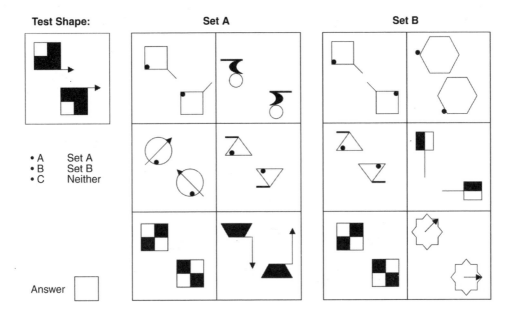

Q12.

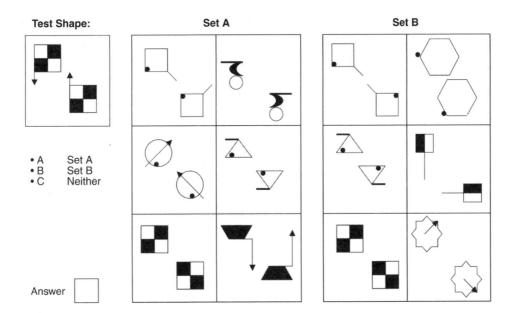

Q13.

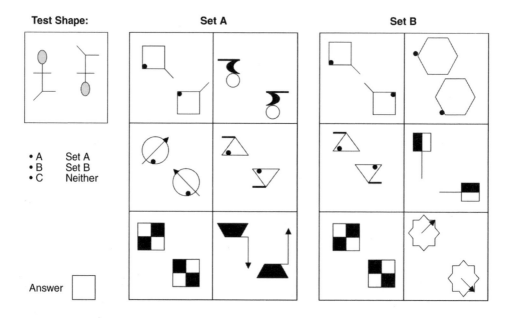

Q14.

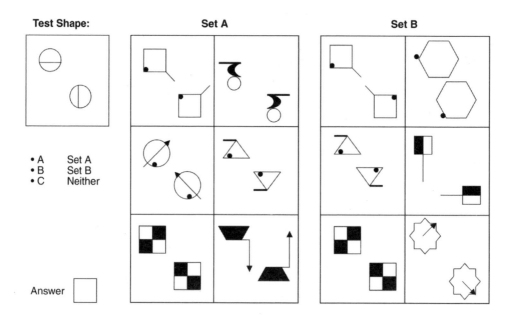

Q15.

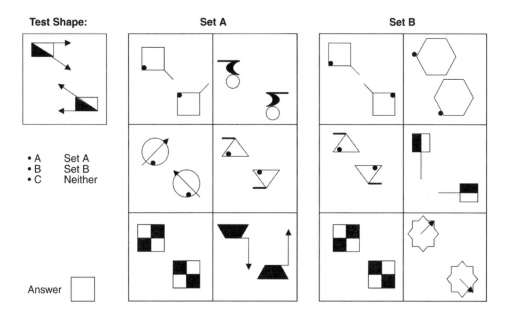

Q16.

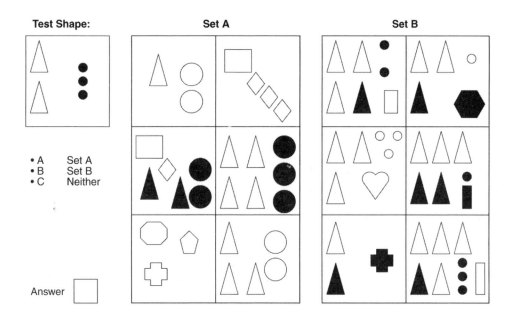

Q17.

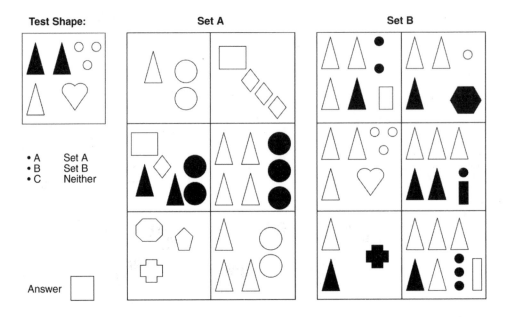

Test Shape: Set A   Set B

- A   Set A
- B   Set B
- C   Neither

Answer

Q18.

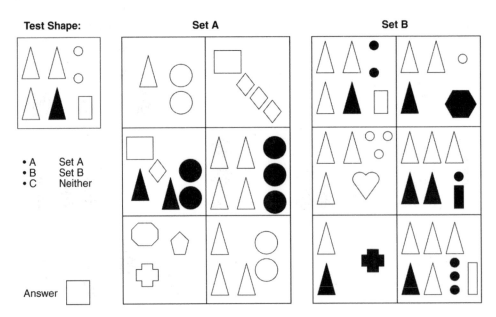

Test Shape: Set A   Set B

- A   Set A
- B   Set B
- C   Neither

Answer

Q19.

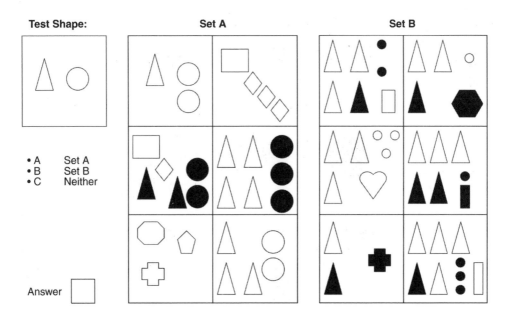

Q20.

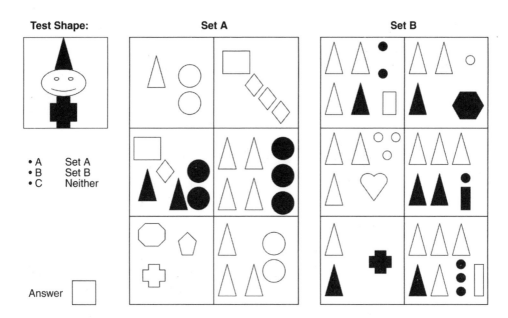

Q21.

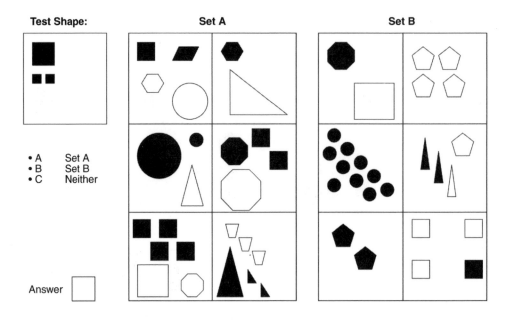

Test Shape:

- A   Set A
- B   Set B
- C   Neither

Answer

Q22.

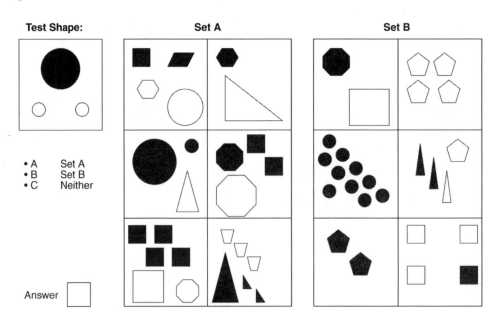

Test Shape:

- A   Set A
- B   Set B
- C   Neither

Answer

Q23.

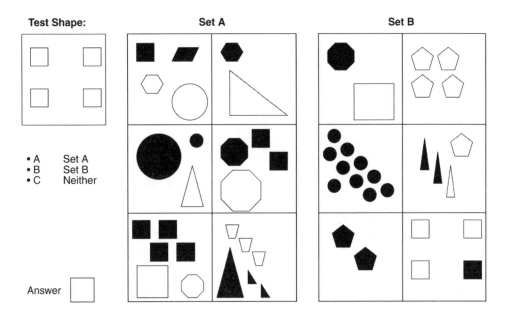

Q24.

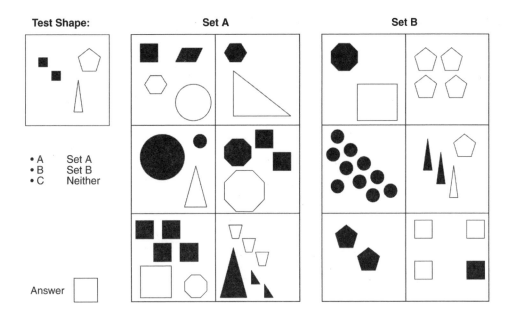

Q25.

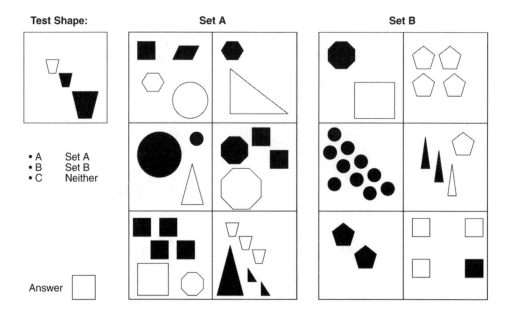

Q26.

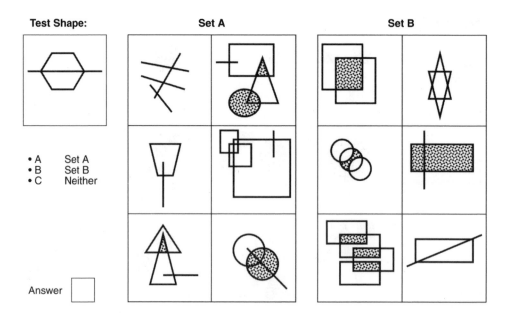

Q27.

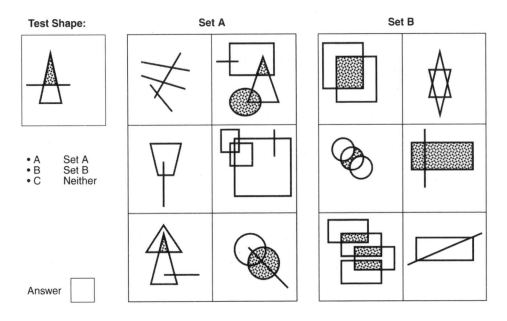

Test Shape:

- A Set A
- B Set B
- C Neither

Answer

Q28.

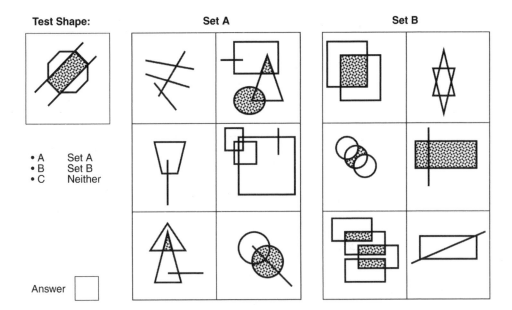

Test Shape:

- A Set A
- B Set B
- C Neither

Answer

Q29.

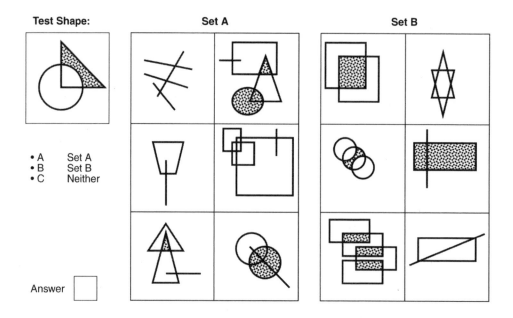

Test Shape:

- A   Set A
- B   Set B
- C   Neither

Answer [ ]

Q30.

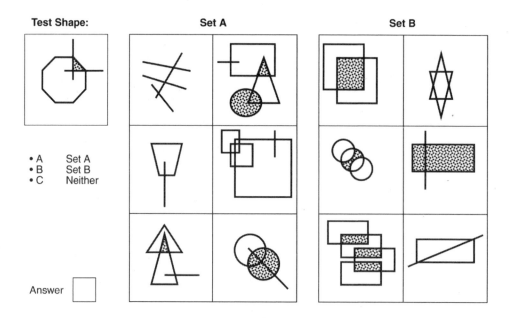

Test Shape:

- A   Set A
- B   Set B
- C   Neither

Answer [ ]

Q31.

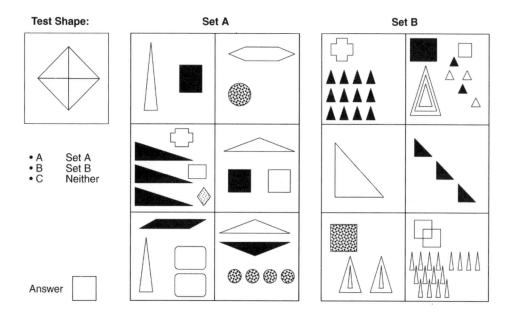

Q32.

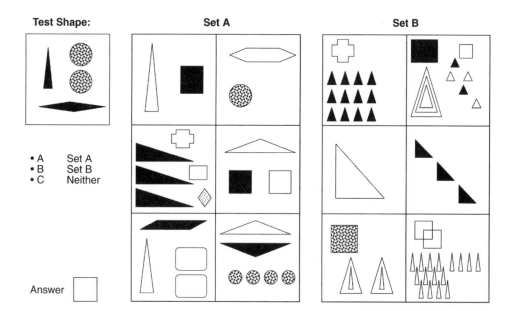

Q33.

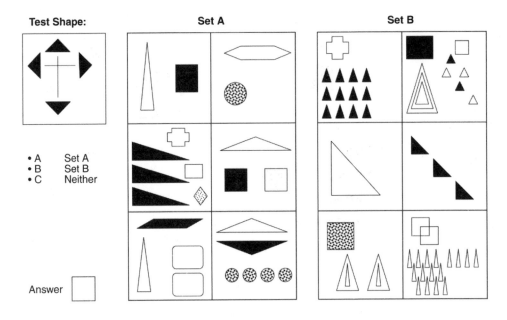

Q34.

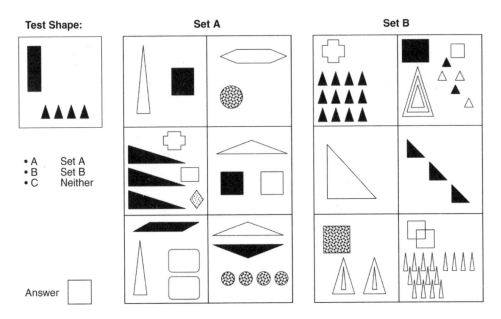

Q35.

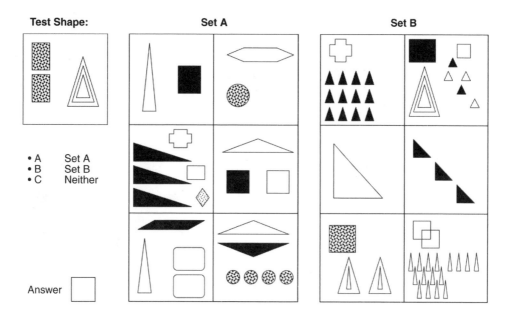

Q36.

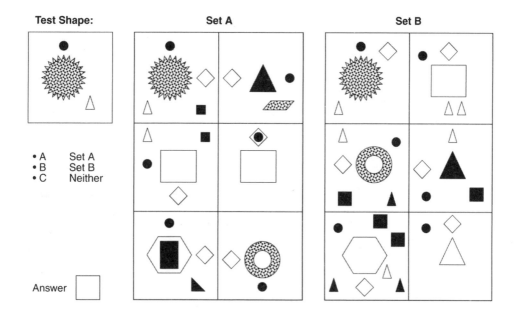

Q37.

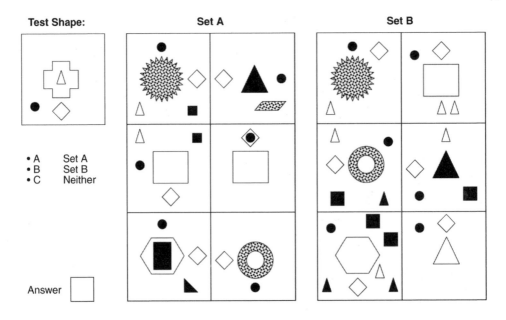

Test Shape: **Set A**   **Set B**

- A   Set A
- B   Set B
- C   Neither

Answer

Q38.

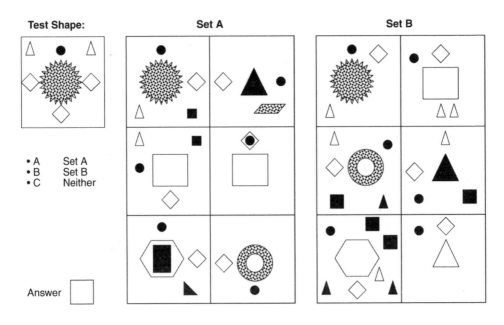

Test Shape: **Set A**   **Set B**

- A   Set A
- B   Set B
- C   Neither

Answer

Q39.

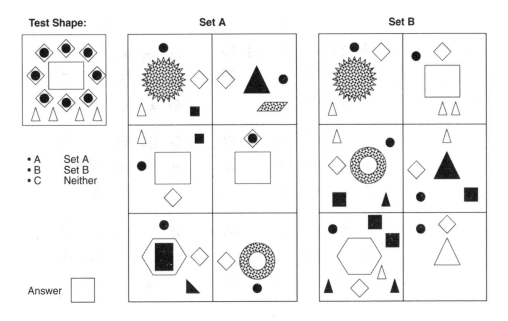

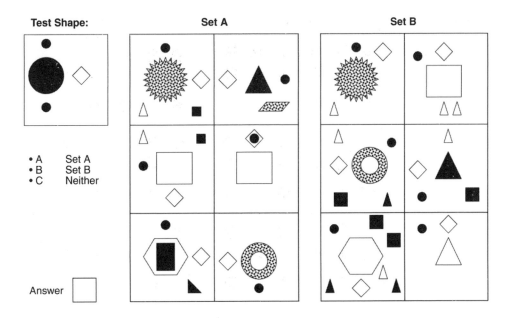

Q40.

Q41.

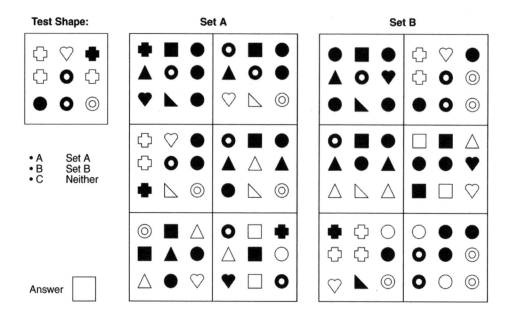

Q42.

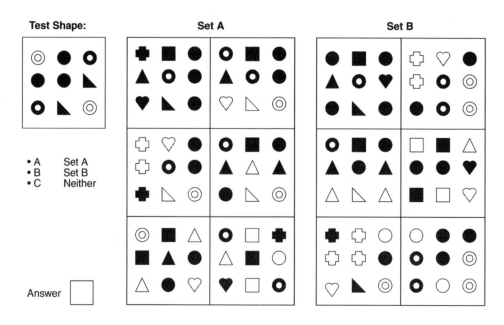

Q43.

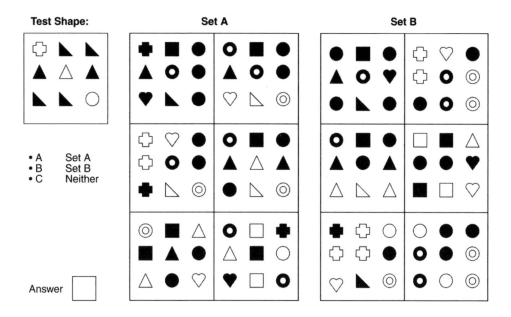

Q44.

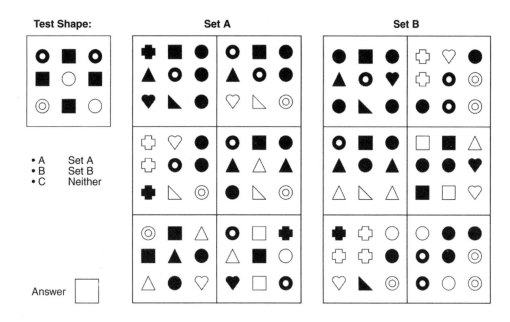

Q45.

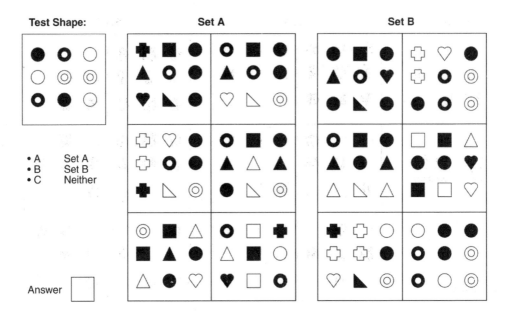

Q46.

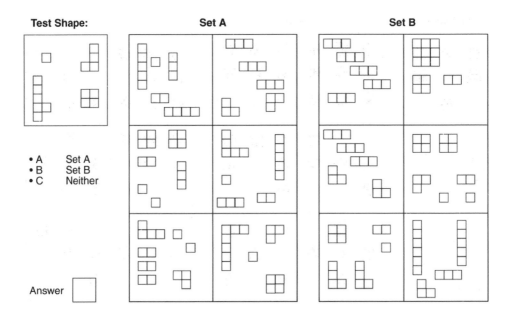

Q47.

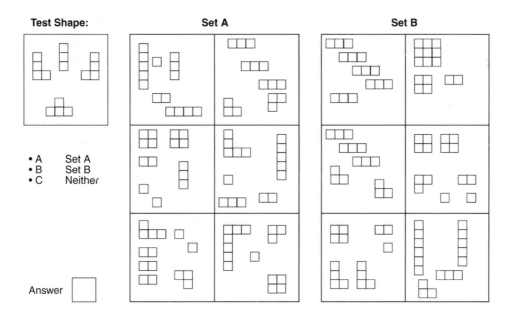

Test Shape:

Set A

Set B

- A   Set A
- B   Set B
- C   Neither

Answer

Q48.

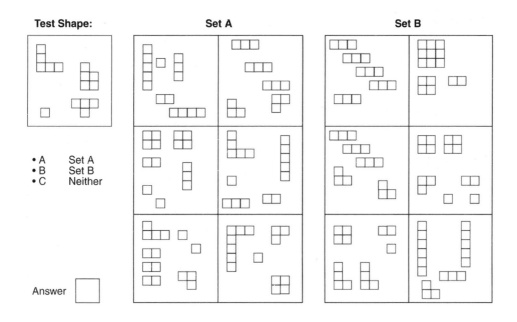

Test Shape:

Set A

Set B

- A   Set A
- B   Set B
- C   Neither

Answer

Q49.

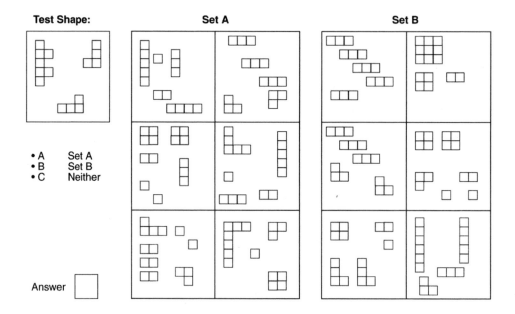

Test Shape:

- A   Set A
- B   Set B
- C   Neither

Answer [ ]

Q50.

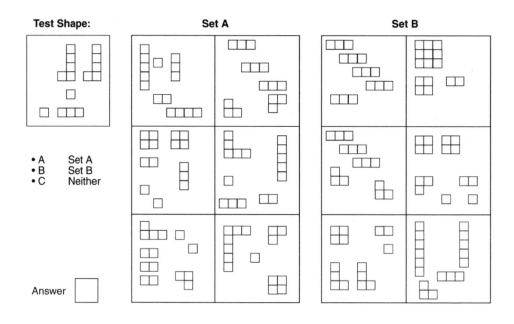

Test Shape:

- A   Set A
- B   Set B
- C   Neither

Answer [ ]

Q51.

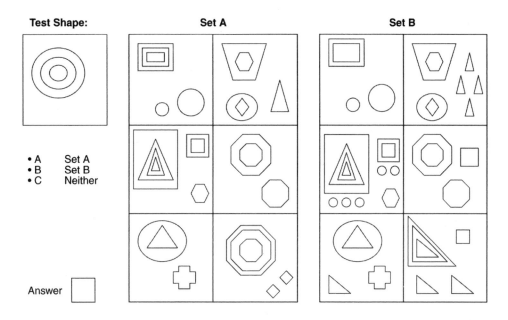

Q52.

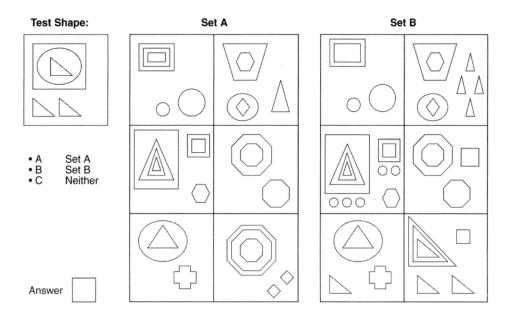

Q53.

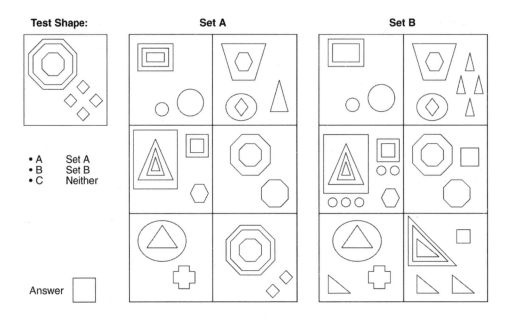

Q54.

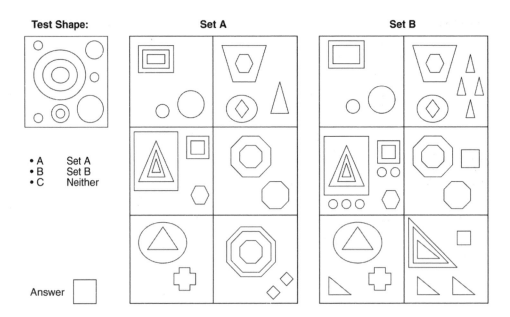

Q55.

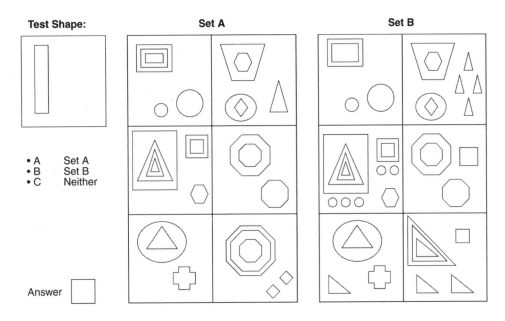

Q56.

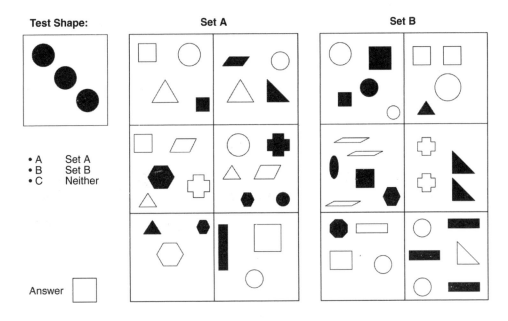

Q57.

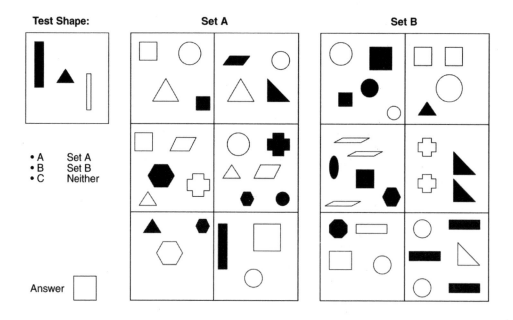

Test Shape: **Set A**   **Set B**

- A   Set A
- B   Set B
- C   Neither

Answer

Q58.

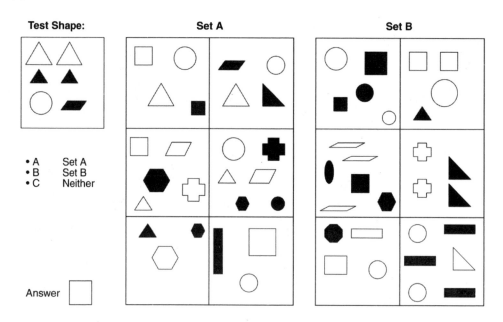

Test Shape: **Set A**   **Set B**

- A   Set A
- B   Set B
- C   Neither

Answer

Q59.

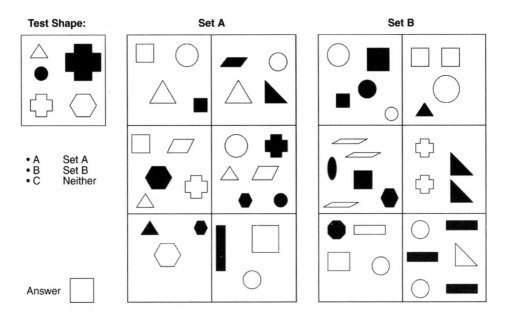

Q60.

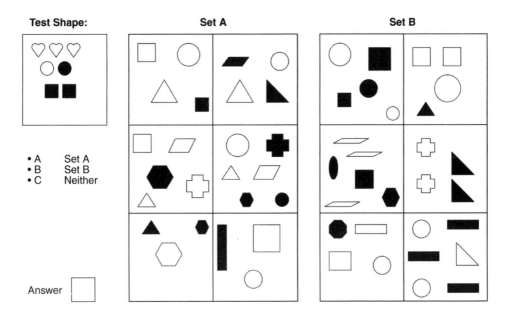

Q61.

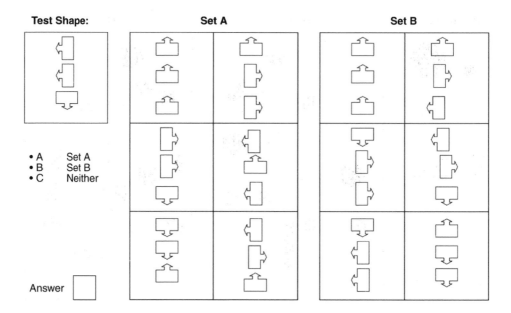

Q62.

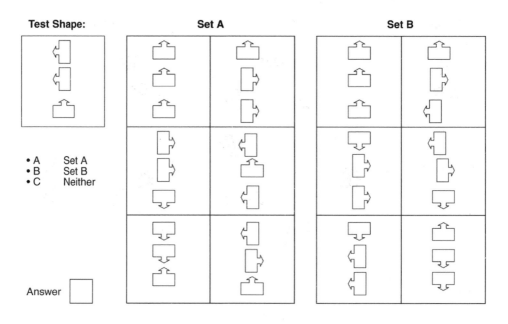

Q63.

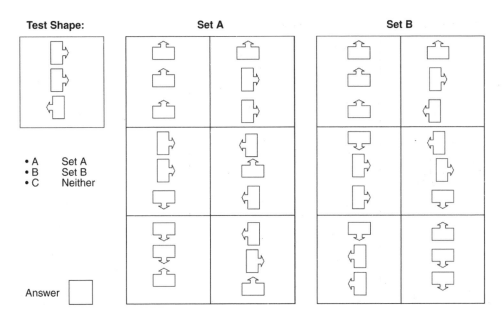

Q64.

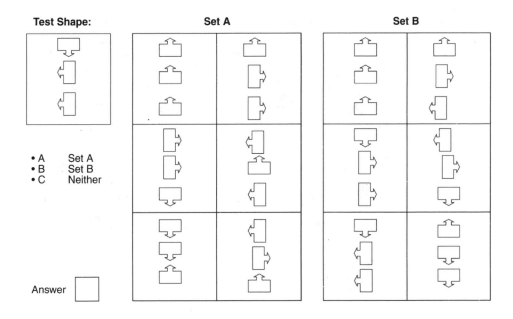

Q65.

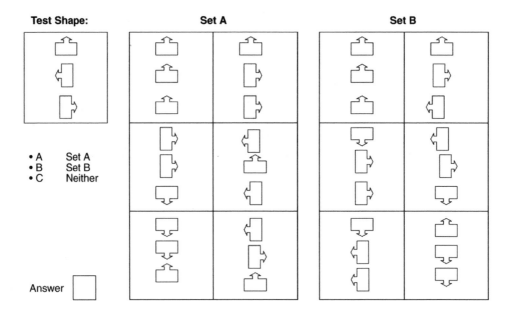

Q66.

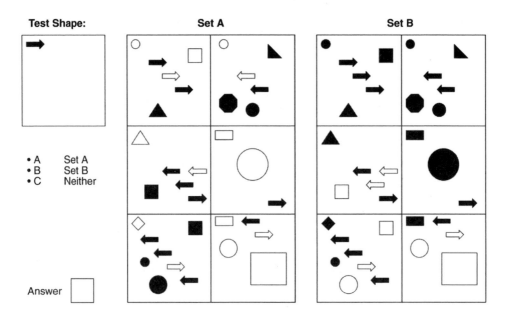

Q67.

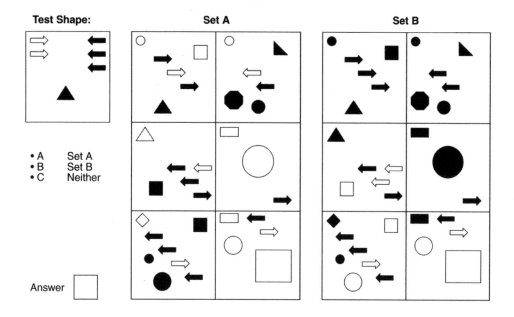

Test Shape:

- A   Set A
- B   Set B
- C   Neither

Answer

Q68.

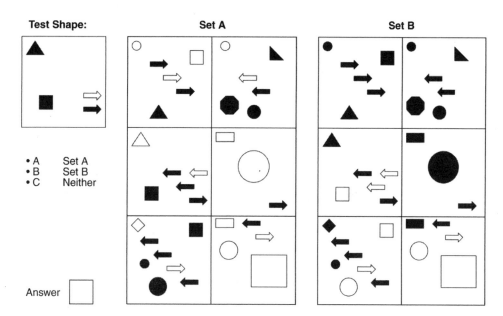

Test Shape: **Set A**   **Set B**

- A   Set A
- B   Set B
- C   Neither

Answer

Q69.

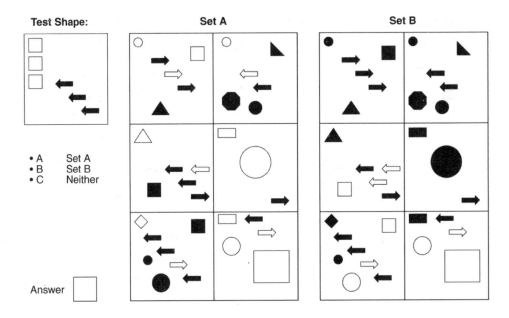

Q70.

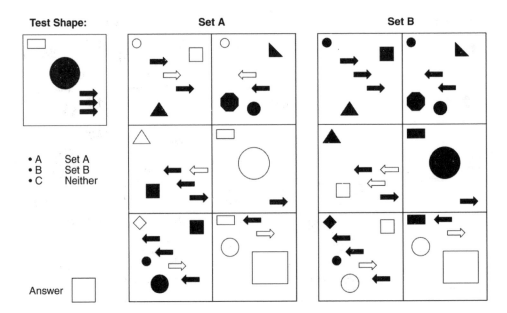

Q71.

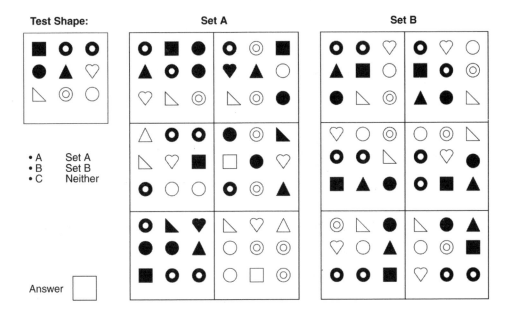

Test Shape:

- A   Set A
- B   Set B
- C   Neither

Answer

Q72.

Test Shape:

- A   Set A
- B   Set B
- C   Neither

Answer

Q73.

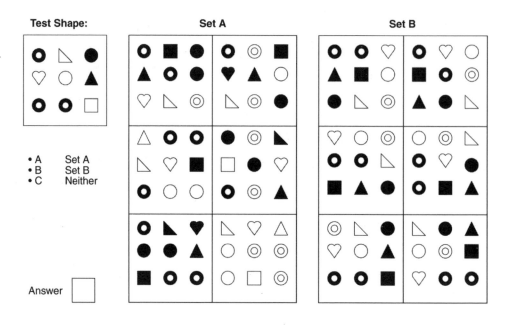

Q74.

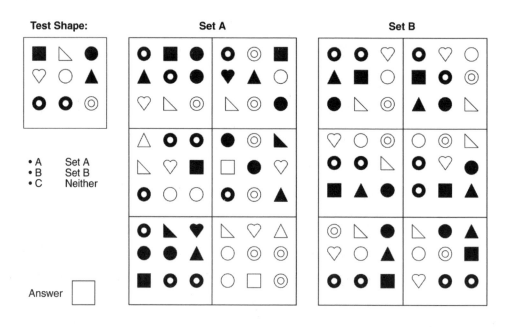

Q75.

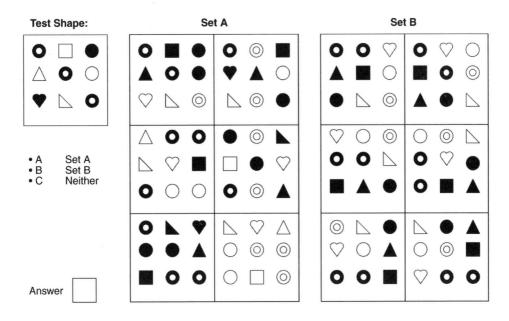

Q76.

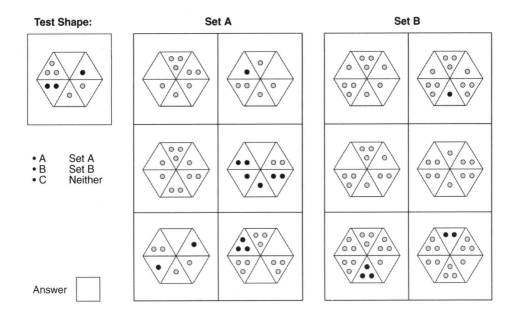

Q77.

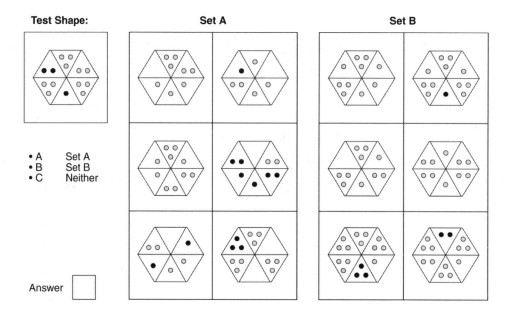

Q78.

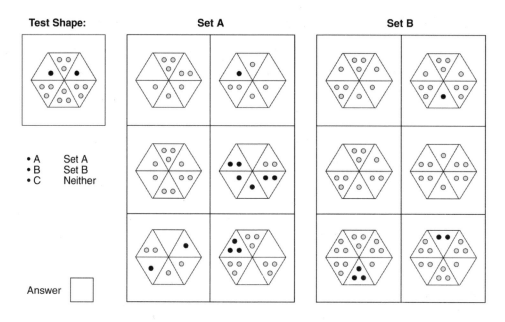

Q79.

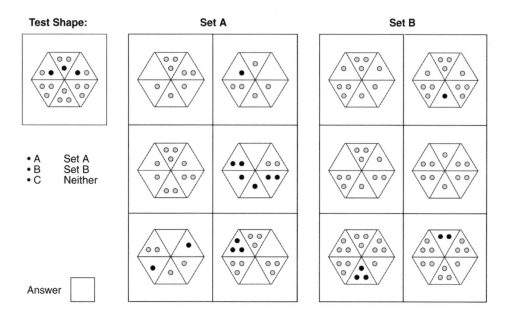

- A   Set A
- B   Set B
- C   Neither

Answer

Q80.

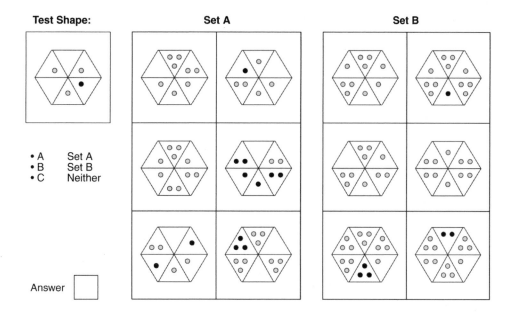

- A   Set A
- B   Set B
- C   Neither

Answer

Q81.

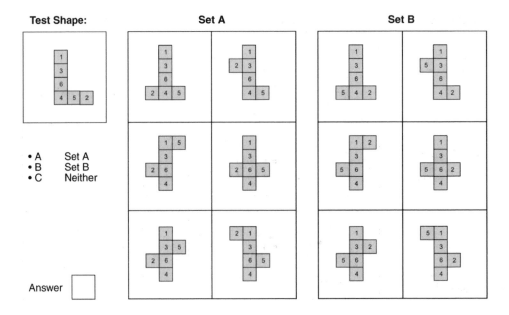

Q82.

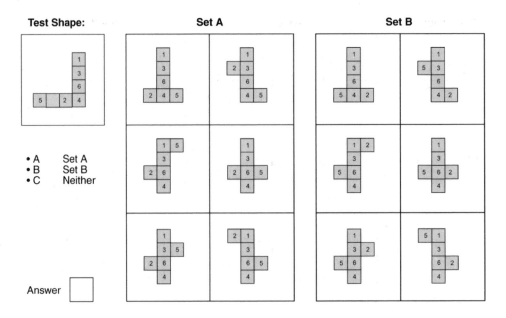

Q83.

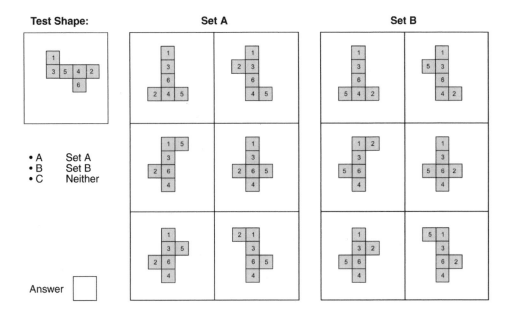

Test Shape: **Set A**   **Set B**

- A   Set A
- B   Set B
- C   Neither

Answer

Q84.

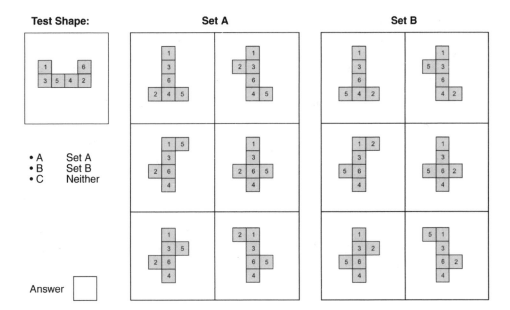

Test Shape: **Set A**   **Set B**

- A   Set A
- B   Set B
- C   Neither

Answer

Q85.

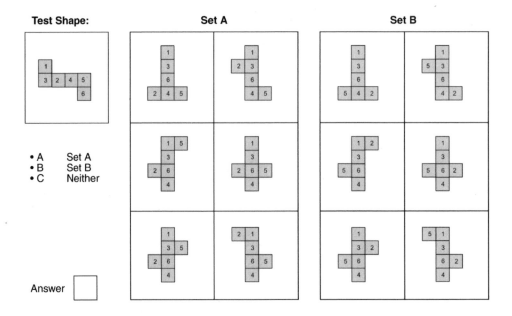

Q86.

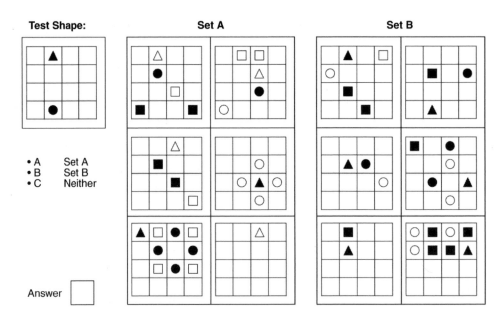

Q87.

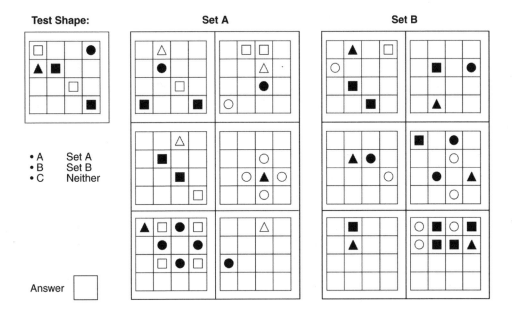

Test Shape: **Set A**   **Set B**

- A   Set A
- B   Set B
- C   Neither

Answer

Q88.

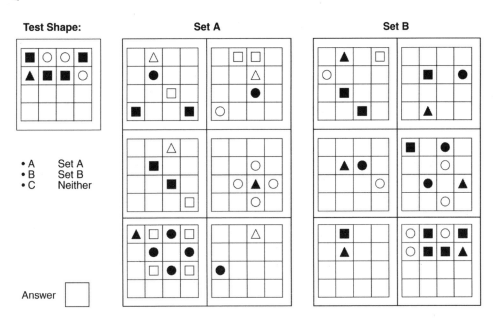

Test Shape: **Set A**   **Set B**

- A   Set A
- B   Set B
- C   Neither

Answer

Q89.

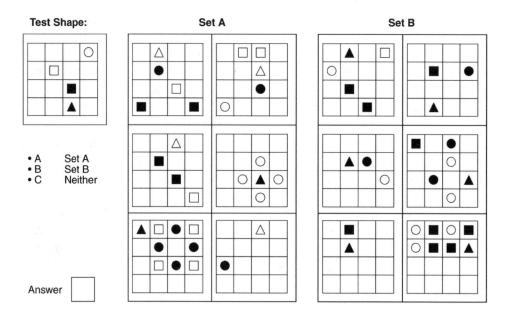

Q90.

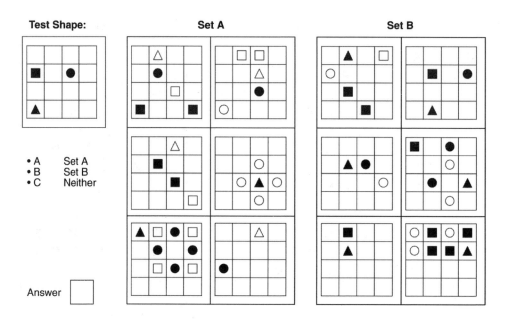

Q91.

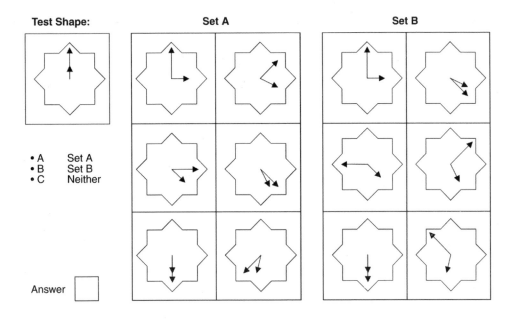

Test Shape:

- A   Set A
- B   Set B
- C   Neither

Answer

Q92.

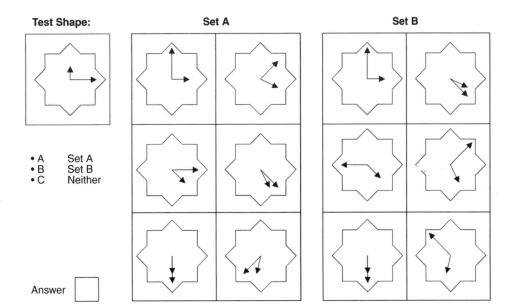

Test Shape:

- A   Set A
- B   Set B
- C   Neither

Answer

Q93.

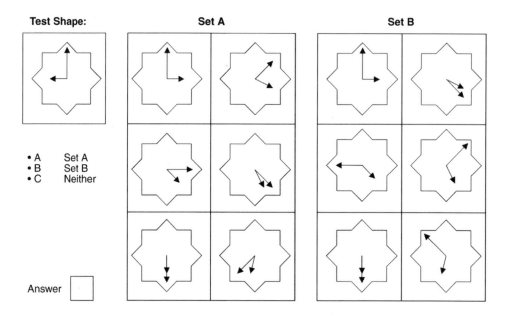

Q94.

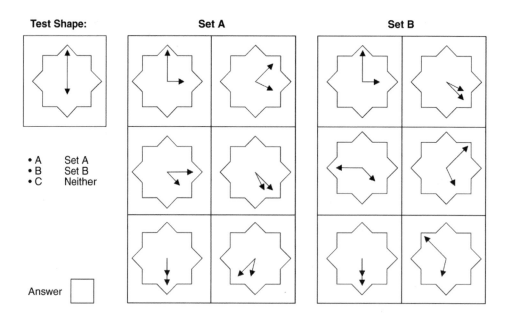

Q95.

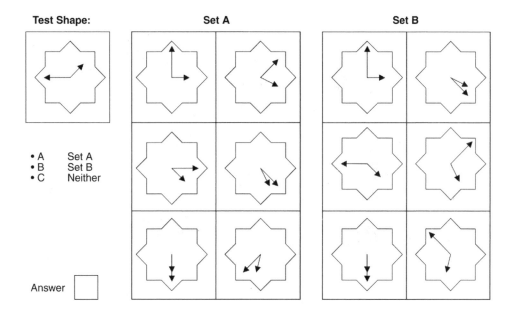

- A   Set A
- B   Set B
- C   Neither

Answer

Q96.

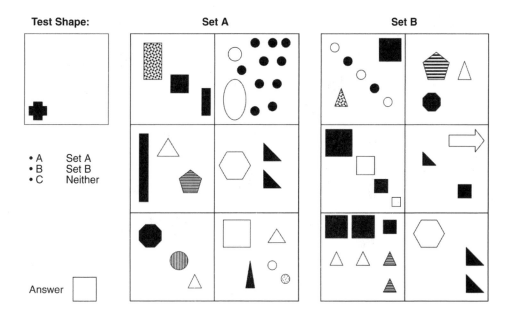

- A   Set A
- B   Set B
- C   Neither

Answer

Q97.

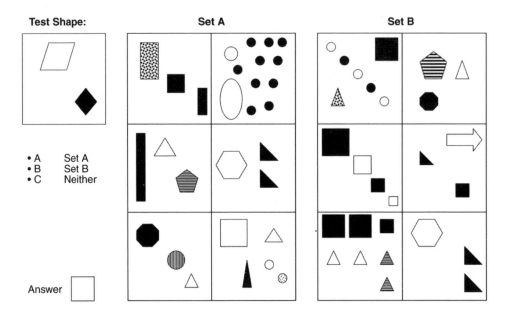

Q98.

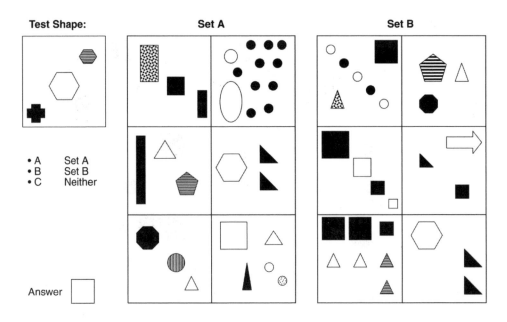

Q99.

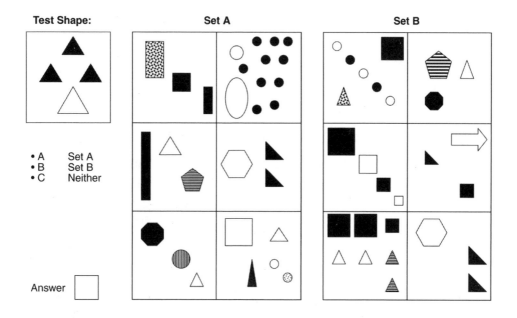

Q100.

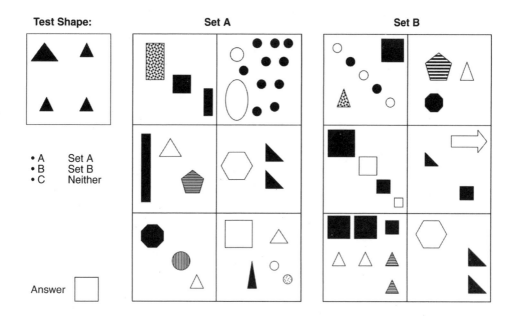

Mini-tests

Mini-test 1

Q101.

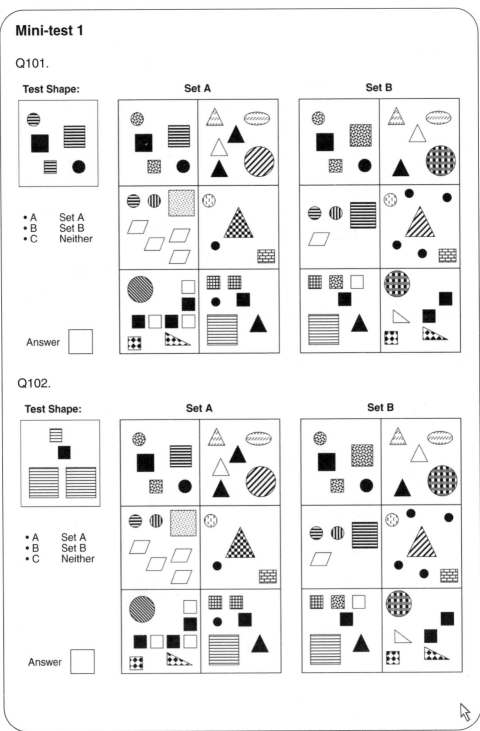

Test Shape: | Set A | Set B

- A   Set A
- B   Set B
- C   Neither

Answer

Q102.

Test Shape:

- A   Set A
- B   Set B
- C   Neither

Answer

Q103.

Test Shape: **Set A**   **Set B**

- A   Set A
- B   Set B
- C   Neither

Answer

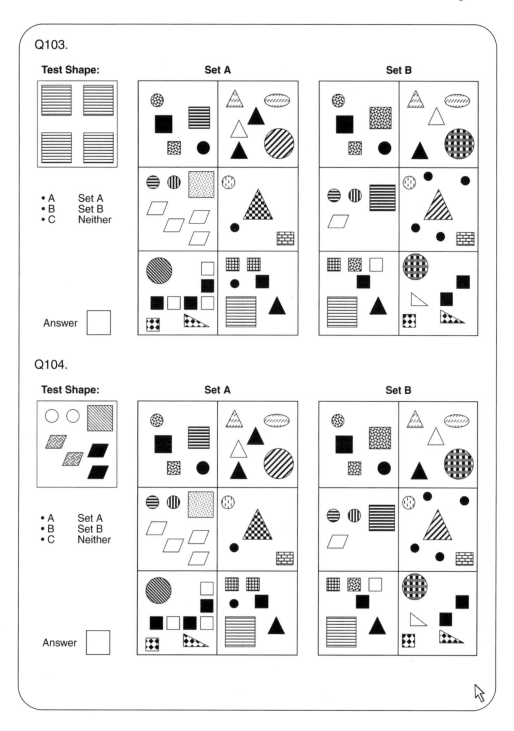

Q104.

Test Shape: **Set A**   **Set B**

- A   Set A
- B   Set B
- C   Neither

Answer

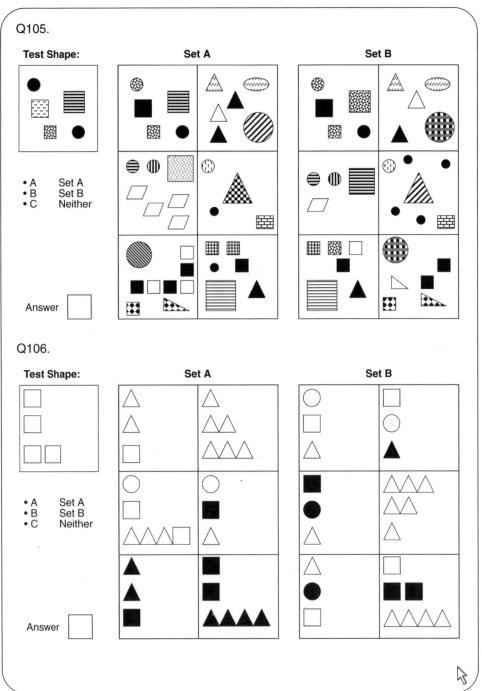

Q107.

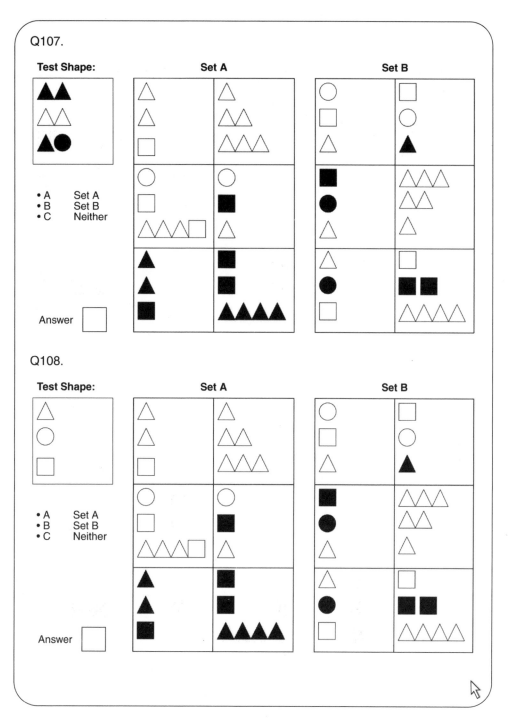

Q108.

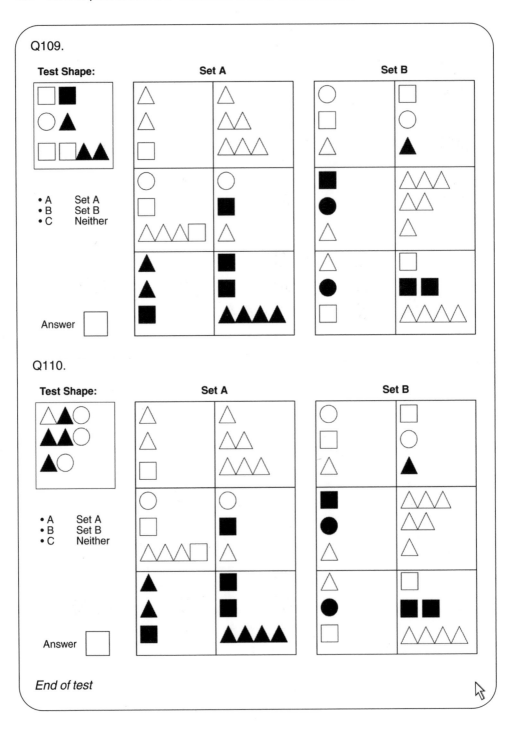

Q109.

Test Shape:

Set A

Set B

- A   Set A
- B   Set B
- C   Neither

Answer

Q110.

Test Shape:

Set A

Set B

- A   Set A
- B   Set B
- C   Neither

Answer

End of test

Mini-test 2

Q111.

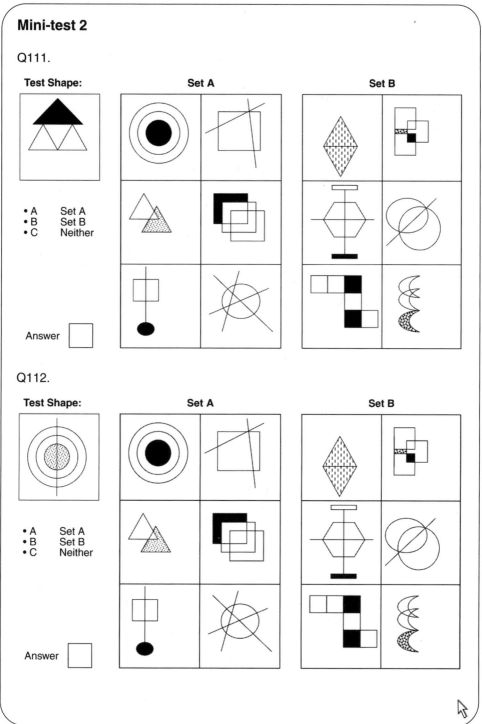

Test Shape:

Set A

Set B

- A   Set A
- B   Set B
- C   Neither

Answer

Q112.

Test Shape:

Set A

Set B

- A   Set A
- B   Set B
- C   Neither

Answer

Q113.

Test Shape:

Set A

Set B

- A　Set A
- B　Set B
- C　Neither

Answer

Q114.

Test Shape:

Set A

Set B

- A　Set A
- B　Set B
- C　Neither

Answer

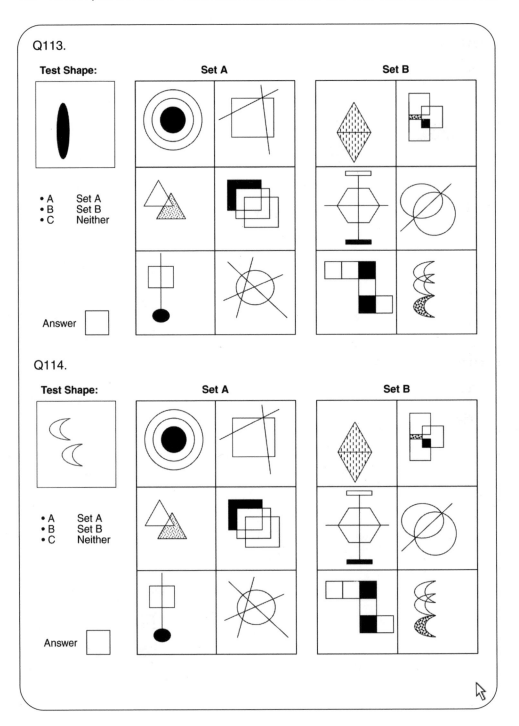

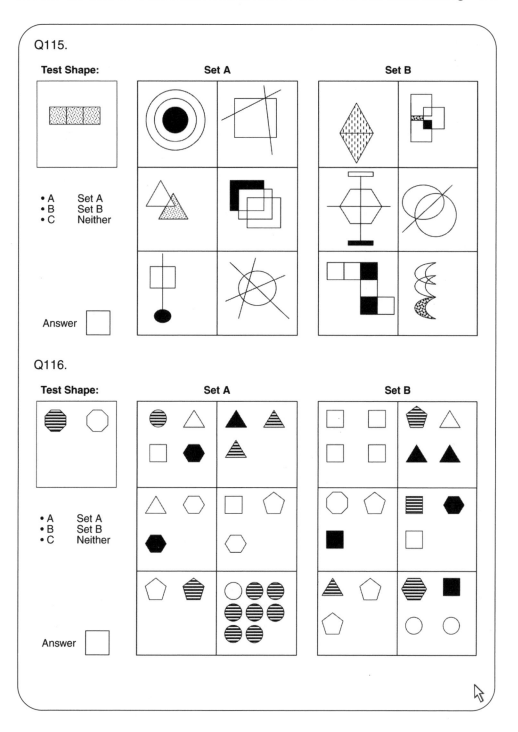

Q115.

Test Shape:

Set A

Set B

- A   Set A
- B   Set B
- C   Neither

Answer

Q116.

Test Shape:

Set A

Set B

- A   Set A
- B   Set B
- C   Neither

Answer

Q117.

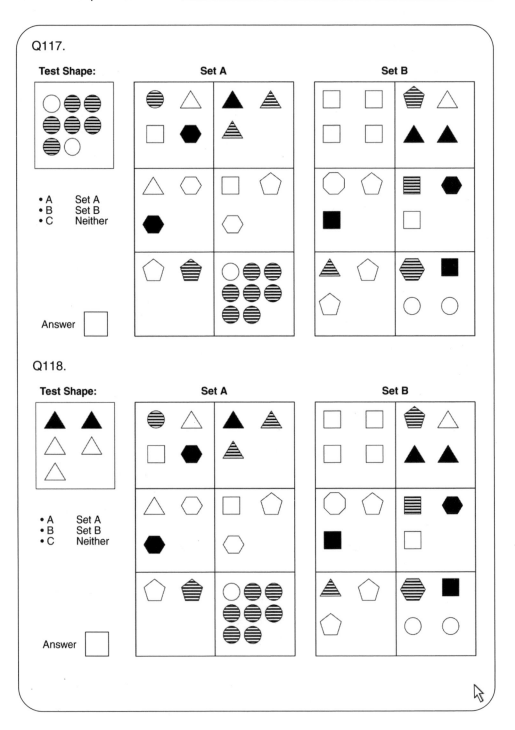

Test Shape:

- A   Set A
- B   Set B
- C   Neither

Answer

Q118.

Test Shape:

- A   Set A
- B   Set B
- C   Neither

Answer

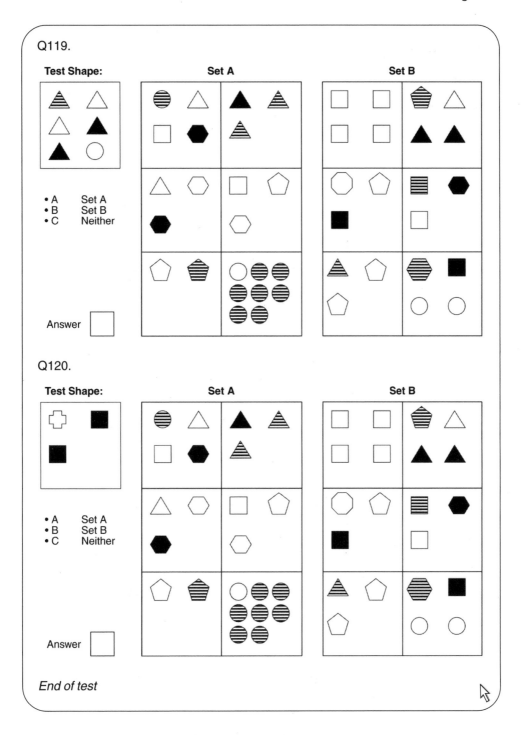

Q119.

Test Shape:

- A   Set A
- B   Set B
- C   Neither

Answer

Q120.

Test Shape:

- A   Set A
- B   Set B
- C   Neither

Answer

End of test

Mini-test 3

Q121.

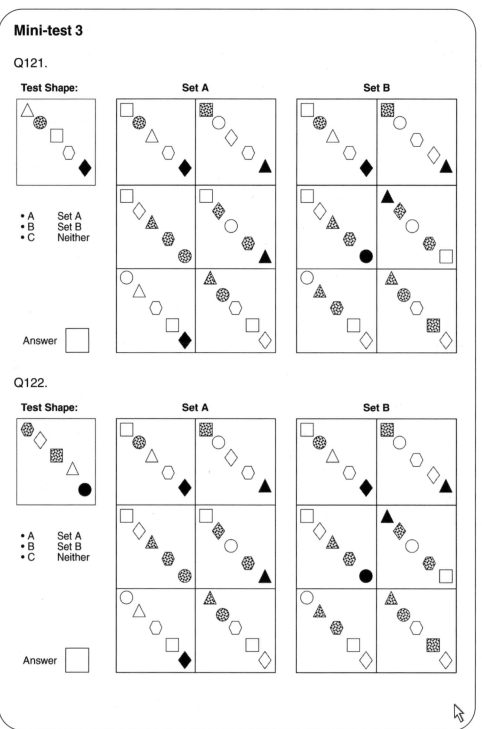

Q122.

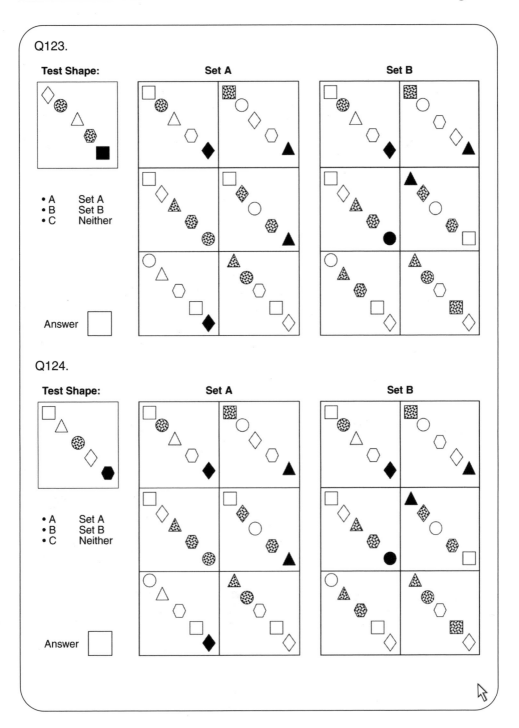

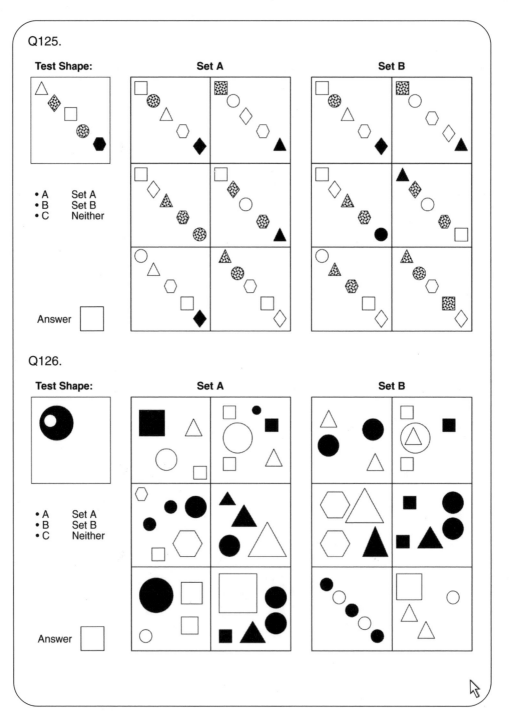

Q125.

Test Shape:

Set A

Set B

- A   Set A
- B   Set B
- C   Neither

Answer

Q126.

Test Shape:

Set A

Set B

- A   Set A
- B   Set B
- C   Neither

Answer

Q127.

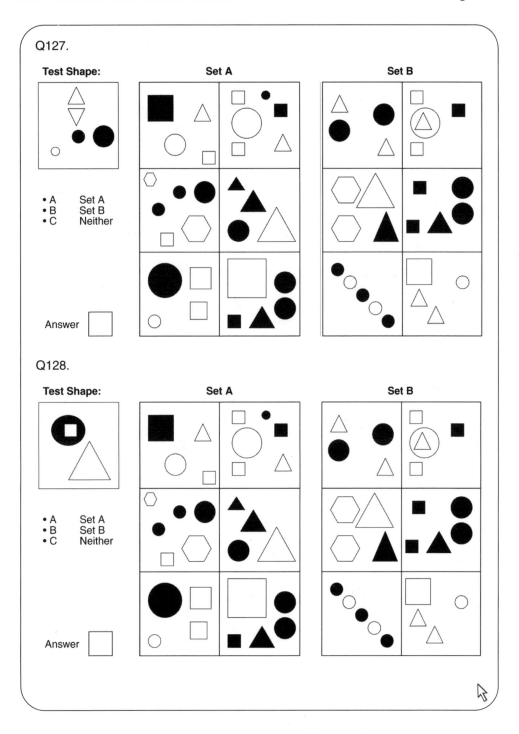

Test Shape:

• A   Set A
• B   Set B
• C   Neither

Answer

Q128.

Test Shape:

• A   Set A
• B   Set B
• C   Neither

Answer

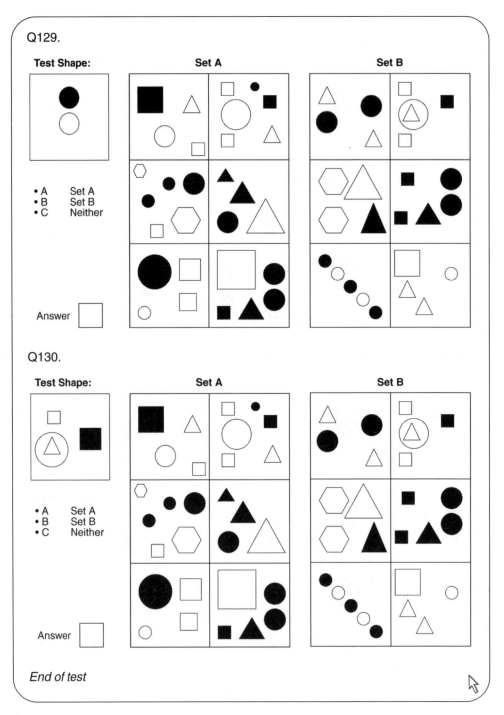

Q129.

Test Shape:

Set A

Set B

- A   Set A
- B   Set B
- C   Neither

Answer

Q130.

Test Shape:

Set A

Set B

- A   Set A
- B   Set B
- C   Neither

Answer

End of test

Mini-test 4

Q131.

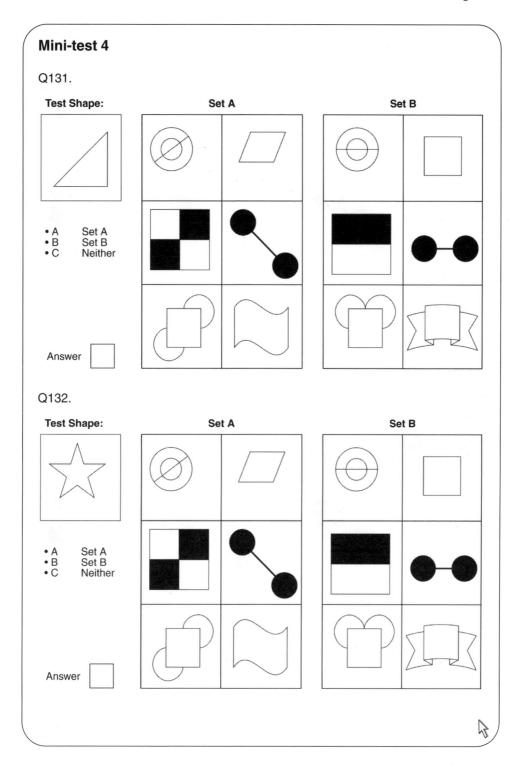

- A Set A
- B Set B
- C Neither

Answer

Q132.

- A Set A
- B Set B
- C Neither

Answer

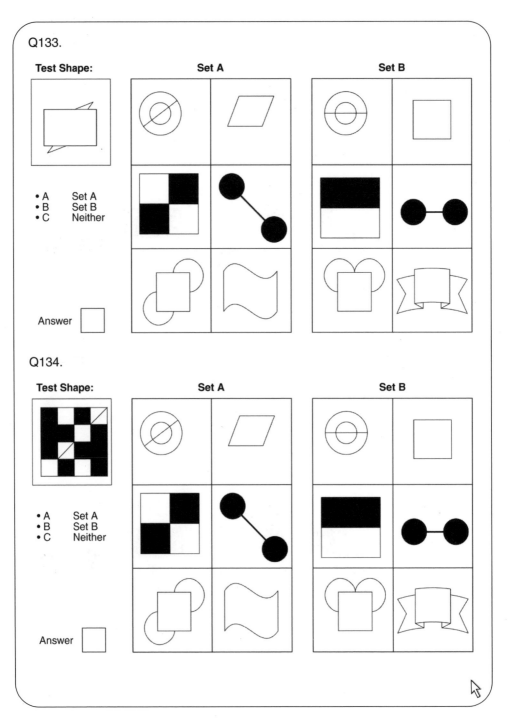

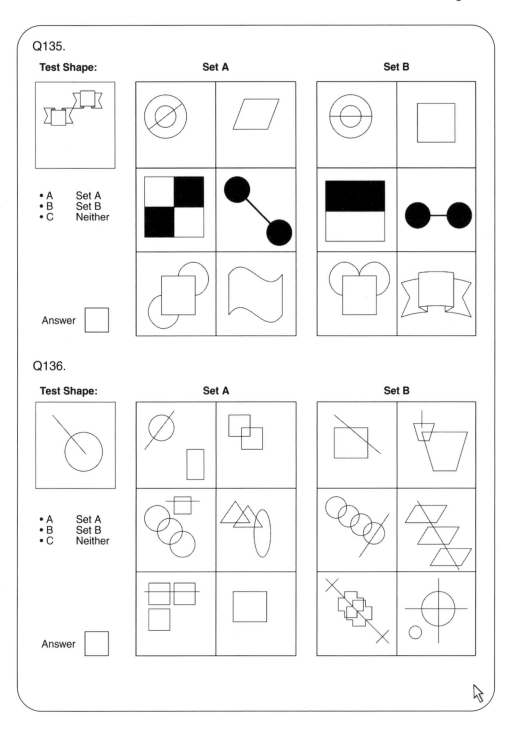

Q135.

Test Shape: **Set A**   **Set B**

- A   Set A
- B   Set B
- C   Neither

Answer

Q136.

Test Shape: **Set A**   **Set B**

- A   Set A
- B   Set B
- C   Neither

Answer

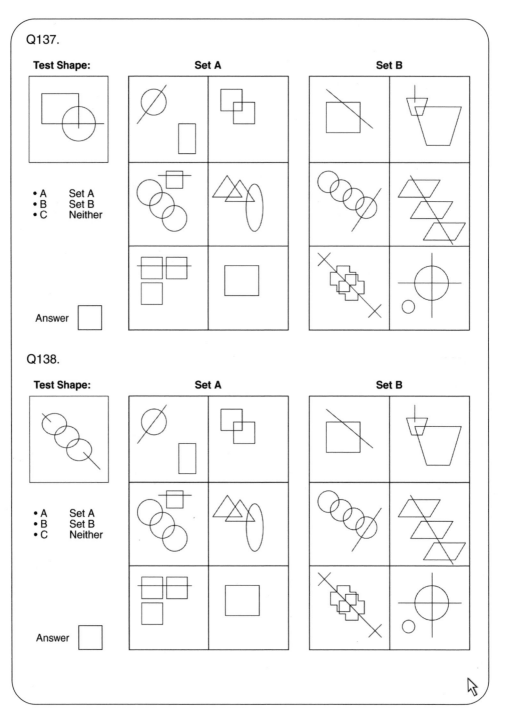

Q137.

Test Shape: **Set A**   **Set B**

- A   Set A
- B   Set B
- C   Neither

Answer

Q138.

Test Shape: **Set A**   **Set B**

- A   Set A
- B   Set B
- C   Neither

Answer

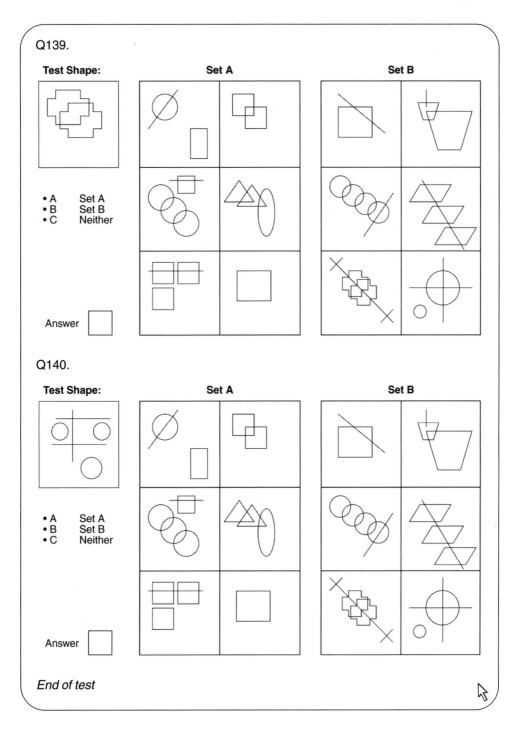

Q139.

Test Shape:

Set A

Set B

• A   Set A
• B   Set B
• C   Neither

Answer

Q140.

Test Shape:

Set A

Set B

• A   Set A
• B   Set B
• C   Neither

Answer

End of test

Mini-test 5

Q141.

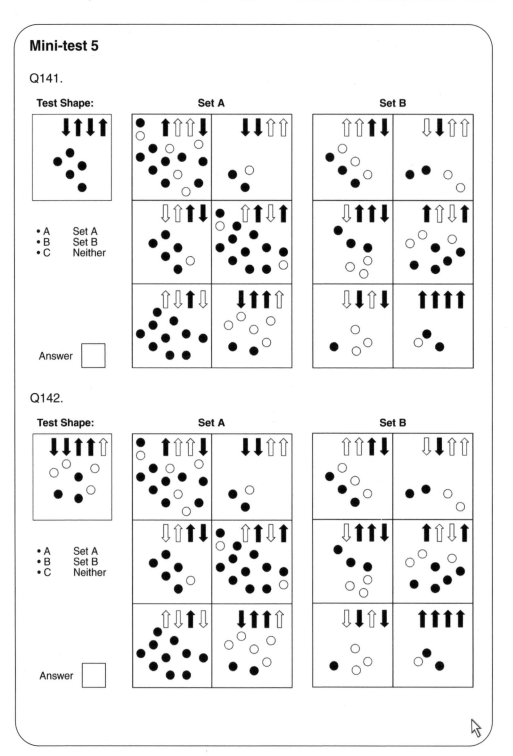

Q142.

Test Shape:

Set A

Set B

- A   Set A
- B   Set B
- C   Neither

Answer

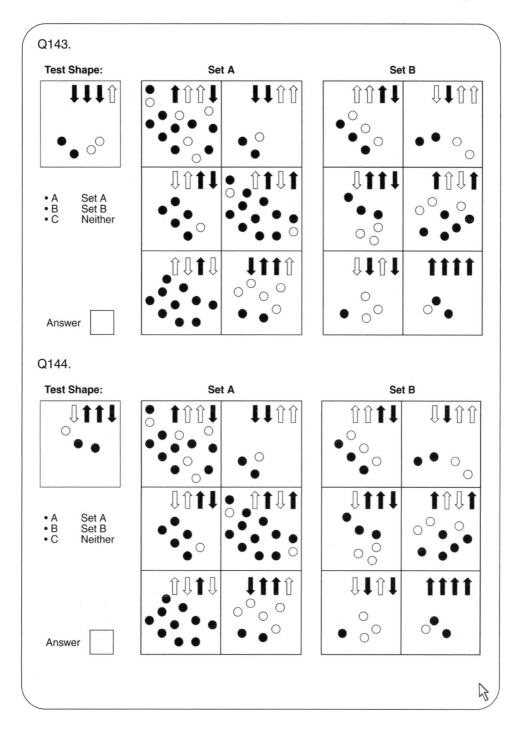

Q143.

Test Shape:

Set A

Set B

- A   Set A
- B   Set B
- C   Neither

Answer

Q144.

Test Shape:

Set A

Set B

- A   Set A
- B   Set B
- C   Neither

Answer

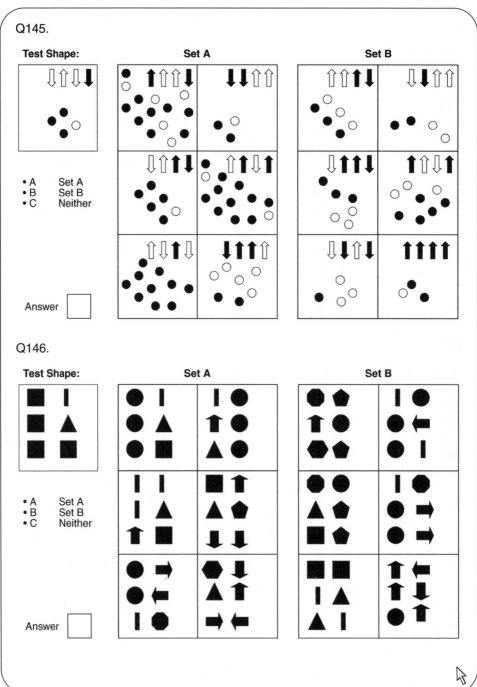

Q147.

Test Shape:

Set A   **Set B**

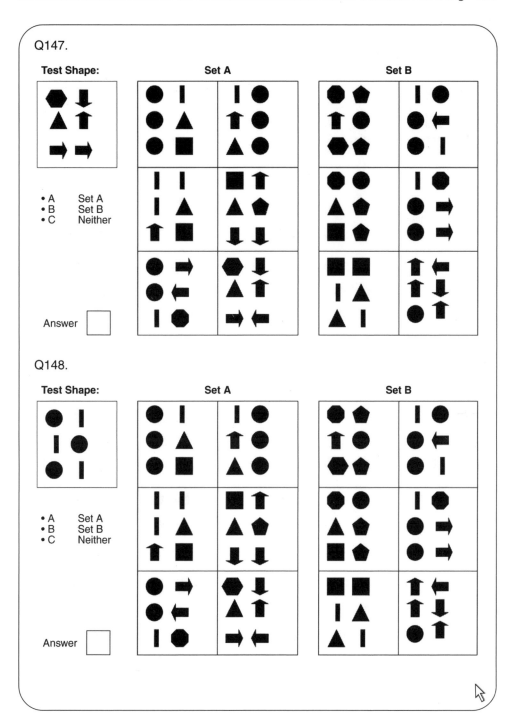

- A   Set A
- B   Set B
- C   Neither

Answer ☐

Q148.

Test Shape:

Set A   **Set B**

- A   Set A
- B   Set B
- C   Neither

Answer ☐

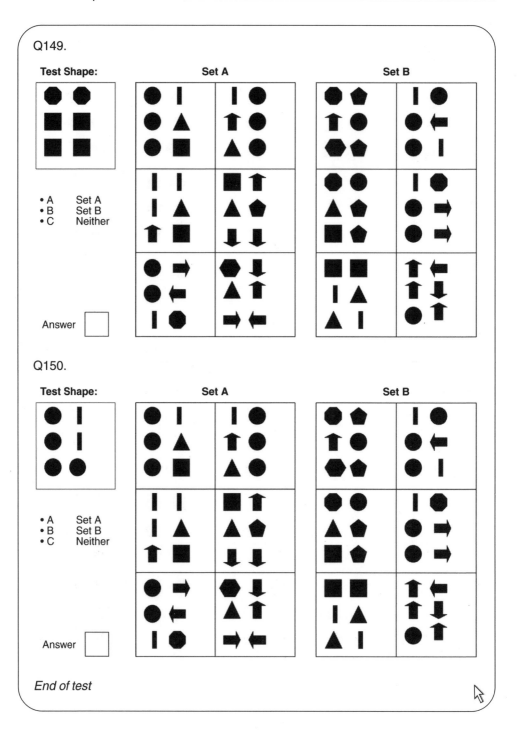

Q149.

Test Shape: Set A   Set B

- A   Set A
- B   Set B
- C   Neither

Answer ☐

Q150.

Test Shape: Set A   Set B

- A   Set A
- B   Set B
- C   Neither

Answer ☐

End of test

Non-cognitive analysis

The fifth sub-test that makes up the UKCAT is very different in nature from the other four and so we have saved it till last. In fact it is not a test in the true sense of the word (more a questionnaire) and is scored very differently from the other sub-tests. Its stated aim is to expand the range of information available on candidates by providing a report on attributes and characteristics regarding the candidate's personal style. Take this to mean that they will use your responses to build a psychometric profile of your attitude and personality. You have 30 minutes in which to complete this section of the UKCAT and you are required to consider a list of statements and indicate your personal response to each of them. Be sure to download and work through the sample questions available as a PDF on the UKCAT website.

Many people rush this type of exercise and do not give the statements it comprises sufficient consideration. While people may be reluctant to call them tests and they say no answer is right or wrong, your answers may well help them decide if your application should be accepted or rejected, so take the questions seriously.

It is essential in this type of exercise that you answer the questions truthfully but it is equally essential that you keep at the front of your mind the context of the question. You are applying for a place at medical school and it is in this context that you are answering the questions. With each question ask yourself: 'As an applicant to medical school, how would I respond in that situation?' Take the first example of the practice questions below: 'I would describe myself as tactful.' You should be able to answer this question positively. You might be able to think up some situation when you would not describe yourself as tactful, perhaps when out with your friends or at home with your family. But this would be the totally wrong response in the context of the question. How you sometimes act with your friends or family is irrelevant to your future role in the medical profession. In such a position tact is essential and candidates who cannot describe themselves as tactful may not be selected.

Responding truthfully to the questions will sometimes mean that you admit to something that risks counting against you. For example, if you have not undertaken voluntary work and you are asked if you have, be prepared to say so. It is unlikely that a few negative-scoring answers will significantly affect your overall score and anyway if you lie and it is discovered at a later stage your application may be rejected.

Look out and take extra care if any questions include double negatives. They can be very misleading and you can easily answer them in a way that you did not intend. An example of this sort of question might be: 'Do you agree or disagree with the statement: It is not true that I'm 18 years of age.' This sort of question can be confusing, especially if you are suffering anxiety during the real test. The way to approach this sort of question is to break it down into parts. Begin by answering the factual bit of the question, in this instance 'are you 18 years of age'. Now add the 'it is not true' part of the question. This in effect changes your answer. If you are 18 then you would disagree that it is not true that you are 18 years of age.

When answering the questions it is best not to give too many responses that imply strongly held views. If you do, you might risk the impression that you are someone too strident in your opinions, with many strongly held views. It is also best not to give too many non-committal responses either, as this might indicate that you find it difficult to make up your mind or commit yourself. It is fine to give some of these strongly held or non-committal responses, but try not to indicate too many.

Be sure that you are confident recognizing the synonyms of key personality attributes desirable in medics. The UKCAT website refers to, for example, 'empathy and robustness' (there are other key attributes so research them) and you should be entirely familiar with the meaning of these terms and their synonyms (empathy includes the synonyms share someone's feelings, talk the same language, relate to, feel for, put yourself in someone else's shoes and sympathize. Robustness includes practical, hands on, realistic, pragmatic, matter-of-fact, sensible, unsentimental, common sense and down-to-earth). You need to be familiar with the synonyms so that despite any nervousness during the UKCAT you can confidently identify the statement as something which you as an applicant medic can agree with or disagree with.

It is important to be consistent in your response. These tests often return to investigate the same issue a number of times (each may be worded differently). You should try to answer these related questions consistently. It can be a bit tricky because these related questions are spread out through the body of questions. To help you practise spotting and consistently answering related questions we have identified in the explanations a good few but not all the related questions.

In the real non-cognitive analysis test some of the questions require you to read additional information which is viewed by clicking an 'exhibit' key. Obviously we do not offer this feature but in these practice questions we have provided a number of background scenarios. When you come across one, you should answer the related questions that follow only in the context of the information contained in the scenario.

Below you will find 100 practice questions. To each you must indicate your personal response. Remember to give honest, considered responses. Be truthful while presenting as many of your positive attributes as possible. Do this by asking yourself in every instance: 'How would I respond to this question as an applicant to medical school?' Use the examples to develop your understanding of yourself and the qualities that you possess that will help make you a great applicant to medical school.

We cannot provide model answers to these questions because in many instances the answers will depend on you. In the answers chapter we have provided an explanation for each of the questions by indicating the likely way in which they will be interpreted and we have indicated the questions that you should have answered consistently. Note that answering questions consistently does not mean that you should have agreed or disagreed with every example of that type but that your approach to the issue is consistent (and a consistent approach might mean you agree with one statement but disagree with another).

Allow yourself 30 seconds for each of the following 100 practice questions.

Q1.   I would describe myself as tactful.

Strongly agree ☐

Agree ☐

Neither agree nor disagree ☐

Disagree ☐

Disagree strongly ☐

Q2.   I am not more practical than compassionate.

Strongly agree ☐

Agree ☐

Neither agree nor disagree ☐

Disagree ☐

Disagree strongly ☐

Additional information for Q3:

Society takes the view that healthcare has to be rationed. As a society we simply cannot afford to treat all conditions.

Q3.   Given the fact that healthcare must be rationed I reluctantly conclude that someone who engages in high-risk activities can't expect the same level of medical care as someone who lives life more moderately.

I agree with this conclusion. ☐

Generally I agree with this conclusion. ☐

Generally I would not agree with this conclusion. ☐

I particularly agree with this conclusion. ☐

I do not particularly agree with this conclusion. ☐

Q4.   I struggle to pay attention to small detail.

I totally disagree with the statement. ☐

I don't agree with the statement. ☐

I partially agree with the statement. ☐

I agree with the statement. ☐

I totally agree with the statement. ☐

Q5.   The only reason I do not steal is because I would not want others to steal from me.

Disagree strongly ☐

Disagree ☐

Neither agree nor disagree ☐

Agree ☐

Strongly agree ☐

Q6.   People who know me would not describe me as passionate about things.

This is not particularly true about me. ☐

This is particularly true about me. ☐

This is not true about me. ☐

Generally this is true about me. ☐

This is true about me. ☐

Q7.   If I was asked to do something critical I would hurry to complete the job I was doing in order to begin the new assignment.

Strongly agree ☐

Agree ☐

Neither agree nor disagree ☐

Disagree ☐

Disagree strongly ☐

Q8.   Only those qualified in the field should contribute to a debate.

I totally agree with the statement.   ☐

I agree with the statement.   ☐

I partially agree with the statement.   ☐

I don't agree with the statement.   ☐

I totally disagree with the statement.   ☐

Q9.   I prefer to leave a fast-changing situation for others to deal with.

I totally disagree with the statement.   ☐

I don't agree with the statement.   ☐

I partially agree with the statement.   ☐

I agree with the statement.   ☐

I totally agree with the statement.   ☐

Q10.   I do not find it frustrating to listen to someone who speaks painfully slowly.

This is true about me.   ☐

Generally this is true about me.   ☐

Generally this is not true about me.   ☐

This is particularly true about me.   ☐

This is not particularly true about me.   ☐

Q11.   People have said they find it hard to get to know me.

Strongly agree ☐

Agree ☐

Neither agree nor disagree ☐

Disagree ☐

Disagree strongly ☐

Q12.   If after leaving a shop I realized they had given me too much change I would turn around, re-enter the shop and point out their mistake.

Disagree strongly ☐

Disagree ☐

Neither agree nor disagree ☐

Agree ☐

Strongly agree ☐

Additional information for Q13 and Q14:

Mary is an extremely challenging customer. She presented herself at casualty two or three times a week and was usually offensive and sometimes violent. She was prone to self-harm and suffered mental health problems.

Q13.   If a colleague was being disrespectful to Mary their behaviour would be excusable so long as it was out of character and they did not take the same attitude with other patients.

This is false.

This is mostly false.

This is mostly true.

This is true.

Q14.   After Mary had left, your colleague realized that she had dropped some money, just a few coins to a total value of under a couple of pounds; you decided to put them in the hospital fundraising tin at the main reception.

This was an ok thing to do.

This was not really the best thing to do but understandable in the circumstances.

This was not the best thing to do.

This was the wrong thing to do.

Q15.   I am not that interested in hearing about alternative lifestyles.

I totally disagree with the statement.
☐

I don't agree with the statement.
☐

I partially agree with the statement.
☐

I agree with the statement.
☐

I totally agree with the statement.
☐

Q16.   I am known for my astuteness.

Strongly agree
☐

Agree
☐

Neither agree nor disagree
☐

Disagree
☐

Disagree strongly
☐

Q17.   At some time or another everyone makes a mistake and when I make one I try my hardest to put right the situation and then tell someone in authority what happened and what I did to put it right.

Strongly agree
☐

Agree
☐

Neither agree nor disagree
☐

Disagree
☐

Disagree strongly
☐

Q18.   I would prefer others described me as serious rather than lucid.

Strongly agree ☐

Agree ☐

Neither agree nor disagree ☐

Disagree ☐

Disagree strongly ☐

Q19.   If someone was really rude to me I might show my disdain but nothing more.

Strongly agree ☐

Agree ☐

Neither agree nor disagree ☐

Disagree ☐

Disagree strongly ☐

Q20.   The end justifies the means.

This is false. ☐

This is mostly false. ☐

This is mostly true. ☐

This is true. ☐

Q21.   If I were asked to help organize an outing for some people with learning difficulties
I would say I am too busy.

I totally disagree with the statement.   ☐

I don't agree with the statement.   ☐

I partially agree with the statement.   ☐

I agree with the statement.   ☐

I totally agree with the statement.   ☐

Q22.   I believe that it is better to help someone you know such as a neighbour rather than
a stranger.

This is true about me.   ☐

Generally this is true about me.   ☐

Generally this is not true about me.   ☐

This is particularly true about me.   ☐

This is not particularly true about me.   ☐

Q23.   People may say one thing but they often mean something else.

I totally disagree with the statement.   ☐

I don't agree with the statement.   ☐

I partially agree with the statement.   ☐

I agree with the statement.   ☐

I totally agree with the statement.   ☐

Q24.   I prefer to work independently.

I totally agree with the statement.   ☐

I agree with the statement.   ☐

I partially agree with the statement.   ☐

I don't agree with the statement.   ☐

I totally disagree with the statement.   ☐

Q25.   I like to talk about things that many people find personal.

I totally disagree with the statement.   ☐

I don't agree with the statement.   ☐

I partially agree with the statement.   ☐

I agree with the statement.   ☐

I totally agree with the statement.   ☐

Q26.   If already very busy and you were asked to complete an additional lengthy task, you would take on the new assignment without complaint and complete it only when you got all your other jobs done.

Strongly agree   ☐

Agree   ☐

Neither agree nor disagree   ☐

Disagree   ☐

Disagree strongly   ☐

Q27. I have never lied in my life.

Disagree strongly ☐

Disagree ☐

Neither agree nor disagree ☐

Agree ☐

Strongly agree ☐

Q28. The views of someone with long service are no more important than those of someone who has only been in an organization for a short time.

I totally agree with the statement. ☐

I agree with the statement. ☐

I partially agree with the statement. ☐

I don't agree with the statement. ☐

I totally disagree with the statement. ☐

Q29. I believe that a single sincere voice can be louder than a crowd's.

This is not particularly true about me. ☐

This is particularly true about me. ☐

Generally this is not true about me. ☐

Generally this is true about me. ☐

This is true about me. ☐

Q30.   On the occasions I have felt frustration with others I wished I had not done so.

I totally disagree with the statement.   ☐

I don't agree with the statement.   ☐

I partially agree with the statement.   ☐

I agree with the statement.   ☐

I totally agree with the statement.   ☐

Q31.   People who know me would describe me as sensitive.

This is not particularly true about me.   ☐

This is particularly true about me.   ☐

This is partially true about me.   ☐

Generally this is true about me.   ☐

This is not true about me.   ☐

Q32.   I don't much enjoy social events at which I will not know anyone.

I totally disagree with the statement.   ☐

I don't agree with the statement.   ☐

I partially agree with the statement.   ☐

I agree with the statement.   ☐

I totally agree with the statement.   ☐

Q33.   I am comfortable in providing a justification for the conclusions I have reached.

I totally agree with the statement. ☐

I agree with the statement. ☐

I partially agree with the statement. ☐

I don't agree with the statement. ☐

I totally disagree with the statement. ☐

Q34.   It is not true that it is best not to tell someone something they do not want to hear.

Strongly agree ☐

Agree ☐

Neither agree nor disagree ☐

Disagree ☐

Disagree strongly ☐

Q35.   In my spare time I would rather pursue my hobby on my own than attend a club with others who share the same interest.

I totally disagree with the statement. ☐

I don't agree with the statement. ☐

I partially agree with the statement. ☐

I agree with the statement. ☐

I totally agree with the statement. ☐

Q36.   I best cope with distressing situations by being emotionally detached.

This is not particularly true about me.   ☐

This is particularly true about me.   ☐

This is not true about me.   ☐

Generally this is true about me.   ☐

This is true about me.   ☐

Q37.   I do not steal because I am afraid of getting caught.

Disagree strongly   ☐

Disagree   ☐

Neither agree nor disagree   ☐

Agree   ☐

Strongly agree   ☐

Q38.   In a few very rare circumstances I might make a racist remark.

This is true about me.   ☐

Generally this is true about me.   ☐

Generally this is not true about me.   ☐

This is particularly true about me.   ☐

This is not particularly true about me.   ☐

Q39.   I am prone to vagueness and sometimes lose all track of time.

I totally disagree with the statement.　☐

I don't agree with the statement.　☐

I partially agree with the statement.　☐

I agree with the statement.　☐

I totally agree with the statement.　☐

Q40.   Some people want a career in which they might make a difference, others can think of no better reward than a large salary. I agree with the former.

I totally agree with the statement.　☐

I agree with the statement.　☐

I partially agree with the statement.　☐

I don't agree with the statement.　☐

I totally disagree with the statement.　☐

Q41.   If I found some money on the street and could not see who it belonged to I might put it in a charity box.

Disagree strongly　☐

Disagree　☐

Neither agree nor disagree　☐

Agree　☐

Strongly agree　☐

Q42.   It would be right to say I am thick-skinned.

This is not particularly true about me. ☐

This is particularly true about me. ☐

This is not true about me. ☐

Generally this is true about me. ☐

This is true about me. ☐

Q43.   To be non-judgemental is not to be without an ethical code.

Strongly agree ☐

Agree ☐

Neither agree nor disagree ☐

Disagree ☐

Disagree strongly ☐

Q44.   Some people believe that nowadays if you still smoke after all the negative press and warnings about the habit and you go on to get a smoking-related illness then you should not expect the National Health Service to treat you at public expense.

This is true about me. ☐

Generally this is true about me. ☐

Generally this is not true about me. ☐

This is particularly true about me. ☐

This is not particularly true about me. ☐

Q45. I find it difficult to get used to people.

Strongly agree ☐

Agree ☐

Neither agree nor disagree ☐

Disagree ☐

Disagree strongly ☐

Q46. In a life-saving situation it may not be possible to deal considerately with people.

Strongly agree ☐

Agree ☐

Neither agree nor disagree ☐

Disagree ☐

Disagree strongly ☐

Q47. Until they give me reason to act otherwise I usually take what people say at face value.

I totally disagree with the statement. ☐

I don't agree with the statement. ☐

I partially agree with the statement. ☐

I agree with the statement. ☐

I totally agree with the statement. ☐

Q48. I prefer to work in a situation where most important decisions are made by (and responsibility rests with) senior management.

I totally agree with the statement.

I agree with the statement.

I partially agree with the statement.

I don't agree with the statement.

I totally disagree with the statement.

Q49. You were late for your shift, and although no one noticed, when you saw your manager at break time you would notify them of your late start.

This is what I would do.

This is what I may do; it would depend on the circumstances.

I may not do this. It would depend on how many times I had been late before.

I would not do this.

Q50. People who know me would describe me as demonstrative rather than reserved.

Strongly agree

Agree

Neither agree nor disagree

Disagree

Disagree strongly

Q51. People may say one thing and from my experience they do not usually mean something else.

I totally disagree with the statement. ☐

I don't agree with the statement. ☐

I partially agree with the statement. ☐

I agree with the statement. ☐

I totally agree with the statement. ☐

Q52. A person who can't speak English can't expect the same level of service as someone who can.

This is true about me. ☐

Generally this is true about me. ☐

Generally this is not true about me. ☐

This is particularly true about me. ☐

This is not particularly true about me. ☐

Q53. It is never necessary to lie.

Disagree strongly ☐

Disagree ☐

Neither agree nor disagree ☐

Agree ☐

Strongly agree ☐

Q54.   It would be right to say I am thin-skinned.

This is not particularly true about me.   ☐

This is particularly true about me.   ☐

This is not true about me.   ☐

Generally this is true about me.   ☐

This is true about me.   ☐

Q55.   I am sometimes so distracted by my private thoughts that I make small mistakes.

I totally disagree with the statement.   ☐

I don't agree with the statement.   ☐

I partially agree with the statement.   ☐

I agree with the statement.   ☐

I totally agree with the statement.   ☐

Q56.   If you were sent to find a senior member of staff and deliver an urgent message but when you located the person you found them deep in conversation with a colleague, you would interrupt their conversation immediately even if it appeared rude.

Strongly agree   ☐

Agree   ☐

Neither agree nor disagree   ☐

Disagree   ☐

Disagree strongly   ☐

Q57.   People who know me would say first and foremost I am an enthusiastic person.

This is not particularly true about me.

☐

This is particularly true about me.

☐

This is not true about me.

☐

Generally this is true about me.

☐

This is true about me.

☐

Q58.   I would rather be a councillor than a counsellor.

I totally disagree with the statement.

☐

I don't agree with the statement.

☐

I partially agree with the statement.

☐

I agree with the statement.

☐

I totally agree with the statement.

☐

Q59.   I would describe my approach to the suffering of others as unfeeling.

This is not particularly true about me.

☐

This is particularly true about me.

☐

This is not true about me.

☐

Generally this is true about me.

☐

This is true about me.

☐

Q60. I often do things spontaneously.

Strongly agree ☐

Agree ☐

Neither agree nor disagree ☐

Disagree ☐

Disagree strongly ☐

Q61. I wear my emotions on my sleeve.

This is not particularly true about me. ☐

This is particularly true about me. ☐

Generally this is not true about me. ☐

Generally this is true about me. ☐

This is true about me. ☐

Q62. If I was in a national supermarket store and someone in an obvious state of desperation was shoplifting food, I would inform the nearest shop assistant.

Disagree strongly ☐

Disagree ☐

Neither agree nor disagree ☐

Agree ☐

Strongly agree ☐

Q63. Working as a part of a team is a more important part of the role of a health professional than keeping abreast of the latest advances in medical knowledge.

I totally agree with the statement.

I agree with the statement.

I partially agree with the statement.

I don't agree with the statement.

I totally disagree with the statement.

Q64. I prefer work that is familiar and routine because it helps with my confidence.

I totally disagree with the statement.

I don't agree with the statement.

I partially agree with the statement.

I agree with the statement.

I totally agree with the statement.

Q65. I would find it slightly irritating if I held out my hand to someone and they
declined to shake it.

This is true about me.

Generally this is true about me.

Generally this is not true about me.

This is particularly true about me.

This is not particularly true about me.

Q66.   I would not find it irritating if I had to interrupt what I was doing in order to do something else.

Strongly agree ☐

Agree ☐

Neither agree nor disagree ☐

Disagree ☐

Disagree strongly ☐

Q67.   I have regretted some things I have said and done.

Strongly agree ☐

Agree ☐

Neither agree nor disagree ☐

Disagree ☐

Disagree strongly ☐

Q68.   Morals are something the well-off can afford but if you are worried where the next meal will come from then they may be a luxury you can't afford.

This is false. ☐

This is mostly false. ☐

This is mostly true. ☐

This is true. ☐

Q69.   Before I say something I often find myself pausing to check that what I am going to say is the correct thing.

I totally disagree with the statement.

I don't agree with the statement.

I partially agree with the statement.

I agree with the statement.

I totally agree with the statement.

Q70.   I am known for my shrewd power of judgement.

Strongly agree

Agree

Neither agree nor disagree

Disagree

Disagree strongly

Q71.   It would not irritate me if someone would not make eye contact with me when I spoke to them.

This is true about me.

Generally this is true about me.

Generally this is not true about me.

This is particularly true about me.

This is not particularly true about me.

Q72.   People who know me would call me unemotional rather than unassuming.

Strongly agree ☐

Agree ☐

Neither agree nor disagree ☐

Disagree ☐

Disagree strongly ☐

Q73.   People would describe my approach to people as bold and decisive rather than delicate and diplomatic.

Strongly agree ☐

Agree ☐

Neither agree nor disagree ☐

Disagree ☐

Disagree strongly ☐

Additional information for Q74 and Q75:

It has been a very stressful day and you and your colleagues are finding it hard to cope.

Q74.   Under the circumstances it would be acceptable to use bad language in front of patients.

This is false. ☐

This is mainly false. ☐

This is mostly true. ☐

This is true. ☐

Q75.   Under the circumstances it would be acceptable to let off steam by using bad language but only in front of your colleagues.

This is false.

This is mainly false.

This is mostly true.

This is true.

Q76.   Honesty is always the best policy.

Disagree strongly

Disagree

Neither agree nor disagree

Agree

Strongly agree

Q77.   If there is an attractive woman in the team, it is only natural that the men present will try to impress her.

I totally agree with the statement.

I agree with the statement.

I partially agree with the statement.

I don't agree with the statement.

I totally disagree with the statement.

Q78. I prefer to eat familiar food rather than try something new that I have not eaten before.

I totally disagree with the statement. ☐

I don't agree with the statement. ☐

I partially agree with the statement. ☐

I agree with the statement. ☐

I totally agree with the statement. ☐

Q79. If I had to classify myself as either emotional or insensitive then I would choose the former.

This is not particularly true about me. ☐

This is particularly true about me. ☐

This is not true about me. ☐

Generally this is true about me. ☐

This is true about me. ☐

Q80. I believe that charity should begin and largely end at home.

This is true about me. ☐

Generally this is true about me. ☐

Generally this is not true about me. ☐

This is particularly true about me. ☐

This is not particularly true about me. ☐

Q81.   I would rather people described me as approachable than polite.

Strongly agree   ☐

Agree   ☐

Neither agree nor disagree   ☐

Disagree   ☐

Disagree strongly   ☐

Q82.   Others may think of me as naïve but not wary.

Strongly agree   ☐

Agree   ☐

Neither agree nor disagree   ☐

Disagree   ☐

Disagree strongly   ☐

Q83.   If you hear one of your colleagues being teased over their sexuality the correct thing to do is to let people know that you don't think it's a fitting way to behave.

This is false.   ☐

This would normally be true but if you had only just started in the role then you might ignore it to begin with.   ☐

This would only be true if you felt the person being teased objected to the treatment.   ☐

This is true.   ☐

Q84. Nearly everyone would be OK with taking some paper and the odd pen from work for, for example, a relative's, or the neighbour's, children and no one would really count it as stealing.

Disagree strongly ☐

Disagree ☐

Neither agree nor disagree ☐

Agree ☐

Strongly agree ☐

Q85. Out of youthful exuberance I might be cheeky but I would not be disrespectful and would never be malicious.

Strongly agree ☐

Agree ☐

Neither agree nor disagree ☐

Disagree ☐

Disagree strongly ☐

Q86. There are some sorts of people I know I am not going to get on with.

This is true about me. ☐

Generally this is true about me. ☐

Generally this is not true about me. ☐

This is particularly true about me. ☐

This is not particularly true about me. ☐

Q87.   I would rather work in a situation where things go to plan and I find it an effort to deal with a situation if the unexpected occurs.

I totally disagree with the statement.

I don't agree with the statement.

I partially agree with the statement.

I agree with the statement.

I totally agree with the statement.

Q88.   When painful choices have to be made I would not commit myself until all the facts are known.

Strongly agree

Agree

Neither agree nor disagree

Disagree

Disagree strongly

Q89.   People would say I show greater integrity than a non-judgemental attitude.

Strongly agree

Agree

Neither agree nor disagree

Disagree

Disagree strongly

Q90.   A compromise is rarely the right decision.

Strongly agree ☐

I totally agree with the statement. ☐

I agree with the statement. ☐

I partially agree with the statement. ☐

I don't agree with the statement. ☐

I totally disagree with the statement. ☐

Q91.   In some very rare circumstances it might be right to steal.

Disagree strongly ☐

Disagree ☐

Neither agree nor disagree ☐

Agree ☐

Strongly agree ☐

Q92.   I would still do my best to see the job through if I found it harder to assist in a child's post-mortem, rather than someone who had died in their seventies.

Strongly agree ☐

Agree ☐

Neither agree nor disagree ☐

Disagree ☐

Disagree strongly ☐

Q93. I am prone to be impulsive and regret some of the things I do afterwards.

Strongly agree ☐

Agree ☐

Neither agree nor disagree ☐

Disagree ☐

Disagree strongly ☐

Q94. People who know me would describe my approach to people more as matter-of-fact rather than down-to-earth.

Strongly agree ☐

Agree ☐

Neither agree nor disagree ☐

Disagree ☐

Disagree strongly ☐

Q95. Unlike the vast majority of people, if when you made a cash withdrawal from an ATM (automatic teller machine) the machine dispensed £10 too much you would visit the branch of the bank the next day and hand the overpayment in.

This is false. ☐

This is mostly false. ☐

This is mostly true. ☐

This is true. ☐

Q96.   You have to pay attention to people's motives as to why they are saying something.

I totally disagree with the statement.   ☐

I don't agree with the statement.   ☐

I partially agree with the statement.   ☐

I agree with the statement.   ☐

I totally agree with the statement.   ☐

Q97.   My motivation to work to a very high standard might suffer if I were in a role that involved delivering the same procedure over and over again.

Strongly agree   ☐

Agree   ☐

Neither agree nor disagree   ☐

Disagree   ☐

Disagree strongly   ☐

Q98.   I am able to talk about things that many people find personal.

I totally disagree with the statement.   ☐

I don't agree with the statement.   ☐

I partially agree with the statement.   ☐

I agree with the statement.   ☐

I totally agree with the statement.   ☐

Q99.   I expect to take joint responsibility for actions at work.

I totally agree with the statement.

I agree with the statement.

I partially agree with the statement.

I don't agree with the statement.

I totally disagree with the statement.

Q100. It is true that we should all try not to say one thing and do another but in reality it is often acceptable not to do this.

This is false.

This is mostly false.

This is mostly true.

This is true.

Answers and explanations

Chapter 2   Verbal reasoning

Warm up questions

Q1.   Answer: Cannot tell
Explanation: The passage states that it is now possible to relocate without affecting earning power but the reason for this new development is not given in the passage. It might be because of new technology but we cannot rule out the possibility that there are other causes; for example, it is conceivably the introduction of new legislation that allows workers a better work–life balance might be the reason. Because we cannot establish new technology as the reason we must conclude that we cannot tell if the statement is true or false.

Q2.   Answer: False
Explanation: Two reasons for the increase in popularity are mentioned in the passage, and although the passage dwells mainly on one of them, commuter towns, the issue of second-home hotspots is also raised as a reason for the increase in popularity.

Q3.   Answer: True
Explanation: Although the passage does not mention a traditional high street with local shops, it is reasonable to conclude that this concept might form part of 'an idea of an unspoilt civic centre'. The statement starts with 'an idea' not 'the idea' and states it 'could include' not 'does or should include'. These are weak assertions and allow for many possibilities and for this reason the correct answer is true.

Q4.   Answer: Cannot tell
       Explanation: The passage states that the most sought-after domesticated varieties
       prefer a ph of 6.5, but we cannot tell or infer from the information given if other
       varieties of wild asparagus also share this characteristic.

Q5.   Answer: True
       Explanation: Inedible means indigestible, unpalatable or poisonous. It is not
       expressly stated in the passage that the berries are indigestible, unpalatable or
       poisonous for humans but if we look to the context of the passage then it is clear
       that we can infer this information. The passage is about asparagus and its edible
       spears and it is stated that people all over the world enjoy eating them. The context
       of the passage therefore is asparagus and people growing it or picking it to eat.
       Given this context we can infer that the berries are inedible for humans. It might
       be that the berries are inedible for other species too but we cannot infer this from
       the passage.

Q6.   Answer: False
       Explanation: The passage states that wild asparagus grows in Europe, northern
       Africa and central Asia but it also states that cultivated asparagus grows in Canada
       so we can infer that the statement is false.

Q7.   Answer: True
       Explanation: The passage states 'when each year an average of 500,000 immi-
       grants entered the country' and we can conclude from the 'when' that the figure is
       no longer half a million a year. We cannot know if the current figure is higher or
       lower but it is reasonable to infer that it is no longer 500,000.

Q8.   Answer: True
       Explanation: Immigration can mean either the inward or outward movement of
       people but only inward migration increases a country's population (outward
       migration would result in a decrease in the population).

Q9.   Answer: False
       Explanation: The passage states that 'Some employers stand to gain much from
       the improved supply of labour and savings made from not having to train young
       people' and it is reasonable to conclude that such employers are 'winners' in a
       climate of large-scale inward migration.

Q10.   Answer: Cannot tell
       Explanation: The passage state that Jupiter has a rocky core but no information is
       provided regarding the other gaseous planets and this information cannot be
       inferred from the passage.

Q11.   Answer: False

Explanation: A synonym of a word is one that has the same meaning and in the passage the words huge and giant are treated as synonyms in reference to describing the size of the huge/giant gaseous planets Jupiter, Uranus and Neptune. But we cannot conclude that the words moon and satellite are used as synonyms. They occur in the passage in relation to the discoveries of the Voyager probes where it is written 'all were found to have distinctive rings, satellites (or moons)' and there are two possible interpretations here. One is that the words are inter-changeable and we can call them either satellites or moons but it is equally possible that the author intended to introduce a difference between the two terms and in some instances it would be correct to use the term moon and in another the term satellite. In this second situation the words would not be synonyms and for this reason it is false to conclude that in the passage the terms moon and satellite are treated as synonyms.

Q12.   Answer: Cannot tell

Explanation: The order of the gaseous planets from the sun is not explicitly stated. Neptune is stated as taking the longest (165 years) to rotate the sun but we cannot infer from this that it is the furthest from the sun. We know that Uranus and Neptune both lie beyond Jupiter in terms of being further from the sun.

Q13.   Answer: True

Explanation: It is stated in the passage that the dollar has traded at lower than its historic rate against the Chinese and Indian currencies and that this is bound to continue and has occurred for a reason other than indebtedness of the US economy. For this reason it is true that even if the US economy were free of debt it is probable that the dollar would have weakened and stayed weak against at least some of the world's currencies.

Q14.   Answer: False

Explanation: The passage is about the weakness of the US dollar and not about the possibility or otherwise of a US recession. What the author meant by the term inevitable, therefore, is that it was inevitable that the dollar would weaken.

Q15.   Answer: Cannot tell

Explanation: It is clear from the opening sentence that people expected the dollar to weaken and that they expected this to happen sooner than it did, but it is not possible to infer the time frame for these predictions. We are told that an economy like that of the United States can live beyond its means for years but not that people were predicting the correction for years.

Q16. Answer: Cannot tell
      Explanation: Aside from the benefits of saving on infrastructure investment costs
      and power loss to resistance in transmission wires, the passage does not describe the
      motive for the investment in the local generation of the community's energy needs.

Q17. Answer: Cannot tell
      Explanation: The energy needs of the community are not quantified and so we are
      unable to establish whether or even when the wind turbines are turning and the
      solar panels generating hot water for the hundreds of homes that this amounts to
      most of the community's energy needs.

Q18. Answer: False
      Explanation: It is stated in the passage that the community's local generation of
      power has led to savings on the investment cost of additional transmission lines in
      the national network. In other words, the network has not had to be expanded
      because of local generation. If the national network were practically non-existent
      then local generation would do more than save on further expansion – it would
      help avoid the initial enormous investments in building centralized power plants
      and transmission lines in the first place. We can infer therefore that it is false to
      describe that network as practically non-existent.

Q19. Answer: Cannot tell
      Explanation: If more than 30 million jobs were lost to India then the case that
      many skilled jobs will be moved will not be strengthened unless those extra lost
      jobs were skilled. Moving low-skilled jobs would not strengthen the case and we
      are not told if the extra jobs involved are skilled or unskilled.

Q20. Answer: True
      Explanation: Three reasons why companies are moving jobs to India are iden-
      tified in the passage; because it is easier to fill highly skilled, English-speaking
      positions there, because, for the time being, wages for these roles are notably
      lower there than wages in Europe and America and because companies want to
      position their businesses where they believe the future lies.

Q21. Answer: False
      Explanation: This claim is not examined in the passage and none of the passage is
      relevant in terms of either supporting or contradicting it. It is false therefore that
      the claim can be rebutted by the contents of the passage.

Q22.   Answer: False
       Explanation: Before we could infer that the sum of the annual running costs of the
       listed electrical appliances amounted to the average household's net electricity
       bill we would need to know that the list was exhaustive and listed every item. We
       do not know this so we cannot infer that the sum of the listed items provides the
       total net annual bill for the household.

Q23.   Answer: False
       Explanation: The main point of the passage is not an account of the saving that
       could be made if we were more frugal with our use of electrical appliances but to
       provide an illustration of how much we spend using everyday appliances and
       (secondary point) how much we could save if we were more frugal in using them.

Q24.   Answer: Cannot tell
       Explanation: Two examples are provided of the sort of things we would need to do
       to reduce waste (not leave unnecessary lights on, not leave appliances unneces-
       sarily on standby), and while these examples would not have much of an impact
       on our daily lives they are only an example of the sort of thing we would need to
       do in order to make the saving indicated. Before we could determine the extent to
       which the difference would impact on our daily lives we would need details of all
       the things we would need to do.

Q25.   Answer: False
       Explanation: The passage describes beautiful things that we cannot see and if we
       cannot see all beauty then it is not in the eye of the beholder but in some of the
       other senses too.

Q26.   Answer: Cannot tell
       Explanation: The passage states that an idea can be beautiful and lack physical
       structure while a smell can be beautiful and lack physical appearance (it still has a
       physical structure). In the context of the opening sentence the term 'form' could
       mean either appearance or structure and so we cannot tell if by saying a thing of
       beauty can completely lack physical form it is meant that it lacks physical
       structure or physical appearance.

Q27.   Answer: True
       Explanation: The word image confuses the case made in the passage because we
       see images with our eyes and this implies a contradiction with the claim that we
       can find a scent beautiful despite it being impossible to see it.

Q28.   Answer: True

Explanation: The opening sentence of the passage states that over $50 billion was spent online last year and it is hardly surprising that criminals want a share of the action, and it is reasonable to rephrase this as online shopping offers the criminal the promise of rich pickings.

Q29.   Answer: False

Explanation: The passage states that most people do not secure their virtual shops to the same degree as their physical shops, and while the physical shop will be attended and have locks and alarms fitted, their virtual shop will have no more than a firewall, antivirus and anti-spyware software. These virtual securities are therefore not the equivalent of shop assistants, locks and alarms but are inferior in terms of security.

Q30.   Answer: Cannot tell

Explanation: While antivirus and anti-spyware software does update automatically and this may well mean that the business owner will believe their security will remain up to date, we cannot establish this from the information contained in the passage so the correct answer is cannot tell.

Q31.   Answer: Cannot tell

Explanation: The views of the author cannot be established from the passage.

Q32.   Answer: False

Explanation: We are told that profits of British pubs have fallen by 20% and many have reported a further worsening of their financial state since the introduction of a new law and a series of tax increases, but it is not possible (or reasonable) to infer from this that some pubs are operating at a loss or not at a profit.

Q33.   Answer: Cannot tell

Explanation: We are told that the smoking ban has led to a marked decrease in pub custom but cannot infer from this that pub customers have been encouraged to drink and smoke less because they may simply be drinking and smoking the same amount but at home instead of in the pub.

Q34.   Answer: True

Explanation: Even though the passage states that millions of law-abiding people have used recreational drugs, it is clear that users, if found in possession of these drugs, are breaking laws as they face penalties of imprisonment or fines. To be a user unavoidably involves being in possession and so someone who has used recreational drugs can only now be law abiding if they are no longer using them. But if they are using recreational drugs then it is not true that they are law abiding.

Q35. Answer: True
Explanation: The passage offers the opinion that using these drugs in your own home should be no one else's business but your own and this would include the courts and police.

Q36. Answer: Cannot tell
Explanation: It is stated in the passage that dealing in these drugs can result in imprisonment for up to 14 years, but the drugs in question are those classified as class C drugs, the lowest classification. We are not informed of the penalties for dealing in the other categories so we cannot know if the statement is true or false.

Q37. Answer: Cannot tell
Explanation: We are told that 20 years after the eruption only 4,000 of the original population of 12,000 remain. We cannot infer from this that therefore only 4,000 live on the island because it is possible, for example, that people arrived from elsewhere to live on the island, making the population greater than 4,000.

Q38. Answer: False
Explanation: The evacuation averted a greater disaster but the death of 19 people and the irrevocable loss of the way of life that existed before the eruption are still a disaster.

Q39. Answer: Cannot tell
Explanation: It is true that there must be a mistake but the mistake could lie in either the date 1997 or the figure of 20 years, so we cannot tell if the mistake lies with the date 1997 as the question states.

Q40. Answer: Cannot tell
Explanation: We are told that the first manned landing was made in 1969 and that probes made soft landings in the 1960s, but we cannot tell from the information given if any landings (unmanned) occurred before that time.

Q41. Answer: Cannot tell
Explanation: The passage stated that the later missions visited highlands but we cannot tell from this whether or not the landing occurred in a mountainous region.

Q42. Answer: True
Explanation: The passage is about the manned lunar landings and the search for suitable sites for those landings. The soft landings performed by probes are described in terms of the search for suitable sites for the manned landings. Given the context, reference to a suitable site in the second sentence can be taken to mean suitable for manned missions.

Q43. Answer: False
Explanation: We suffer a suspension of judgement only when we spend money that we intended to use for something essential or unintentionally create an unauthorized overdraft.

Q44. Answer: True
Explanation: The passage states that there is a widely held perception that electronic money and credit are somehow not as real or valuable as notes and coins and that retailers play on this emotional weakness. It is reasonable to take this to mean that electronic money and credit have a lower psychological value than cash in your hand.

Q45. Answer: Cannot tell
Explanation: The passage does not indicate if unregulated sites are also unlicensed.

Q46. Answer: True
Explanation: The effects of rising food prices are uneven and for some of the landless poor and, in some places, poor food-importing nations, the burden is greatest.

Q47. Answer: True
Explanation: The subject of the passage is the rise in world food prices and how the effect of this is that some countries and individuals have benefited from this while others are suffering.

Q48. Answer: True
Explanation: The passage states that governments of the poorest food-importing countries are counterbalancing the rapid rises in the prices of staple foods with improved food subsidy programmes. To counterbalance something is not to compensate it nor to stop or bring to an end the rise in food prices.

Q49. Answer: True
Explanation: The term estimate means approximation and does not usually imply a commitment to spend. The passage states that the decision to proceed with the project has still to be made, so it is reasonable to conclude that in this instance the estimated build cost does not include a commitment to spend.

Q50. Answer: False
Explanation: The passage states that the construction work has been priced at a figure higher than the annual gross domestic product of one-quarter of the world's nations, not the sum of the annual gross domestic product of one-quarter of the world's nations.

Q51.   Answer: True
Explanation: The plan is described as widening both sides of 240 miles of motorway so it does involve 480 miles of construction – 240 miles of road each side of the motorway.

Q52.   Answer: Cannot tell
Explanation: We cannot tell if the current advantages of PFIs will always remain and we cannot infer from the passage that PFIs are used to fund the building of every type of public building (the passage only lists schools, hospitals, social housing and prisons).

Q53.   Answer: True
Explanation: The fact that PFIs count as off-balance-sheet expenditure is described as the most important for the government and for this reason, if the other advantage was no longer to exist, the government might still prefer to use PFIs.

Q54.   Answer: False
Explanation: It would in fact be more open to misinterpretation. The private sector bears the cost of building, not the government. The government leases the building and is able to spread out the cost of the lease.

Q55.   Answer: False
Explanation: Reference to the holiday resort that provides a school for local children is offered as an example of a tour operator who is contributing to the local community. The example of cynical exploitation relates to the real-food movement.

Q56.   Answer: True
Explanation: Historically a bandwagon was literally a wagon carrying a band (playing music) and a metaphor is when a word or phrase is used in a context when it is not literally the case.

Q57.   Answer: Cannot tell
Explanation: The passage states only one motive for why tourists prefer to use the services of a tour operator who is contributing to the local community and ecosystem, and that is that they want a guilt-free holiday. We cannot tell if the tourist has other motives.

Q58.   Answer: False
Explanation: We are told that the jet stream determines the boundary between Arctic and Atlantic air and we are informed that in north America and northern Europe when the jet stream moves south cold air is experienced and when it moves north warm air is experienced, but this does not allow us to infer that Arctic air is relatively cold and Atlantic air relatively warm.

Q59. Answer: Cannot tell

Explanation: We are unable to identify where this part of the world is from the information given. It could be in northern Europe but it could just as easily be in North America or anywhere on the Atlantic side of the northern hemisphere.

Q60. Answer: False

Explanation: The key qualities of the jet stream on which the explanation of the changeable nature of the weather in the northern hemisphere depends are that it separates the Arctic and Atlantic air and moves around more in the spring and autumn. Neither of these qualities is affected should it in fact not be true that the jet stream is a two-mile-high column of wind.

Mini-test 1

Q1. Answer: False

Explanation: The case for smaller families in the developed world is not dependent on the question of whether or not the population of the developed world is growing or contracting but on the higher carbon dioxide emission lifestyle of people living in the developed world.

Q2. Answer: Cannot tell

Explanation: The passage states that having a child in the developed world has a greater environmental impact than having a child in the developing world. Before we can know that a child not born in the developing world will effect a major cut in a family's future carbon dioxide emissions we would need information about the level of carbon dioxide output produced by the family. If they produced no or very little carbon dioxide then having fewer children would not result in a major cut in their family's future carbon dioxide output.

Q3. Answer: False

Explanation: You are only likely to get this question wrong if you are sacrificing accuracy too much to speed. The passage states that of the 4 million workers who have paid into a pension scheme for the bulk of their working life, only those who have paid into a final salary scheme will enjoy retirement on two-thirds of their final salary and the rest will have to manage on far less because their pension scheme lacked the final salary guarantee.

Q4. Answer: Cannot tell

Explanation: We are told that workers need two-thirds of their final salary to be comfortable in their retirement but we are not told the amount needed to be secure. It is reasonable to infer that the amount needed to be secure (safe) is less than the amount needed to be comfortable. But we cannot infer that 40 per cent of final salary is either sufficient or insufficient to be secure in retirement so the correct answer is cannot tell.

Q5.   Answer: False

Explanation: We are told that the population of workers is 15 million (4 million contributing to a pension scheme and a remaining 11 million who have made no or very little contribution to a scheme other than the compulsory state scheme). We can also establish from the passage that the total population of the country to which the passage refers must be greater than 15 million because it also includes some retired people (see the first sentence which reads 'to enjoy a comfortable retirement, many retired people recommend retiring on two-thirds of final salary'). The correct answer therefore is false.

Mini-test 2

Q1.   Answer: False

Explanation: The fact that the French national health service is probably the best in the world is left aside so is not a factor attributed to the lower level of heart disease. The passage therefore attributes three factors to the lower level of death caused by heart disease: remaining active, consuming more fruit and vegetables and enjoying more red wine.

Q2.   Answer: False

Explanation: It is true that twice as many may still amount to very few but the last sentence of the passage states that 'this allows significant numbers of people to live until their centenary' and just a few people living until their centenary would not be described as a significant number.

Q3.   Answer: False

Explanation: The passage states that if extreme weather was occurring more frequently then it is feasible that the forecast might include the prediction that the frequency of these events will continue to be higher than the historic average. It is therefore not a mistake to believe that the exceptional can be forecast in the long term.

Q4.   Answer: Cannot tell

Explanation: Neither the date when the passage was written nor the year of the summer to which the passage refers is indicated, so it is not possible to tell from the passage if the summer of 2007 was very wet and windy.

Q5.   Answer: Cannot tell

Explanation: It is clear from the passage that the frequency of exceptional events can be predicted, but this is not to predict specific weather events such as an incidence of extreme flooding. While the forecast failed to predict these events last summer, it cannot be established from the passage whether or not it is possible to predict such events as a matter of principle.

Mini-test 3

Q1. Answer: False

Explanation: The passage states that in almost zero gravity and no wind, very large droplets or, in other words, globules of water can form so it is false to say that the passage disproves this.

Q2. Answer: False

Explanation: The passage states that 'in every situation droplets do collide and these combine to form larger droplets that may well survive'.

Q3. Answer: True

Explanation: English is described as a dominant, apparently all-conquering, language and as more and more of the world speak it, it will break up into dialects and then distinct languages.

Q4. Answer: False

Explanation: The passage does answer the question (although the answer is incomplete). It is stated that in the case of a language spoken by a small linguistic community it becomes extinct when there is no one left in that community and it describes how a dominant language might become extinct if it breaks down into dialects which then evolve into new languages.

Q5. Answer: True

Explanation: Ambivalent means in two minds and the passage offers first an account of the theory that English will evolve into dialects and then new languages but also describes this view as controversial because speech is standardized and dialects prevented from forming.

Mini-test 4

Q1. Answer: Cannot tell

Explanation: We are only informed that there were a total of 23 student volunteers and cannot infer from this how this number was split between the various roles.

Q2. Answer: True

Explanation: All the volunteers were male and the passage provides no indication that women might act differently. For this reason it is true that it is wrong to deduce from the passage that women volunteers would act differently.

Q3. Answer: False

Explanation: Three of Philip Zimbardo's factors are identified in the passage: conformity, anonymity and boredom.

Q4.　Answer: True

Explanation: The passage is about how Japan can maintain its competitiveness given the projected fall in its population and the disproportionately elderly character of that population. The proposed answer is through innovation. Although the passage also considers how Japan can remain innovative, unless it engages in new ways of thinking and changes in worldwide values this is a secondary issue and the 'big' question posed is one of competitiveness.

Q5.　Answer: False

Explanation: No abilities are attributed to India or China in the passage, nor can you infer from the tone of the passage that the predicted success of these nations is due to their ability to engage in new ways of thinking.

Mini-test 5

Q1.　Answer: True

Explanation: The passage states that the S section of the English dictionary is the largest in terms of the number of entries and that 'the longest section in the Italian dictionary and the section that contains the most entries is the S section'.

Q2.　Answer: Cannot tell

Explanation: The passage states that the S section contains the largest number of entries but we cannot infer from this that the section is also the longest. It is possible that another section has fewer entries but is longer because of the extent of the definitions.

Q3.　Answer: Cannot tell

Explanation: We are told that the Q section of the English dictionary is the shortest but this does not mean that it necessarily has close to the fewest number of entries. The Q section of the Italian dictionary contains close to the shortest number of Italian entries but we are not told how many foreign word entries the J, K, Y and W sections of the Italian dictionary contain (we are told that they are very short as they only contain foreign words used in Italian) and they may be shorter than the Q section.

Q4.　Answer: False

Explanation: The list is correct in that the names begin with successive letters of the alphabet and alternate between boy and girl names but there are only eight names and in a typical year nine named storms would occur.

Q5.   Answer: Cannot tell

Explanation: We are told that initially only girls' names were used but later this was changed so that the names alternated from boy to girl names. But we cannot establish when this change took place. The question implies that weather forecasts are no longer broadcast over shortwave radio but if this practice stopped there is nothing in the passage to suggest when or whether it stopped before the change to the naming of storms with both boy and girl names.

Mini-test 6

Q1.   Answer: False

Explanation: The passage states that their colours hark back to the days when flags were extensively used for identification and communication. So their previous use gave rise to the colours and symbolic designs used today and not the rectangular shape.

Q2.   Answer: False

Explanation: You are informed in the passage that the flag of the Republic of Ireland was inspired by the tri-colour of the French revolution and that the tri-colour was blue, white and red. It is possible to infer from the passage that the tri-colour design was the inspiration for the flag of the Republic and that they adopted different colours from those adopted by France.

Q3.   Answer: True

Explanation: We can tell that this statement is true because in the passage the use of the symbolic designs and their meanings is mentioned. For example, the crescent moon and cross are referred to as identifying the official religion of a nation.

Q4.   Answer: False

Explanation: The passage states that the new threat to personal liberty is how to prevent complete strangers finding out our personal details. While this is quite the opposite problem of the old issue of secrecy, it does not mean that the old problem of finding out the personal details that organizations are holding on us no longer exists. It could be that we now face two threats and for this reason the statement is false.

Q5.   Answer: True

Explanation: Penultimate means last but one and the sentence states 'if the person for whom you are searching is active on a social network site or an internet specialist interest forum then you may well be able to identify a database of friends and contacts and by reading recent postings obtain a flavour of their views and preferences'. From this it is clearly the case that the penultimate sentence of the passage illustrates the sort of things that people post on the internet.

Mini-test 7

Q1.   Answer: False

Explanation: Satellite images being used to locate a fabled and lost city is not an example of the scientific debunking of popular belief but the scientific confirmation of popular belief (it could be taken as an example of the scientific whittling away of mystery).

Q2.   Answer: Cannot tell

Explanation: The passage asks the question 'Do scientific investigations of our past add to our understanding...?' This raises the possibility that science can play a positive role but the passage does not provide an answer to the question raised so we cannot tell from the passage if science can in fact play a positive role,

Q3.   Answer: False

Explanation: It is stated that 5 per cent of Canadian land is suitable for the growing of crops while 10 per cent of Russian land is arable and we are also told that Russia is a bigger nation than Canada. But before we can infer from this that Russian arable production is greater than that of Canada we would need to know that the Canadian productivity per hector was not far higher than Russian productivity. Without this information we cannot rule out the possibility that Russian productivity is in fact lower than that of Canada despite Canada having less arable land.

Q4.   Answer: Cannot tell

Explanation: Cover means extend over while astride means on both sides. If there is a difference in the meaning of these two phrases then it is one of fact (the extent to which Russia covers the northern parts of the continents of Europe and Asia) and we are not provided with sufficient information to decide which description, covers or sits astride, is the more correct.

Q5.   Answer: True

Explanation: Polar means Arctic or Antarctic, cold or freezing, and both countries are described as having a sizable extent of frozen wilderness. The passage states that the majority of Russians live in the temperate part of the country while the bulk of Canadians have settled in the clement conditions found within 400 km of the border. From these statements we can infer that the author of the passage would agree that the polar regions of both countries are relatively sparsely populated.

Mini-test 8

Q1.   Answer: Cannot tell

Explanation: The bases of the statements made in the passage are not explained, nor can they be inferred from the contents of the passage.

Q2.   Answer: True

Explanation: If the sentence read swell rather than wave it would be consistent with the definition of the difference between waves and swell provided at the start of the passage.

Q3.   Answer: False

Explanation: Providing an explanation of what happens after death is attributed to all religions in general and no exception for Buddhism is made.

Q4.   Answer: True

Explanation: The passage is not illustrated with details from Hinduism (it is only stated that it is the oldest of the major religions). Details from Buddhism (does not identify a supreme god), Sikhism (its sacred test is called the Adi Granth), Judaism (the synagogue is the place for communal prayer), Christianity (celebrate baptism) and Islam (celebrate important events in the life of the Prophet) do illustrate the passage.

Q5.   Answer: False

Explanation: The main theme of the passage is an examination of more than the ceremonies, festivals and observances of the world's major religions and the lives of the prophet or prophets and the lives of the followers. The main theme is an examination of the sense of community, the shared set of values that shape daily life, the definition of the meaning of life and sets of beliefs as to how the world began and what happens after death that religion provides as well as the ceremonies, festivals and observances of the world's major religions and the lives of the prophet or prophets and the lives of the followers.

Chapter 3   Decision analysis

Warm up questions

Synonyms, antonyms, expanded or contracted terms and terms that are similar

Q1.   Answer: D self-important

Explanation: Turn around means find the opposite of the term. Humble means, for example, unpretentious, ordinary and modest. It can also mean to belittle or bring someone down. But its antonym is self-important.

Q2.   Answer: C excavate

Explanation: Enlarge means increase so we are looking for a term that means something greater than what is usually meant by deepen. Deepen means make deeper and synonyms of deepen include dig, hollow or excavate (lessen is its antonym). Of the suggested answers, excavate is used to mean something on quite a big scale and so is in this sense an enlargement of deepen.

Q3.   Answer: B corrupting
        Explanation: To decrease is to reduce something. Poisonous means venomous, fatal or corrupting; its antonym is cleansing. Of the three suggested answers that have the same or similar meanings, corrupting is the less extreme.

Q4.   Answer: A friendly
        Explanation: In this context find an equivalent means find a synonym and from the suggested answers only friendly is a synonym of social.

Q5.   Answer: B fool
        Explanation: Block can mean a lump, an obstruction and a building (a block of flats); we can suggest someone is a fool by calling them a blockhead but not a block.

Q6.   Answer: C offer
        Explanation: To request is to ask for and demand and seek are synonyms; to offer something is the opposite of asking for something.

Q7.   Answer: C very good
        Explanation: Unsurpassed means the best and of the suggested answers the lesser term to unsurpassed is very good (not the best but still very good). Even better would be to increase unsurpassed.

Q8.   Answer: A scanned
        Explanation: Past means in the past tense and to scan something is to copy it and scanned is the past tense of scan.

Q9.   Answer: B superfluous
        Explanation: Requirement, obligation and essential are all equivalents of necessity. Superfluous means unnecessary and is the opposite of necessity.

Q10.   Answer: D mask
        Explanation: Synonyms of display include show, reveal and extend while to mask something is to cover it up, which is the opposite meaning.

Q11.   Answer: A paradox
        Explanation: Enigma means mystery, puzzle or paradox. Axiom and platitude are both sayings considered true.

Q12.   Answer: B like chalk and cheese
        Explanation: Resemble means look alike or are similar. Like, comparable and kindred are synonyms. The saying 'like chalk and cheese' means different and is the opposite of resemble.

Q13.   Answer: C chop
Explanation: All the suggested answers are valid ways of saying carve, but to etch or engrave are methods of fine carving while to chop something is at the extreme of the meaning of carve and so is in a sense an extension.

Q14.   Answer: A perimeter
Explanation: Akin means of the same kind or similar and so you must find a word similar in meaning to margin. Both perimeter and margin mean edge.

Q15.   Answer: D stroke
Explanation: To shrink is to diminish and in this context we are looking for a term that diminishes the meaning of slap. Suggested answers whack, knock and punch all have the same or very similar meanings – a slap – while stroke means something much more gentle.

Q16.   Answer: B group
Explanation: Analogous means similar or equivalent to, so we are looking for a term with the same or a similar meaning. Assorted, not assort, means mixed, miscellaneous and sundry. Assort means group together, rank or arrange.

Q17.   Answer: D dissect
Explanation: To thunder and boom are 'bigger' but related terms to peal, as in a peal of bells; peel means unwrap or skin and to dissect is to do more than peel or skin something.

Q18.   Answer: A sensible
Explanation: Unwise means ill-advised or imprudent and its opposite would be smart or shrewd. Sensible is somewhere in between and so is the correct answer.

Q19.   Answer: B weakness
Explanation: Converse means opposite. Might can mean may (we say, for example, I might or may go) and it also means strength, the opposite of which is weakness.

Q20.   Answer: C atricle
Explanation: Analogous means similar or the same so we are looking for a term with the same or most similar meaning to thing. Belongings are particular things rather than a thing, while an article or object is a thing. Slender is analogous to thin, not thing, and journal is a type of magazine.

Sixty warm-up decision analysis questions

Q1.   Answer: B
Explanation: The code states reverse delete, wooden flooring. Notice that the comma is after delete, so we can take this to mean that the code 323 refers to delete and the reverse of delete is add.

Q2.   Answer: D
Explanation: The code reads add pasta, cigarettes parallel delete. A and C could be right but for the modifier 321 which means parallel. A parallel is a sort of synonym and only answer D offers a parallel to delete = remove.

Q3.   Answer: A
Explanation: The code reads gasoline, akin add, parallel the basket of goods and services. Akin means similar, and we have already seen that parallel means a synonym. The word 'on' is akin to add ('put in' a synonym) in this context; 'list' and 'inventory' are parallels to basket of goods and services. Only A is correct because B does not offer a word akin to add but states add.

Q4.   Answer: B
Explanation: The code reads append popular, parallel elevated, pasta. Append means 'add' and the phrases 'all the rage' and 'very popular' are phrases with similar but greater meaning to popular. A parallel to elevated is promote. Only suggested answer B offers both an append to popular and a parallel to elevated.

Q5.   Answer: C
Explanation: The code reads reverse commodity, mobile phone contract, landscape gardening. Reverse means the antonym or opposite. A commodity is a useful product that can be bought or sold. Both goods and services can be described as commodities (services are not tangible commodities but they are commodities all the same) so these terms cannot be taken to be the antonym. The reverse of commodity is not commodities and the best explanation of the code is C; mobile phones and landscape gardening are not commodities.

Q6.   Answer: D
Explanation: The code reads banking, append service, akin temperate, inflation. To append service we must add something and making it plural services can be taken to be adding something. In this context, temperate means mild or moderate but not pleasant.

Q7.   Answer: A
Explanation: The code reads milk, akin add, inflation, parallel lessen. Only suggested answer A contains a word or phrase akin to add and parallel to lessen.

Q8.   Answer: B
Explanation: The code reads unfashionable, mobile phone contracts, pasta, reverse. Of the code words it only makes sense to reverse unfashionable to fashionable or, in other words, popular. A can be questioned because the code makes no reference to a decision to delete mobile phones or pasta from the list. Out of favour and out of date are synonyms, not antonyms, of unfashionable.

Q9.   Answer: B
Explanation: The code reads reverse delete, lessen wide screen TVs, append unfashionable. To lessen wide screen TVs makes small screen TVs, not TVs in general, append unfashionable could be hate, very unpopular or very unfashionable. In the context of the situation, hate would not be applicable. In the context of the situation, to add TVs to the basket of goods and services because they are very unpopular/unfashionable would be wrong. We can judge therefore that B is correct given the context.

Q10.   Answer: C
Explanation: The code reads soft furnishings, lessen delete, popular, parallel elevated, inflation. Lessen delete can be to 'think about' or 'consider deleting' (but it can't be 'don't delete'). Parallel elevated can be high or very high. The code for popular is unmodified, so very popular is not the best suggestion. This only leaves suggested answer C as correct and including all the codes.

Q11   Answer: A and D
Explanation: The code reads parallel, add, gasoline; notice the comma which implies that the modifier parallel could relate to either add or gasoline. Include is a parallel of add and petrol is a parallel of gasoline, but put on the list is not a parallel of add. B is also questionable because both gasoline and add have been modified. E is likely to be wrong because neither add nor gasoline has been modified.

Q12.   Answer: A, B and C
Explanation: The code reads soft furnishings, delete, refrigerator. The code only provides a single instruction, delete. We should only use this operation once and can use it to either delete (both) soft furnishings and refrigerator or one or the other. D and E are questionable because they imply more than one instruction: to delete one item and keep another.

Q13.   Answer: A, B, C and D
Explanation: The code reads parallel delete, append banking. All the suggested answers offer parallels to delete and all but suggested answer E propose appendages to banking. E, however, does not add to banking – it only suggests everything involved in banking.

Q14.   Answer: A, B, C, D, E
Explanation: The code reads delete, gasoline, parallel temperate, popular, add, cigarettes. The sequence of codes can be combined differently from the way it is presented in the question, so 607 (delete) may relate to either gasoline or cigarettes and 321 602 (parallel temperate) can relate to popular, cigarettes or gasoline. All five suggested answers are valid interpretations of the code sequence. If we look to the context there is nothing stated in the situation that suggests we should favour one or more of the suggested answers over any other. This means that all five of the suggested answers are equally valid interpretations of the code.

Q15.   Answer: B and D
Explanation: The code reads akin milk, the basket of goods and services, add, reverse tiny. Butter, yogurt, white paint and dairy products are all akin to milk. Suggested answer A does not include the code add, so should be rejected, C should be rejected because minute is a synonym of tiny, not the reverse of it. E can be rejected because cows are not akin to milk (ie similar); also, to ask why they are not in the basket is not to follow the code add.

Q16.   Answer: A
Explanation: The code reads vegetable oil alternative diesel green. To describe vegetable oil as a form of diesel (suggested answer C) fails to use the code for alternative. A and B are the only suggested answers that make use of all the codes, but answer B goes against the context of the question (diesel cannot be described as green given the context).

Q17.   Answer: C
Explanation: The code reads octane, alcohol, gasoline, new, high. A does not include gasoline, B uses high twice and D fails to use new.

Q18.   Answer: B
Explanation: The code reads gain, turn around contradiction, may. Turn around contradiction means the antonym of contradiction, which is agreement. We can favour suggested answers A and B over C and D because A and B use terms that are either an antonym of contradiction (agreement) or a term related to its antonym (permission). We can favour A over B because it uses the antonym of contradiction (rather than a related term) and because it introduces fewer clauses unsupported by the sequence of codes (in B we have the suggestion that permission may be denied but try). While it is not incorrect to use additional terms not in the sequence of codes, we can favour the suggested answer that does not introduce them over one that does.

Q19.   Answer: D

Explanation: The code reads diesel, green, enlarge alternative, similar new, more. Enlarge alternative can be alternatives, and similar new can be innovative or recent. Only D uses all the codes and correctly applies the transformers. A does not include more, B fails to enlarge alternative and C fails to include more.

Q20.   Answer: A

Explanation: The code reads investment, new, bio, similar know, fuel. We can reject C because it uses know rather than a word similar to know. Arguably the other three suggested answers all involve words similar to know (no, knows and even now as there is only one letter missing). They also all include the remaining words in the code. We can, however, question D because it states bio-fuels not bio-fuel. This leaves A and B and we can favour A over B because B includes the word high which features in the matrix but does not occur in the question sequence.

Q21.   Answer: C

Explanation: The code reads diesel, oil, vegetable, alternative, enlarge new. Suggested answer B can be questioned because it does not enlarge new; we can eliminate A also because it states vegetables rather than vegetable. Both D and C fully comply with the code but we can judge C to be the best choice as D is not consistent with the context.

Q22.   Answer: A

Explanation: The code reads tell, turn around could. The antonym of could is could not or its abbreviation couldn't. Only suggested answer A offers a correct antonym of could.

Q23.   Answer: C

Explanation: The code reads green, turn around may, ethanol. If you turn around may you get may not. Only suggested answer C offers a correct antonym of may.

Q24.   Answer: B

Explanation: The code reads enlarge alternative, enlarge more, investment, more. Note that the code 526 occurs twice in this sequence and so we can use it twice (once transformed). A and D are less favourable because they use a synonym of more (additional and extra) rather than its enlargement (most). C can be eliminated because it does not include an enlargement of more.

Q25.   Answer: D

Explanation: The code reads gain, similar high, turn around can, tell, new, oil. Soar and gain are similar to high but gains is not. Turn around can is can't. Only D makes use of all the codes and correctly applies the transformations.

Q26.   Answer: A, B and C

Explanation: The code reads green, alternative, ethanol, diesel. All the answers correctly use all parts of the sequence. But we can reject suggested answer D because from the context we know that diesel is not green. As stated in suggested answer E, it is in fact true that ethanol is used as an alternative to gasoline (and not an alternative to diesel) but we are not told this in the context so we cannot know this to be the case. We can arguably reject answer E as incorrect because it includes the word gasoline, which is one of the terms in the matrix but is not included in the sequence.

Q27.   Answer: B and C

Explanation: The code reads similar contradiction, similar investment, bio, fuel. Words/phrases that occur in the suggested answers that are similar to contradiction are inconsistent, disagreement and conflicting evidence. Terms similar to investment include venture, speculation and arguably capital. Suggested answers A and D can be eliminated because they do not make use of the code for similar contradiction. Both B and C make full use of the code sequence and the context does not rule either of them out.

Q28.   Answer: A, B and C

Explanation: The code reads similar few, ethanol, investment, alternative. Answers A B and C all include terms similar to few: minority, hardly any, small amount. D includes the antonym: many. Suggested answers A, B and C therefore correctly utilize the sequence of code and all three are also consistent with the context.

Q29.   Answer: C and D

Explanation: The code reads turn around gain, diesel, fuel, gasoline, turn around new. If we turn around gain we get decrease, dwindle, decline and fall. If we turn around new we get old, traditional or conventional. Only suggested answers C and D include the meaning of all the codes. Answers A and B both fail to include an antonym of new (B also uses the term bio which is in the matrix but does not appear in the question sequence). Both C and D are also consistent with the context and so both can be judged as the best interpretations.

Q30.   Answer: B and D

Explanation: The code reads ethanol, gasoline, fuel, octane, high. Suggested answers B and D both use all parts of the sequence; however, suggested answer A does not include gasoline while answer C fails to utilize the term fuel. Both B and D are also consistent with the context and are equally the best interpretations.

Q31.   Answer: B
Explanation: The code reads he or S, we, know, works. Suggested answer C can be eliminated because it includes the term online, which is in the matrix but not in the question sequence. D can be rejected because it does not make use of the code for we and uses the plural for know. Both A and B correctly apply the code but we can reject A because it does not comply with the context (the threat is internal).

Q32.   Answer: D
Explanation: The code reads he or S, information, expand try, online. Tries and trying are both examples of expanded try. Suggested answers A and B fail to use the code for online. B and C do not include an expanded try. None of the suggested answers contradict the context.

Q33.   Answer: C
Explanation: The code reads he or S, similar to information, prefers, high. Similar to information means, for example, data and details. All but suggested answer D are consistent with the context (D can be eliminated because it describes the business as small); to decide between the remaining suggestions we must judge which is best according to the manner in which they utilize the code. Suggested answer A can be questioned because it does not make use of the code for he or prefers. B is problematic in its use of highest rather than high.

Q34.   Answer: A
Explanation: The code reads works, he or S, seems, reverse week. All suggested answers are consistent with the context so we must look to the utilization of the code to decide which answer to favour. The reverse of week could be many things, including arguably weekend, days, hourly, but it cannot be weekly which means we can reject suggested answer C. We can also eliminate B and D because the code for seems is not used.

Q35.   Answer: B
Explanation: The code reads reverse he or S, know, he or S, we. The last sentence of the context concludes with the term 'his colleagues' so we can reject suggested answer A as not consistent with the context even though it correctly applies the sequence of code. Suggested answers C and D do not make use of the reverse of he.

Q36.   Answer: B
Explanation: The code reads we, reverse believe, expand know, he or S. The reverse of believe is doubt and don't think, expand know can be knows, very familiar terms, realize and recognize. We can reject suggested answers A and C because they do not make use of the code for reverse believe. Both A and D apply the sequence correctly but D is inconsistent with the context, which states that criminal gangs will pay a great deal for the information.

Q37. Answer: C

Explanation: The code reads we, same as ready, online, he or S. Words or phrases the same as ready include, for example, all set and standing by. None of the suggested answers are inconsistent with the context so we look to how they utilize the code to discriminate between them. Suggested answers A and B do not use the code for he so can be rejected. Suggested answer D does not use a term the same as ready.

Q38. Answer: C

Explanation: The code reads past similar to staff, looks, he or S. Past similar to staff means a word or phrase that is similar to staff and in the past tense. Examples used in the suggested answers include 'ex-employee', 'once worked for the organization' and 'personnel who have left the organization'. The context states that you are trying to uncover the identity of an employee, not an ex-employee or someone who had once worked for the organization, so for this reason we can reject suggested answers B and D as inconsistent with the context. We can also prefer C over suggested answer A because A does not include a term similar to staff which is in the past tense.

Q39. Answer: A

Explanation: The code reads staff, similar to no, information, expand ready, he or S, believe, we. All the suggested answers are consistent with the context and so we must look to how the sequence of code is utilized to select a best answer. Thinking laterally, words similar to 'no' used in the example are 'on' (same letters) and 'not' (one extra letter also negative). We can favour suggested answer A over B and D because B and D do not make use of the code for expanded ready. We can prefer A over C because C does not use the code for staff and it uses no rather than a word similar to no.

Q40. Answer: D

Explanation: The code reads contract all, only, know, staff. Contract all can mean few (every single one is a synonym, not a contraction, of all). Only suggested answer D includes a contraction of all. Suggested answer B does not use the code for only, suggested answer C states knows rather than know. Suggested answer A contradicts the context, which states that all but the most secure networks are compromised.

Q41. Answer: B and C

Explanation: The code reads he or S, proves, works. Only answers B and C correctly utilize the three components of the sequence.

Q42. Answer: A and D

Explanation: The code reads we, no, similar to he or S. Similar to he can be him, he's, his and man. Only suggested answers A and D fully comply with the sequence of code. In the case of B we have two terms similar to he and the code for we is not utilized. In suggested answer C also the code for we is not used.

Q43. Answer: A and C

Explanation: The code reads works, we, know, if, he or S. Answers A, B and C correctly apply the code but B is inconsistent with the context, which states that the threat is internal.

Q44. Answer: B, C and D

Explanation: The code reads he or S, we, know. Suggested answer A contradicts the situation, which suggests that something is known of S, for example that he is an employee. The remaining suggested answers are consistent with the context and correctly apply the sequence of code.

Q45. Answer: A and B

Explanation: The code reads contract we, same as believe, proves, expand no. None of the suggested answers contradicts the context so we must establish which ones utilize the code correctly. Contraction of we is I or my, same as believe can be trust, think, my best judgement, and an expansion of no can be nothing and none. Suggested answer C can be discarded because it does not use the code for expand no. Suggested answer D does not utilize the code for we and uses the term prove not proves.

Q46. Answer: C

Explanation: The code reads vote, must, turn around rich, turn around wrong. Turn around rich to get poor and turn around wrong to get right. Only suggested answers A and C make use of the full sequence but A is inconsistent with the context which states that the group champions the disenfranchised.

Q47. Answer: A

Explanation: The code reads equivalent merit, children, better, education. The equivalent to merit could be deserve, value or worth. Only A fully applies the sequence of code.

Q48. Answer: D

Explanation: The code reads must, high, accept, rich. Suggested answers A, C and D correctly apply the sequence of code but only answer D is consistent with the context. C is wrong because the context states that the group campaigns peacefully for its aims. A is wrong because the reason the rich must accept higher taxation is given (the redistribution of wealth).

Q49. Answer: C

Explanation: The code reads industry, must, pollution, similar reform, similar turn around high. Words similar to reform are modernized and transformation. Turn around high gives you low and words similar to low include, for example, lower. Only C correctly applies all parts of the sequence.

Q50.   Answer: A

Explanation: The code reads wrong, similar poverty, public, similar rich. Similar to poverty can be poor or squalor and similar to rich can be wealth and affluence. D can be rejected because it uses the term wronged rather than wrong. B can be rejected because the term shortages is not similar to poverty. C (and also B) can be rejected because it contradicts the spirit of the context.

Q51.   Answer: A

Explanation: The code reads enlarge reform, decrease better, must. Enlarge reform means revolution and change but not civil disobedience. Decrease better can mean OK, reasonable, tolerable and all right. Suggested answers A and C comply fully with the sequence of code but C can be rejected because it goes beyond the peaceful aims stated in the context.

Q52.   Answer: B

Explanation: The code reads poverty, pollution, turn around result. Result means consequence or effect and to turn it around means basis, cause or foundation. Suggested answers A, B and C comply with the sequence of code. The context does not suggest or support the suggestion that pollution or poverty is the cause or effect of one or the other so we can reject these suggested answers. This leaves suggested answer B as the better interpretation in that it is most consistent with the tone of the context.

Q53.   Answer: D

Explanation: The code reads education, children, turn around wrong, similar better. Turn around wrong means right and similar better can mean superior and good (if it were equivalent good would be incorrect). Suggested answers A, B and C do not apply the code sequence correctly. A and C fail to use the code for turn around wrong. B uses the term child rather than children.

Q54.   Answer: C

Explanation: The code reads rich, pollution, equivalent better, similar turn around high. Equivalents of better are improved and healthier. A word similar to the opposite (turned around) of high is lower. Only suggested answer C applies the code sequence correctly.

Q55.   Answer: A

Explanation: The code reads rich, turn around rich, must, better. Turn around rich gives poor. Suggested answers A and D correctly apply all aspects of the code sequence but D is not in line with the spirit of the context. Suggested answers B and C both fail to implement the code sequence fully.

Q56.   Answer: B and C
Explanation: The code reads similar must, poverty, accept. Words and phrases similar to must include ought to or ought not to, should and obliged. Suggested answer A applies the code correctly but is inconsistent with the spirit of the context. Suggested answer D does not make use of the code for accept.

Q57.   Answer: A, B and D
Explanation: The code reads children, wrong, education, turn around rich. Turn around rich to obtain poor, deprived or underprivileged. Suggested answers A, B and D all correctly apply the code sequence and are consistent with the context. Suggested answer C does not make use of the code for wrong.

Q58.   Answer: B and C
Explanation: The code reads high, similar public, reform. Words similar to public include unrestricted community and civic. Suggested answers B and C correctly apply the code sequence and are consistent with the context. Suggested answer A fails to use the code for high while suggested answer D does not include a term similar to public.

Q59.   Answer: A, B, C and D
Explanation: The code reads equivalent merit, reform, industry. Terms that are equivalent to merit include plus points, advantages, great value and worth. All four suggested answers correctly apply the sequence of code and are consistent with the context.

Q60.   Answer: B and D
Explanation: The code reads reform, industry, accept, pollution, similar vote. Suggested answer A does not make use of the code for accept. And suggested answer C uses the term vote rather than a term similar to vote.

Mini-test 1

Q1.   Answer: B
Explanation: The code reads buy, any, similar to price. Similar to price can mean worth, cost, consequence and outlay. We can reject suggested answer A because the code for buy is not used (and because the term price is used rather than a term similar to it). We can judge C as incorrect because the code for 'any' is not utilized. Both suggested answers B and D correctly implement the sequence of code but suggested answer D is not consistent with the context, which states that the auction is of a unique British stamp so we cannot buy any of them (there is only one).

Q2.   Answer: A

Explanation: The code reads million, twenty, Smith, bid. Suggested answers A and D both correctly apply the sequence of code but answer D is inconsistent with the context as it implies that the auction has already taken place and the context states that you are preparing for it.

Q3.   Answer: C and D

Explanation: The code reads similar to buy, investment, stamp. Terms similar to buy include acquired, bought and purchase. Suggested answer A can be rejected because it uses the term buy rather than a term that is similar. Suggested answer B fails to use the code for investment. Both C and D correctly apply the sequence of code and are consistent with the context.

Q4.   Answer: D

Explanation: The code reads twenty, years, expand million, sold, stamp. Expand million to get millions or countless. We can reject suggested answer B as it uses an item from the list of terms 'collectors' that is not in the sequence of code. Suggested answer C can be rejected because we say '20 million is' and not '20 millions are'. Both suggested answers A and D correctly apply the sequence but A is inconsistent with the context which describes the stamp as unique.

Q5.   Answer: B

Explanation: The code reads feature, stamp, cheap at, unique, reverse similar to small, price. Terms that are similar to the reverse of small include eye-catching, striking, titanic and conspicuous. Suggested answer A fails to use the code for cheap at. Suggested answer D uses the term cheap whatever rather than cheap at. Suggested answers B and C both correctly apply the sequence of code but C refers to 'the price' and this is inconsistent with the context from which we can infer that the auction has not yet taken place so the price paid is not yet known.

Mini-test 2

Q1.   Answer: A and C

Explanation: The code reads admit, children, parents, assignments. Suggested answer B does not use the code for admit and D uses a term that occurs in the dictionary but is not in the sequence of code. Both suggested answers A and C apply the code correctly and are both consistent with the context.

Q2.   Answer: B

Explanation: The code reads nothing like big, websites, model, offer. Terms nothing like big are small and modest (full-length is like big rather than nothing like it). Suggested answer A does not use a term nothing like big. Answer C does not utilize the term website or model (and uses the term grade which is in the dictionary but not in the sequence of code). Suggested answer D does not utilize the code for offer.

Q3.   Answer: D

Explanation: The code reads students, like admit, easy, cheat. Terms that are like admit include declare, come clean, say and confess. Suggested answers B and C do not utilize the code for easy. Both suggested answers A and D apply the code correctly but suggested answer A contradicts the context which states that cheating is widespread.

Q4.   Answer: C

Explanation: The code reads nothing like students, students, help. We can take nothing like to mean the opposite and the opposite of students can be teachers (but not learners). Suggested answer B and D fail to utilize a term nothing like student. Both suggested answers A and C comply with the code sequence and both are consistent with the context so we must decide which of the two in our judgement is best. Suggested answer C is the more relevant to the main issue of the context (also suggested answer A is to some extent implausible as it is not often you hear students complaining that they get too much help).

Q5.   Answer: A

Explanation: The code reads siblings, help, grade, parents, like increase. In the context a term like increase can be higher, boost, and inflation. Suggested answer D is nonsensical – we cannot correctly say that we can enlarge grades – and so can be rejected. Suggested answer B is questionable because it uses the term helped rather than help. Suggested answer B can also be rejected, along with answer C, because it is unclear what relevance it has to the context. Parents and siblings obviously can help students boost their grade through perfectly legitimate assistance. The point of the context is that grades may be boosted by parents and siblings helping in ways that amount to cheating. We can reject answers B and C, therefore, because parents and siblings can legitimately help students and this help can result in higher grades. This leaves answer A which complies with the code sequence and is consistent with the context.

Mini-test 3

Q1.   Answer: C

Explanation: The code reads treasure, join wood rock, similar to me. A term similar to me can be my, I, and mine. By joining wood and rock we can get coal and arguably a wooden box covered with rock. Suggested answer A can be rejected because even if we accept that joining wood and rock could give a rocky outcrop above the tree line, the context described the billionaire as an agoraphobic (someone fearful of open spaces) and we can suppose that he would not venture out onto such an exposed location. Suggested answer B does not make use of the code for a term similar to me. D uses a term (dig) that occurs in the lexis but is not included in the sequence of code.

Q2.   Answer: D

Explanation: The code reads stop, three, type of card game. The only types of card game in the suggested answers are bridge and poker. We can question suggested answer A because a casino is not a type of card game. We can reject suggested answer B because the code is supposed to be directions to the treasure and three men could not be permanently playing a game of cards (the context states that he confided in no one so they could not be accomplices). We can reject suggested answer C because the context described the man as severely moral and we can surmise that such a person would not oblige another to play a game of poker.

Q3.   Answer: B and D

Explanation: The code reads rock, look, equivalent to flat. Terms that are equivalent to flat include smooth and apartment. We can question suggested answers A and C because they do not utilize a term equivalent to flat (C uses the term flat not an alternative). A uses the term top which is not an equivalent to flat.

Q4.   Answer: B

Explanation: The code reads similar to wood, similar to circle, equivalent to broken rock. All the suggested answers include a term similar to wood; wooden, planks, tree and timber. Suggested answers A and D do not include a term similar to circle. Only suggested answer B contains a term that is the equivalent to broken rock, namely stones. In the context we are told that the treasure was buried and so if suggested answers A and C are referring to the location of the treasure then they both contradict the context.

Q5.   Answer: A

Explanation: The code reads turn around mountain, join primitive plant cow, city. We can turn around mountain to get plane or valley and while only suggested answers B and C include the code for city by joining the primitive plant moss and cow we get the name of the city Moscow in suggested answer A (we can surmise that the set of street maps to most of the world's capital cities includes the city of Moscow which would allow us to identify it as a city). We can question B and D because in the case of B a hill top and in the case of D a flat patch are not terms that mean the opposite of mountain and in neither is the code for 'turn around primitive plant cow' utilized. In C rainforest is not a primitive plant and again the code for join primitive plant and cow is not utilized. Given that we can identify Moscow as a city from the set of street maps the best answer is A.

Mini-test 4

Q1.   Answer: D
Explanation: The code reads flight, nose, stable. All four suggested answers comply with the sequence of code so we must rely on the context to decide which is in our judgement the best. The context states that 'The ultimate design involves a snub nose.' From this we can conclude that a snub nose is better than a pointed nose design and blunt is another word for snub. We can dismiss suggested answers A and C on the grounds that they described pointed nose designs as the better and we can identify D as the best interpretation because it states that a blunt nose is better and then goes on to explain why this is the case.

Q2.   Answer: A and B
Explanation: The code reads design, construct, akin to choice. Terms that are akin to choice include best, choose and select. Suggested answer C does not include a term akin to choice and uses a term that occurs in the vocabulary but is not in the question's sequence of code. Suggested answer D includes the terms delta and wing which are not in the question's sequence of code. Both A and B correctly apply the sequence and both are consistent with the context.

Q3.   Answer: C
Explanation: The code reads folds, tape, strength, minimize, drag. Suggested answer B uses the word design which occurs in the vocabulary but the code is not present in the sequence. Suggested answer D does not utilize the term tape. Both suggested answers B and C correctly apply the sequence of code but answer B contradicts the context which states that the use of tape is not allowed.

Q4.   Answer: A and C
Explanation: The code reads akin to slant, lift, increase, wing or wings, upwards. Terms that are akin to slant include incline and camber. Suggested answer B does not include a term akin to slant. Suggested answer D fails to include a word for upwards). Both A and C utilize all parts of the sequence and do not contradict the context.

Q5.   Answer: B
Explanation: The code reads expand important, design, wing or wings, nose. Expand important to get fundamental and vital (significant and central are equivalents to important rather than an expansion of it). Suggested answer A uses a term that occurs in the vocabulary but is not in the code sequence. Suggested answers C and D use equivalents to important rather than an expansion. Also, D is in conflict with the context which describes both the nose and wing as key.

Chapter 4   Quantitative reasoning

1.   D. 29,900. 6,450 + 7,600 + 8,450 + 7,400 = 29,900

2.   D. 25%. 6,450 + 7,600 + 8,450 + 7,400 + 5,550 = 35,450, (35,450 / 131,250) = 0.270, therefore approximately 25%.

3.   C. 1/7. 9,600 + 7,950 = 17,550, (17,550 / 131,250) = 0.134, approximately 1/7.

4.   A. 4 : 5. Schoolchildren: 7,600 + 8,450 + 7,400 = 23,450, retired: 7,450 + 7,100 + 6,450 + 4,500 + 2,750 = 28,250. The ratio 23,450 : 28,250 is about 4 : 5.

5.   E. 81.0. Add up all the times = 810, then divide by the number of children, 10. 810 / 10 = 81.0.

6.   B. 81. Put the numbers in numerical order then take the number in the middle. As there are an even number, split the difference between the two central numbers, 80 and 82, giving 81.

7.   E. Two and a half times greater. Range in east = 95 – 65 = 30, range in west 145 – 70 = 75. 75 / 30 = 2.5.

8.   C. 121.Mode is the most frequent. There are two occurrences of 121.

9.   D. Black £20. 30 calls for a total of 300 minutes, therefore the charges would be as follows: Green £10: (30 × 10p) + (300 × 0.4p) = 420p; Green £20: (30 × 10p) + (300 × 0.35p) = 405p; Black £10: (30 × 8p) + (300 × 0.5p) = 390p; Black £20: (30 × 6p) + (300 × 0.4p) = 300p.

10.   B. 60%. The total cost of calls would be £3.90 (see above) leaving £6.10 unused. (6.10 / 10.00) = 0.61, or approximately 60% wasted.

11.   B. 10. The total number of calls was 325 and the total duration 3,243 minutes, therefore the average was (3,243/325) = 10.0

12.   D. Black £20. The price per minute for the Black £20 is now = 0.4p + (0.4p × (70/100)) = 0.68p. The cost for 300 minutes is now = 300 × 0.68p = 204 and the total cost = (30 × 6p) + 204p = 384p. Still the cheapest (see question 9 above).

13.   B. 4. 19,000 people in a population of 200,000 as a percentage = (19,000 / 200,000) = 0.095, 9.5%. Anything bigger than 9.5% will therefore employ more than 19,000 people, i.e. 12%, 18%, 10% and 14%.

14. A. 8 times. If 12% work in manufacturing and 2% in agriculture, there are 6 times as many in manufacturing and they produce a third more per person, so in total they generate 6×1.33 times more, ie 8.

15. E. 62.5m. Half of £100m is £50m. $50m \times 1.25 = 62.5m$.

16. A. 1,000. Number of people in hotels and catering $= 10\%$ Of $200,000 = 20,000$. Number of employers $= 20,000 / 20 = 1,000$.

17. A. 0.55. 6 out of 11 products have at least 1.5g of salt, $6 / 11 = 0.545454$ equivalent to 55%.

18. B. 117%. Each 100 g contains 2 g of salt, so 350 g contains $3.5 \times 2 g = 7$ g. Divided by the recommended maximum allowance of 6, this gives $7 / 6 = 116.6666$, ie 117%.

19. D. £3.30. The price of the Paella is $1.1 \times 1.50 = £1.65$. The Fish Curry costs twice as much $= £3.30$.

20. C. 66.25 cents $1.50 \times 2.65 = 3.975$, $1.25 \times 2.65 = 3.3125$. $= 0.6625$.

21. D. 53%. $106 - 50$ over 1.6 m gives 56 people 1.6 m or less; $56/106$ gives 53%.

22. D. 89. There are 62 people born in this country, 50 taller than 1.6m and 14 left-handed, making a total of 126. As there are only 106 people in the survey there are an 'extra' 20 people. As three people are in all three groups they have been counted twice more, accounting for six of these 'extra' people. This leaves 14 extra who have been counted twice. $14 + 3 = 17$ from an original group of 106, leaving 89.

23. E. Cannot tell. There is no information about how many in the groups overlap.

24. A. 6. This is really a question of simultaneous equations. Let BL equal the number born in England and left-handed, L = number just left-handed. $L + BL + 3 + 2 = 14$, therefore, $BL + L = 9$. Also $L = 2 \times BL$, therefore $L = 6$ and $BL = 3$.

25. E. $3X + 2Y = 1285$, $2X + 3Y = 1040$, where X is cod, Y is chips and the price is in pence.

26. B. £5.47. Cost of cod originally, from the simultaneous equations in Q25, is £3.55 and a portion of chips, £1.10. $3.55 + 20\% = 4.26$, $1.10 + 10\% = 1.21$, therefore total cost is $4.26 + 1.21 = 5.47$.

27. D. 1 : 1.18. The new price divided by the old price is $5.47 / 4.65 = 1.1763$ which rounds up to 1.18.

28.   B. €16.74. Cost in euros of cod is $1.20 \times 3.55 = 4.26$, a portion of chips is $1.20 \times 1.10 = 1.32$. Therefore the total cost $= (3 \times 4.26) + (3 \times 1.32) = €16.74$.

29.   C. 6. The square root of 26 is 5.099 which rounded *up* is 6.

30.   A. 11. The average is 54.81 and so 11 students have less than this score.

31.   C. 30. If three students fail then 23 out of 26 pass, ie 88.5% pass. If the mark is set at 30, three students, those with 26, 28 and 29 points, will fail.

32.   E. 4. Range is $91 - 26 = 65$. 10% of this is 6.5 which, added to the lowest score, gives 32.5 as the pass mark. Four students are below this.

33.   E. $(95 \times 87.5 \times 4.75) / 30$. The number of gallons required would be $95 / 30$ and the price per gallon would be 87.5×4.75. This can be rearranged to give $(95 \times 87.5 \times 4.75) / 30$.

34.   C. Belgium, Finland, United Kingdom, Italy.

35.   D. 22.5%. The information about the car and distance is a red herring. The increase is $1.07^3 = 1.225$, ie 22.5%

36.   B. 342.5p. Cost in the Netherlands $= (210/30) \times 4.75 \times 100.3 = 3334.975$. In Germany $= (210/30) \times 4.75 \times 90 = 2992.5$, $3334.975 - 2992.5 = 342.5$.

37.   A. Nearly twice as much. $1.25^3 = 1.953$, ie almost twice.

38.   B. 15%. $P = Av^3$, rearranged gives $v = {}_3\sqrt{(P/A)}$. If P increases by 50%, v increases by ${}_3\sqrt{(1.5)} = 1.1447$, ie 14.5%, or 15%.

39.   A. $\sqrt{0.4}$. Without the fuel the plane weighs 40% of the original weight, ie a factor of 0.4. If the speed is proportional to the weight, the new speed will be $\sqrt{0.4}$ times the original.

40.   D. $2.5^{1.5}$. This is a little complicated. The power when full is given by $P_f = A v_f^3$, but $v = B\sqrt{W}$, where B is some constant and W the weight, which can also be written as $v = BW^{0.5}$. So $P_f = A(BW_f^{0.5})^3$. The final weight is equal to 0.4 times the original weight, ie $W_e = 0.4W_f$. Power when empty is $P_e = A(B (0.4W)^{0.5})^3$. Therefore $P_f / P_e = A(BW_f^{0.5})^3 / A(B (0.4W)^{0.5})^3 = (1 / 0.4)^{3 \times 0.5} = 2.5^{1.5}$.

41.   E. Cannot tell. As the number with the substance present in the 780 samples is unknown, it is impossible to tell.

42.   C. About 46. Five hundred were identified as having the substance present, 8% of these would be wrong, ie 40. The remaining 280 were identified as having no substance present, of these 2% would be wrong, ie 5.6. 40 + 5.6 is about 46.

43.   D. About 20 more. Allcheck: of the 390 positive, 5% would be wrong giving 19.5, of the 390 negative about 10% wrong, giving 39. This makes a total of around 60 wrong. Truespot: of the 390 positive, 8% would be wrong giving 31.2, of the 390 negative about 2% wrong, giving 7.8. This makes a total of around 40 wrong. Therefore about 20 more wrong for Allcheck. Hopefully, no one sues.

44.   B. About 465. Let P be the number that actually have the substance present, then $0.95P$ would be the number identified by Allcheck as positive. Because the result can only be positive or negative, $800 - P$ are negative, but Allcheck would identify 10% of these as positive, $0.1(800 - P)$. The total number identified as positive would be $0.95P + 0.1(800 - P) = 475$. Rearranging gives $0.85P = 395$, therefore $P = 395 / 0.85 = 464.71$, about 465.

45.   A. 30. The average can be estimated reasonably accurately by saying that, for example, the group of students who play between 10 and 14 hours are 2 students who play 12 hours each (halfway between 10 and 14). This then equates to $2 \times 12 = 24$ 'student hours'. The total number of student hours can then be summed and divided by the number of students to give the average $= 6,560 / 220 = 29.8$ or about 30. Or you can just estimate. Much quicker.

46.   C. 14. $2 + 12 = 14$.

47.   E. 5/9. The average, as seen in question 45, is 30. There are $77 + 38 + 8 = 123$ students who play more than this. 123 divided by the total number of students gives $123 / 220 = 0.559$. $5/9 = 0.555$. Near enough.

48.   D. 27. The heaviest users will have the largest effect on the number of student hours and they reduce their playing by 10%. A large proportion remains unchanged, so a reasonable guess would be about a 10% reduction in average time, ie $30 - 3 = 27$. If you choose to calculate, it should come out to 27.2.

49.   C. $A = 21.5$, $B = 22.22$, $C = 22.5$, $D = 20.5$, $E = 21.5$.

50.   C. Minus 9%. An increase of 10% is equivalent to multiplying by 1.1, so the increase in BMI would be given by $1.1 / 1.1^2$, ie 0.909, or a reduction of 9%.

51.   A. 9 kg. $B = M / H^2$, so $H = \sqrt{(M / B)} = \sqrt{(80 / 28)} = 1.69$ m. To have a BMI just within the 'normal' range a value of 24.9 is needed. $M = BH^2 = 24.9 \times 1.69^2 = 71.1$. Person A needs to lose just under 9 kg.

52.   C. 1/5. $M = BH^2$, so original weight is $24.9 * 1.8^2 = 80.7$ kg. Weight at a BMI of 30 is 97.2 kg. The difference is 16.5 which is 16.5 / 80.7 or 1/5 of the original.

53.   E. Region 2, year 1. Around 3%.

54.   A. Year 1. A 4.4% difference compared to year 3 with 3.5%, for example.

55.   B. £7,000. Difference in percentage in year 3 = 3.5%. 3.5 of £200,000 = £7,000.

56.   C. $1.05 \times 1.03 \times 1.075 \times 1.023 \times 0.99$. Compound interest and reducing by 0.1% is equivalent to multiplying by 0.99.

57.   E. Cannot tell. Several people may have answered no to all questions.

58.   D. 32. 51 buy a paper every day and 32 have been to France, so the maximum number that could have done both would be 32.

59.   A. 20. Yes, sometimes it is that easy. It is the intersection between the two specified groups.

60.   C. 50. The total number of people in the overlapping groups, who have answered yes to *two or more questions*, is 60. However, the 10 people in the centre have answered yes to three questions, so only 50 have answered yes to two.

61.   D. ½. Around 32% are intending to vote for one party and 32% for the other, so those intending to vote are split equally.

62.   A. August. This month has the least total number intending to vote, and hence the largest number abstaining, 32% and 30% compared to 34% and 32% in December, for example.

63.   B. 42.5% and 23.5% respectively. A total of 62% are voting, which means that 38% are abstaining. If 10% of these now vote, there are an additional 3.8% to distribute among the parties in proportion to their current voting intentions, ie $40/62 \times 3.8$ to one and $22/62 \times 3.8$ to the other. An increase respectively of 2.5% and 1.5%, more or less.

64.   E. April to May. The difference in points went from 10 to 0.

65.   D. $(200 - 1.20) \times 0.97 \times 1.20$. You start with 200, then, before doing anything you lose £1.20. Then you lose 3%, ie have 0.97 times the original which is then converted to euros by multiplying by 1.20.

66. E. Concurrency. For a large enough sum, the fee is irrelevant. You can then calculate the number of euros by subtracting the commission from the exchange rate, thus: HH: $1.20 \times 0.97 = 1.164$; BB: 1.18; XC: $1.22 \times 0.98 = 1.1956$; FEC: $1.22 \times 0.97 = 1.1834$; CON: 1.20. Therefore Concurrency will buy you the most euros.

67. A. 3%. The biggest is £177.60 and the smallest £173.20, the difference being £4.40. This is 4.4 / 150 of the original, or 2.9333%.

68. C. ¼. With no losses, £10 becomes €12.50, but from the table you would receive only €9.60, ie €2.90 less. 2.9 / 12.5 = 0.232, or nearly a quarter.

69. E. 5/9. The total is 32% + 23% = 55%; this is approximately equivalent to 5/9 = 0.555 recurring.

70. B. PP increases to 20% and 3A decreases to 12%. This is now a ratio of 20 : 12, or 1.67 : 1.

71. E. 95%. It would be theoretically possible for the major brands to have market shares of 0.0032%, 0.0017%, 0.0015%, 0.0023% respectively, thus maintaining the ratios, but for the own brands to have captured the part of the market, 5%, not occupied by the newcomer. Unlikely, I know, but likelihood wasn't the question.

72. C. 17%. If the current total sales represent a value of 100, then the current sales of Pepper Pop are 15. Increasing this by 15% gives new sales of 17.25, 2.25 bigger and new total sales of 102.25. Therefore the new market share of PP is (17.25 / 102.25) $\times$ 100 = 16.9%.

73. B. $1.1^{0.75}$. Factor for the increase in dosage is $D_2/D_1 = (0.5H^{0.5}W_2^{0.75}) / (0.5H^{0.5}W_1^{0.75}) = (W_2^{0.75}) / (W_1^{0.75}) = (1.1W_1)^{0.75} / W_1^{0.75} = 1.1^{0.75}$.

74. E. Cannot tell. No original weight is given, so no proportional increase can be determined.

75. E. 150 ml. 70 in = 177.8 cm, 10 stone = 63.6 kg. $D = 0.5 \times 177.8^{0.5} \times 63.6^{0.75} = 150$.

76. B. 32%. 20% more is equivalent to multiplying by 1.2, so the overall increase is given by: $1.2^{0.75} \times 1.15 = 1.318$, or 32%.

77. C. 10–14.9. 473 observations. The 237th value will fall in the 10–14.9 group as this contains the observations from 173 to 327.

78.　A. 12.5 minutes. You could check by adding up all the midpoints, ie 2.5, 7.5, 12.5 etc multiplied by the number (5,905.5) and dividing by the total number (473). But, as you only have about 30 seconds per question you just have to judge that the average is in the middle of the 10–14.9 group.

79.　E. Cannot tell. No information is given about the distribution of the 154 observations within the 10–14.9 group; they could all be before 12.5 minutes or all after.

80.　D. 600 litres. 473 trips at an average of 12.5 minutes a trip = 5,912.5 minutes. Multiply this by the 0.1 litres per minute to get 600 litres, roughly.

81.　B. 60. Velocity is the rate of change of distance with time. You could either determine the formula that relates distance and time, distance, $s = 5t^2$, and differentiate to get $ds/dt = v = 10t$, therefore at 6 seconds $v = 60$. Or you could look at the distance at 7 seconds and 5 seconds and estimate the velocity at 6 seconds as being the difference in distance divided by the difference in time $= (245 – 125) / (7 – 5) = 60$.

82.　A. 10. The same process as above can be used to determine the velocities at 1, 2, and 3 seconds, 10, 20 and 30 m/s respectively, to give an acceleration of 10 m/s^2.

83.　C. Between 2 and 3 seconds. After 2 seconds the first object will have travelled 20 m, the second, which has now been travelling for 5 seconds, 25.4 m. After 3 seconds the first has now reached 45 m and the second, 30.2. Somewhere between these two times the first overtook the second.

84.　E. None of the above. It has greatest acceleration just after it is released, just after 0 seconds.

85.　B. 0.7. The mode is 99.9, which subtracting 99.2 leaves 0.7.

86.　D. 25. There are three numbers greater than 99.9 so the total calculated will be 300 less than it should. The average is determined by dividing the total by 12, in this case. The result will therefore be 300 / 12 = 25 too small.

87.　C. 5/6. With numbers this close to 100 the effect of a 2% increase is to add 2. Thus any number previously above 98 will now exceed 100. Only two numbers are below this threshold, therefore 10 out of 12 or 5/6 will be above 100.

88.　A. Answer + 100. As all the numbers input are missing 100, the answer will similarly be missing 100.

89.　B Havanaisday. Multiplying the number of claims by the cost of claim gives the lowest figure for Havanaisday.

90.   E. £163. There are 37.7 claims per 100, but this is divided over the 100 cars, so the cost per car = (37.7 / 100) × 433 = 163.

91.   A. 2/5. Original cost = 36.4 × 223 = 8,117. New cost = 25 × 200 = 5,000. Fractional saving = (8,117 – 5,000) / 8,117 = 0.384, nearly 0.4 or 2/5.

92.   A. £25. 1 in 12 cars breaks down at a cost of £250, so the cost per car is 250 / 12. The company wants to make 20% more than the cost, ie a factor of 1.2, so the premium would be (250 / 12) × 1.2 = 25.

93.   B. 4.429. To get from Robbers to Yangs you have to multiply by 4.429 (104.93/23.69).

94.   A. 56%. The first exchange rate drops by 20%, ie 0.8 times the original value, the others increase by 25%, ie 1.25 the original. Therefore going from one that has dropped to one that has increased the difference is 1.25 / 0.8 = 1.5625, or 56%.

95.   A. Up 1/4. The value of the denominator (the bottom of the fraction) compared to the numerator (top) has dropped to a factor of 0.8. The relative value is therefore 1 / 0.8 = 1.25, ie up a quarter.

96.   C. In the first transaction the tourist loses 3 Dollally (3%). In the second he or she loses 3 Bart or 3 / 33.15 = 0.09 Dollally.

Mini-test 1

97.   D. 1/40. The maximum sales were 33,000, the minimum, 900. 33,000/900 = 36.67, so the fraction is about 1/40.

98.   A. 500%. In the same way that a 100% increase is equivalent to doubling, the sales have gone from 1,100 to 6,600, ie 6 times as much or a 500% increase.

99.   E. £45m. The total sales over the year add up to £104.7m. The total costs = 12 × £5m = 60m, so the total profits are 104.7 – 60 = 44.7.

100.   A. 1.001^{12}. A 0.1% increase is the same as multiplying by 1.001; do this 12 times (once for each of the 12 months) and you have 1.001^{12}. Compound interest in action.

101.   D. Drug D. Has the quickest average recovery time at 13.78.

102.   D. Drug D. 13.5, apparently.

103.   E. Unchanged. In effect, if all the values move towards the 'centre' value by the same proportion, this value will remain unchanged.

104.   D. Cannot tell. There is no information on whether other values change, whether the minimum remains unchanged and the maximum is reduced etc. (OK, so they were easier, or maybe you're getting better, well done.)

Mini-test 2

105.   B. A and E. As you are not required to give any units, the quickest way to determine speed is probably to calculate in miles per minute. A and E both then give the highest values of 1.0.

106.   C. s = 65 / (1 + (11/60)). There are 60 minutes in one hour, so 11/60 represents the fraction of the hour for 11 minutes, so the total time taken is 1 + (11/60). Speed is distance divided by time, as suggested by the units, miles per hour. Be careful of the right number and position of the brackets.

107.   C. + 25%, –17%. If you reduce the time by 20% it is now 0.8 times the original value, but because you need to divide by the time to calculate the velocity you get 1 / 0.8 = 1.25, ie a 25% increase. Similarly, when you increase the time by 20% you get 1 / 1.2 = 0.8333, a 17% decrease.

108.   A. 26.82 m/s. There are 95 minutes, 95 × 60 = 5,700 seconds. 95 miles = 95 × 1,609 = 152,855 metres. Speed = 152,855 / 5,700 = 26.82 m/s.

109.   B. 360. From the graph the average can be seen to be about 15. 15 × 24 = 360.

110.   E 9/24. Nine of the hours *exceed* 15 TeraBytes.

111.   B. 5 and 6 or 8 and 9. Tricky question. The largest absolute increase was between 8 and 9, going from 10 to 29, but the largest *relative* increase was between 5 and 6, from 2 to 6, a factor of 3 times.

112.   A. 14. The bar chart gives TeraBytes in any particular hour, so to get the transfer rate per second you need to divide by 3,600 (60 × 60). Completing this calculation gives 14 values which are 3 GigaBytes/sec or higher.

Mini-test 3

113.   B. 4/3. If the pressure changes by 3/4 in order to give the same constant result, the volume must correspondingly change by 4/3.

114.   C. + 1/5. To compensate the pressure must increase by 6/5 or increase by 1/5.

115.   A. The volume 0.020 should read 0.200. All the others when multiplied together (PV = const) give a value of 2.

116. A. 10%. The answer should be 0.0022222, but the experimenter will only read 0.002. This gives a percentage error of $((0.0022222 - 0.002) / 0.0022222) \times 100 = 10\%$.

117. D. 3/20. A total of 85% (55 + 30) made some pronouncement, so 15% were undecided. $15/100 = 3/20$.

118. C. 65%. Population Y represents two-thirds of the total population and X, 1/3 (2/3 is twice as big as 1/3 and 2/3 + 1/3 = the entire population). The average value, therefore, is $(1/3 \times 85) + (2/3 \times 55) = 65$.

119. A. Population X for juice A. This has shown a 20-point drop.

120. C. Around 7% more. The preference for the original was 65% as in question 118. In the second test the preference is 63% (following the same analysis as above). However, those 63% generate 10% more revenue, adding around another 6 comparative points to give a score of about 69.3. $(69.3 - 65) / 65 = 6.6\%$ higher.

Mini-test 4

121. E. 5. If you look at team A and team E you can create simultaneous equations: $2W + 2D = 26$ and $2W + 1D = 21$, therefore $D = 5$.

122. A. 9. Each of the five teams plays the four others twice, $5 \times 4 \times 2 = 40$. But each match involves two teams so there are 20 matches. 11 have been played already (there are 22 'results' in the table) so there are 9 to play.

123. B. 192. There are 102 points so far. The maximum number of points is gained when two teams draw giving 5 points each, ie 10 points per game. There are 9 remaining games and so 90 more points.

124. A. 1/5. Team C will have 28 points.

125. A. $y = \sqrt{x}$.

126. B. B and C. Slightly sneaky question, but looking at the average height of the line should give you the answer. Integration would give you the exact results; lines B and C have an average value of 3, line D an average of 2.75.

127. E. 7. The formula for the curve is $y = 0.5x + 2$, so when $x = 10$, $y = 7$.

128. D. 6. This is asking the value of x for which $x^2 / 3 = 2x$. Multiply both sides by 3 ($x^2 = 6x$), then divided both sides by x, $x = 6$.

Mini-test 5

129. B. 87.5. Two students have *more* than this.

130. A. 49. If we follow the same process as above then the failure mark should be just above the second lowest, ie 38.5, then the range will be 49.

131. A. 1. A mode of 55 in the first set and 56 in the second. Easy, huh?

132. B. 3. The top four marks, rounded to the nearest integer, are now: 85, 90, 91, 94, three of which exceed the key, 87.5.

133. A. 18 m/s. $50 - 32 = 18$.

134. C. 1,620 m. Every second the car has gone 27 m further than the horse ($50 - 23 = 27$). After 60 seconds it has gone $60 \times 27 = 1,620$ m more.

135. E. 30.43. The horse will complete the 100 m in $100 / 23 = 4.348$ seconds. The bicycle will travel $16 \times 4.348 = 69.57$ m in that time and will therefore need a head start of $100 - 69.57 = 30.43$ m.

136. B. $s = 100 - 13t$. The distance between them starts at 100. The horse gains $23 - 10 = 13$ m every second, so the distance between them reduces following the equation, $s = 100 - 13t$.

Mini-test 6

137. C. March, April, May, June. The four highest points.

138. A. 11/20. $2.75 / 5 = 0.55$ or $11 / 20$.

139. D. £8,500. The average is 3.4. This gives $0.034 \times 250,000 = £8,500$.

140. B. $C = 50,000 \times 1.05^{(1/12)}$. At the end of the year the amount paid with 5% interest will be 1.05 times the loan amount. The interest for each month multiplied together, ie multiplied by itself 12 times, will give this factor. So the factor for the month must be the 12th root of this factor, ie $1.05^{(1/12)}$. Multiply this by the loan amount to give the total due after one month.

141. A. 300%. The key is how much *more*. The leisure time is 4 times the travel time, so with the 100% you have already you need an *additional 300%* to give the 400% (4 times).

142. B. 3 : 2. The number of hours spent travelling has gone from 1.5 to 3 and the number of hours' leisure from 6 to 4.5, ie a new ratio of 4.5 : 3, or 3 : 2.

143. D. 11 minutes. $(1.20 / 6.50) \times 60 = 11.07$ minutes.

144. Travel costs are now $3.00 - 1.20 = £1.80$ more expensive. So the student must earn at least $£1.80 / 6$ hours, 30p / hour more than before.

Mini-test 7

145. B. Equation 2. The square will generate the largest values at higher values of t.

146. D. 25%. At $t = 5$, $V_1 = 3(5) + 5 = 20$. $V_2 = (5)^2 = 25$. $25 / 20 = 1.25$, ie 25% larger.

147. A. They have the same value when the equations are equal, $5\sqrt{t} = t^2$. Squaring both sides gives $25t = t^4$ and then dividing by t gives $25 = t^3$.

148. A. Equation 1. This is a little tricky to answer in 30 seconds, but familiarity with these equations would allow you to sketch quickly and see that equation 1 must have the highest average value. Equation 4 is a close second, starting at 10 and dropping to 1.8 at $t = 1$.

149. A. 2001. Sometimes it is that easy.

150. E. None of the above. The graph shows levels of satisfaction, not quality of teaching.

151. C. 50. Replacing B by n gives $S = 100 (n) / 2n = 50$.

152. E. 6. It is closing the gap at $3 + 3 = 6$ points per year and is currently $78 - 44 = 34$ points behind. It will therefore take $34 / 6 = 6$ years.

Chapter 5   Abstract reasoning

Questions 1–5
Set A has an odd number of shapes and fewer black ones than shaded.
Set B has an even number of shapes and the same number of black as shaded.

1.   C.
2.   B.
3.   A.
4.   C. No black shapes.
5.   C. Odd, but too many black shapes.

Questions 6–10

Set A: Eight enclosed regions and the rectangles are shaded.
Set B: An odd number of enclosed regions and three-sided regions are shaded.

6.   B.
7.   C. Shaded three-sided regions, but eight regions in total.
8.   A.
9.   C. Not all rectangles shaded.
10.   C. Even number.

Questions 11–15

Set A: One is a reflection of the other, either horizontally or vertically.
Set B: One is a rotation of the other.

11.   A.
12.   C.
13.   A.
14.   B.
15.   C.

Questions 16–20

Set A: At least one triangle means two or more circles will be present. An even number of triangles gives shaded circles.
Set B: The difference between the number of unshaded and shaded triangles gives the number of circles. Circles will be shaded black if a rectangle is present.

16.   A.
17.   A.
18.   C.
19.   B.
20.   C.

Questions 21–25

Set A: The total number of sides of shaded shapes minus the total number of sides on the unshaded shapes adds up to zero. The largest shape counts double.
Set B: The total number of sides is 20. Shaded shapes count double.

21.   C.
22.   A.
23.   C.
24.   C.
25.   B.

Questions 26–30

Set A: Odd number of line intersections. Any three-sided enclosed regions are shaded.

Set B: Even number of line intersections. Any four-sided enclosed region is shaded.

26. C. Four-sided shapes would need to be shaded in set B.
27. C. Even number, but three-sided figure shaded.
28. C. Not all four-sided shapes shaded.
29. B.
30. A.

Questions 31–35

Set A: Number of acute angles = number of non-triangular figures. Shading immaterial.

Set B: Number of right angles = number of triangles. Shading immaterial.

31. B. The 'right angles' of the diamond do not count as they are internally divided by lines. There are four right-angle triangles.
32. A.
33. B.
34. B.
35. C.

Questions 36–40

Set A: The angle between the circle, the centre of the large shape and the diamond is always 0°, 90°, 180° or 270°. There are more four-sided shapes than three-sided.

Set B: The angle between the circle, the centre of the large shape and the diamond is always 45°, 135°, 225° or 315°. There is the same number of four-sided shapes as three-sided.

36. C.
37. B.
38. A.
39. C. Not enough triangles for Set B.
40. A. More four-sided than three as there are no triangles at all.

Questions 41–45

Set A: Three similar shapes form a line, as in noughts and crosses.

Set B: Four similar shapes will form a rectangle.

41. B.
42. B.
43. A.
44. C.
45. C.

Questions 46–50

Set A: Pieces put together will form a right angle triangle, five blocks long and five blocks high.
Set B: Pieces put together will form a five by three rectangle.

46. B.
47. B.
48. A.
49. C.
50. B.

Questions 51–55

Set A: The total number of shapes is odd and more shapes are in multiple groups than singularly.
Set B: The total number of shapes is even, same number in multiple groups as singularly.

51. A.
52. A.
53. C.
54. B.
55. C.

Questions 56–60

Set A: Where there are two shapes the same, the smaller one is shaded. All other shading is random.
Set B: Where there are three shapes the same, there are three shaded shapes.

56. B.
57. C. The smaller one should be shaded.
58. A.
59. C.
60. B.

Questions 61–65

Modular arithmetic. The arrow pointing up represents 0, right is 1, down is 2, left is 3. So, $2 + 2 = 0$, because four quarter-rotations would bring the arrow back to the top.
Set A: Addition.
Set B: Subtraction. The first minus the second.

61. A. 3 plus 3 quarter-turns = 6 quarter-turns or 2 half-turns. $3 + 3 = 6$ (2)
62. B. $3 - 3 = 0$.
63. C
64. B. $2 - 3 = -1$ (3)
65. B. $0 - 3 = -3$ (1)

Questions 66–70

Set A: If the majority of arrows point to the left, the majority of shapes are shaded and vice versa. The top-left shape is white. Arrow shading irrelevant.

Set B: If all arrows point the same way, all shapes are shaded. The top-left shape is shaded. Arrow shading irrelevant.

66.   B.
67.   A.
68.   C.
69.   C.
70.   C.

Questions 71–75

Sequence of figures to be read clockwise from top left in a spiral towards centre:

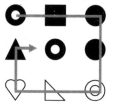

Set A: Same sequence 'A', shading irrelevant.
Set B: Same sequence 'B', figure always shaded the same.

71.   B.
72.   A.
73.   C.
74.   C.
75.   A.

Questions 76–80

Set A: Moving clockwise around the cells in the hexagon from the top, $A - B = C$. Negative numbers are shaded black.

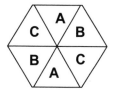

Set B: The total number of spots in the hexagon = 10, using negative numbers shaded black.

76.   A.
77.   C.
78.   B.
79.   B.
80.   A.

Questions 81–85

Set A: Development will make 'right-handed' die, 6 at the top, 1 at the bottom, 3 at the front, 2 on the right and 5 on the left.

Set B: Development will make 'left-handed' die, 6 at the top, 1 at the bottom, 3 at the front, 5 on the right and 2 on the left.

81. C.
82. A. If the 3 overlaps the blank square this will work.
83. A.
84. C.
85. B.

Questions 86–90

Numbering the position in the grid from left to right and then top to bottom gives the first row: 1, 2, 3, 4 and the second row: 5, 6, 7, 8, etc up to the last cell, 16 bottom right.

Set A: Triangle indicates a prime number. Shading is random.

Set B: Triangle indicates an even number. More shapes are shaded than not, triangle is always shaded.

86. B.
87. C.
88. A.
89. C. 15 is not prime.
90. A.

Questions 91–95

Sixteen-'hour' clock.

Set A: When the small hand advances by one 'hour' the long hand advances by two.

Set B: When the small hand advances by one 'hour' the long hand advances by six.

91. C.
92. B.
93. B.
94. C.
95. A.

Questions 96–100

Set A: Total number of sides is 12; shading irrelevant; largest shape leftmost.

Set B: Number of 'black' sides = the rest; largest shape uppermost.

96. A.
97. B.
98. C.
99. C.
100. A.

Mini-test 1

Questions 101–105

Set A: If the two smaller patterned shapes are the same, the larger pattern shape will have stripes, otherwise randomly patterned. All other shapes irrelevant.

Set B: If the two smaller patterned shapes are different, the larger pattern shape will have stripes, otherwise randomly patterned. All other shapes irrelevant.

101. A.
102. C.
103. C.
104. A.
105. B.

Questions 106–110

Triangle = 1, square = 2, circle = 3. Black shapes have negative values.

Set A: Sum of values in top row plus values in middle row equals values in bottom row.

Set B: Top row minus middle row equals bottom row.

106. A.
107. B.
108. C.
109. A.
110. B.

Mini-test 2

Questions 111–115

Set A: Odd number of bounded regions. Zero or one shaded space.

Set B: Even number of bounded regions. One or two shaded spaces.

111. B.
112. B.
113. A.
114. C.
115. C.

Questions 116–120

Set A: The total number of sides is 15. Striped shapes count double. Shapes are in ascending order of number of sides, reading across and down.

Set B: The total number of sides is 16. Striped shapes count double, black shapes count half. Shapes are in descending order of number of sides, reading across and down.

116. C.
117. C.
118. A.
119. B.
120. B.

Mini-test 3

Questions 121–125

Set A: Moving from top left to bottom right, if there is a circle before a triangle, the last shape will be black. Other shading irrelevant.

Set B: Moving from top left to bottom right, if there is a square before a triangle, the last shape will be black. Other shading irrelevant.

121. C.
122. B.
123. A.
124. B.
125. C.

Questions 126–130

Set A: Biggest shape is the smallest. Shading irrelevant.

Set B: Same shapes are also the same size. Shading irrelevant.

126. A.
127. A.
128. C.
129. B.
130. C.

Mini-test 4

Questions 131–135

Set A has 180° rotational symmetry, but no reflective symmetry in vertical axis.

Set B has reflective symmetry in vertical axis, may have 180° rotational symmetry.

131. C.
132. B.
133. A.
134. C.
135. A.

Questions 136–140

Set A: The number of enclosed regions is one larger than the number of line intersections. For example, the second diagram with the two overlapping squares has three regions and two line intersections.

Set B: The number of enclosed regions is the same as the number of line intersections.

136. B.
137. B.
138. C.
139. A.
140. A.

Mini-test 5

Questions 141–145

Set A is based on binary numbers, up arrows are 1, down arrows are zeros. Therefore the first cell represents the number 1,110, or $8 + 4 + 2 = 14$. There are 14 circles. The shading is irrelevant.

Set B has a simple rule. If the number of up arrows is equal to the number of down arrows, there are as many shaded circles as unshaded. If there are more up arrows, there are more shaded circles and vice versa.

141. A.
142. A.
143. C.
144. B.
145. A.

Questions 146–150

Circle = 0, rectangle = 1, up arrow = 2, triangle = 3, square = 4, pentangle = 5, hexagon = 6, down arrow = 7, octagon = 8 and right or left arrow = 9.

Set A: Represents addition. The first two plus the second two = the last two. For example, the first cell has the equation: $01 + 03 = 04$.

Set B: Represents subtraction.

146. C.
147. A.
148. C.
149. B.
150. B.

Chapter 6   Non-cognitive analysis

Q1.   Explanation: Tactful or tact means discretion or diplomatic and these are desirable qualities in applicants to medical school. Check the consistency of your answers with, for example, questions 16, 19, 25, 58 and 69.

Q2.   Explanation: To agree with this statement allows you to be both practical and compassionate while to disagree means that you are more practical than compassionate. The role of a medical professional demands both compassion and a practical, ie sensible, realistic approach. For this reason the better response might be to agree.

Q3.   Explanation: That healthcare might need to be rationed does not imply that it should be rationed according to people's lifestyle and certain lifestyles should be discriminated against in terms of the level of care they receive.

Q4.   Explanation: Your work in the health service will require extensive detail and small differences will make a significant difference to the quality of care that you provide. For these reasons an admission that you struggle to pay attention to small detail is unlikely to support your application.

Q5.   Explanation: If you can think of other reasons why you do not steal, like for example the fact that it is wrong, then you should disagree with this statement. Check your answer for consistency with your response to questions 12, 27, 37, 41, 53 76, 84 and 91.

Q6.   Explanation: There is nothing wrong with compassion but too much and you might risk the impression that you may find the stresses and strains of the medical profession a little too much. This question investigates an aspect of how emotional you are; consider, for example, questions 31, 36, 42, 54, 57, 59, 61 and 79 which also investigate aspects of this trait and check your responses for consistency.

Q7.   Explanation: You should disagree with this statement because you should first establish if you should stop immediately what you were doing and turn to the critical new task rather than first complete your current assignment. Consider your response to, for example, questions 17, 34, 46 and 88 all of which to some extent investigate your attitude towards aspects of the trait robustness.

Q8.   Explanation: The views of someone qualified in the field may carry more weight than someone unqualified but this should not lead you to agree with the suggestion that only the views of those qualified should be allowed to contribute to a debate.

Q9.   Explanation: To leave a situation which might well amount to an emergency would not be the kind of response expected from someone who wants to work in the medical profession.

Q10.   Explanation: In the medical profession you may well have to take the time to listen to people who are only able to speak slowly; for this reason agreement with this statement would suggest you can empathize with others.

Q11.   Explanation: To agree with this statement might suggest that you are reserved, unapproachable and inaccessible in nature and these are not the ideal qualities in someone who wants to work in the medical profession. See questions 45 and 81 for the consistency of your response.

Q12. Explanation: We place medical professionals in very high positions of trust and expect from them exemplary integrity. As a doctor you may well be known in the community in which you shop and for this reason to disagree with this statement might damage your application and your standing in the community that you serve. Check your answer for consistency with your responses to questions 5, 27, 37, 41, 53 76, 84 and 91.

Q13. Explanation: Despite the fact that Mary is a challenging character she deserves the same treatment and respect as every other patient; such behaviour therefore would never be excusable.

Q14. Explanation: The money was not yours to donate or decide how to spend and so the suggested action would have been the wrong thing to do. If you did not answer that it was the wrong thing to do then you may risk the impression that you lack integrity.

Q15. Explanation: Being identified as a sociable sort of person with a genuine interest in people would support your application to medical school and disagreement with this statement might help give that impression. Check the consistency of your answers with your responses to questions 78 and 87.

Q16. Explanation: Astuteness means intelligence and is a desirable quality in applicants to medical school.

Q17. Explanation: You should be happy to disagree with this statement. If you make a mistake, and we all do from time to time, you should be able to report it immediately and when appropriate work hard to correct it.

Q18. Explanation: You might well disagree with this statement because to be serious not only means taking your role seriously but also is to be solemn, stern or even severe, whereas to be lucid is to be articulate, clear and logical and the latter might be the more valuable quality in a medical professional.

Q19. Explanation: To show disdain is to show contempt or to be condescending and these would be inappropriate responses in work no matter the provocation. A patient might be very uncomfortable or worried and consequently may be rude unintentionally, and in these circumstances one should try to understand and sympathize. Check for consistency your answers to, for example, questions 1, 16, 25, 58 and 69.

Q20. Explanation: This common saying implies that it matters little how you achieve something so long as it is achieved. Such a pragmatic stance risks you being judged as lacking principle. Would it be right, for example, to achieve departmental targets by forging the results? This question investigates aspects of the trait integrity – consider, for example, questions 13, 14, 29, 49, 68, 74, 75 and 100 for consistency as they too investigate aspects of this trait.

Q21. Explanation: The wish to help others is an important motivation for many in the medical profession and agreement with this statement would suggest a lack of interest in helping others. It may be that on some occasions you are too busy but to say you are busy when your current commitments are unspecified suggests an unwillingness to help as a matter of principle.

Q22. Explanation: To agree with this statement suggests that you would prefer to help only certain sorts of people and that you might treat someone you do not know differently from someone you do. This is unlikely to be the sort of response a medical school would expect of its preferred candidates. Look to question 2 for consistency in your response.

Q23. Explanation: Disagreement with this statement suggests that you do not find it difficult to trust people and are happy to accept at face value what people say.

Q24. Explanation: Health professionals work both independently and as a part of a team. But this does not mean that the ideal candidate should prefer to work independently, because this would suggest that they favour autonomy over interdependence and the role of health professional is dependent on the services of others and teamwork. This question investigates aspects of self-sufficiency. Check that you have responded consistently with, for example, question 8, 28, 48 and 90.

Q25. Explanation: You might recall the earlier statement which asked 'I am able to talk about things that people find personal', a statement that you should have been able to agree with. However, this statement, 'I like to talk about things that many people find personal', is quite a different matter and suggests a certain lack of sympathy. If people find something personal then they are likely to feel uncomfortable and we do not enjoy making people uncomfortable.

Q26. Explanation: You should disagree with this statement because if you were already very busy then you should inform the person who asked you to undertake the additional work that there is a risk that you may not have time to complete anything else. Check question 1 to see if your response is consistent.

Q27. Explanation: You should be honest enough to answer the statement truthfully, which will almost certainly mean that we all disagree with it. Check your answer for consistency with your responses to questions 5, 12, 37, 41, 53, 76, 84 and 91.

Q28. Explanation: On the basis of the information provided it is quite possible that the views of a new member of a team are equal to or more important than those of a long-standing member of the team. This question investigates aspects of self-sufficiency. Check that you have responded consistently with, for example, questions 8, 24, 48 and 90.

Q29. Explanation: To agree with this statement would support the view that you have integrity and are a principled person.

Q30. Explanation: Most people should be prepared to agree with this statement. Agreement does not mean that you lack patience because the most patient person in the world may wish they were even more so. We all feel frustration with others from time to time and it would be a credit to us if we desired that we did not do so.

Q31. Explanation: It is possible to be too sensitive for a role as a medical professional where you will face many stressful and some distressing situations, so it might be best to avoid the suggestion that the statement is particularly true of you. To say that people who know you would not say you are sensitive might also risk the impression that you lack the compassion essential for the role. Perhaps the best answer, if it is true, is that it is partially true that people say you are sensitive.

Q32. Explanation: Feeling at ease with strangers and being able to confidently start a conversation are skills important to the role of a medical professional and agreement with this statement might risk the impression that you do not excel in this aspect of the role.

Q33. Explanation: Agreement with this statement suggests an assured and self-reliant approach to work, qualities that would be valued in a health professional. This question investigates aspects of self-sufficiency. Check that you have responded consistently with, for example, questions 8, 24, 28, 48 and 90.

Q34. Explanation: You should be able to agree with this statement. Your colleagues and managers will want to know all the facts and if you withhold information because you believe they might not want to hear it then problems could arise. Check to see that your response is consistent with question 1.

Q35. Explanation: In the medical profession people work collaboratively and it is a role that suits the naturally gregarious; for this reason, to disagree with this statement might be the preferred response.

Q36. Explanation: Emotional detachment implies an indifference or aloofness so you should only agree with this statement if you are indifferent towards others or aloof. This question investigates an aspect of how emotional you are; consider, for example, questions 31, 42, 54, 57, 59, 61 and 79 which also investigate aspects of this trait and check your responses for consistency.

Q37. Explanation: Only agree with this statement if you would steal in a situation when you could not possibly get caught. Most people, even if they know they could not get caught, would still not steal as a matter of principle. Check your answer for consistency with your responses to questions 5, 12, 27, 41, 53, 76, 84 and 91.

Q38. Explanation: You should have no difficultly in disagreeing with this statement; there are no circumstances when a racist remark is appropriate.

Q39. Explanation: The work of a health professional requires someone's full attention and concentration and to admit to vagueness or losing track of time is something we should guard against and work hard to avoid.

Q40. Explanation: You should only disagree with this statement if it is true that you are primarily motivated by salary. In the health profession salaries can be good but they are not most people's first and foremost motivation.

Q41. Explanation: You should be able to disagree with this statement. The money is not yours and so it is not for you to decide how it should be used. The correct action would be to take it to the police station so that the person who lost it might report it lost and collect it. Check your answer for consistency with your responses to questions 5, 12, 27, 37, 53, 76, 84 and 91.

Q42. Explanation: To be thick-skinned is to be insensitive or indifferent to the feelings of others. To describe yourself in such a way might risk the impression that you lack compassion and empathy, both of which are desirable qualities in health professionals.

Q43. Explanation: To agree with this statement implies that you believe it is possible both to be non-judgemental and to operate according to an ethical code, and this stance is most certainly expected of you in the medical profession. To disagree allows the possibility that you hold an ethical code that requires you to be judgemental. Check your response to question 89 for consistency.

Q44. Explanation: To agree with this statement suggests that you hold that fault and blame might be attributable to people with certain medical conditions and that state-funded medical care should be withdrawn from sufferers in certain circumstances. To criticize people for their lifestyle and to judge them (or even treat them differently if they suffer certain medical conditions) risks being viewed as lacking empathy. Consider your responses to, for example, questions 10, 22, 38, 52 and 65 all of which to some extent investigate your attitude towards aspects of the trait empathy.

Q45. Explanation: Work as a health professional best suits people who are at ease socially and can build and maintain working relationships effectively. To admit that you find it difficult to get used to people does not suggest that you possess these important qualities. Check questions 11 and 81 for consistency of your responses.

Q46. Explanation: To be caring or thoughtful in your approach to others should not get in the way of a life-saving intervention and if you agree with this statement then you risk the impression that you might in some situations be inconsiderate and such an impression is unlikely to support your application to medical school.

Q47. Explanation: To agree with this statement suggests a confident and trusting approach in your dealings with others.

Q48. Explanation: People in senior roles do carry a disproportionate share of responsibility for the actions taken; however, every member of a team should share a sense of ownership for the successful outcome of the team's work and agreement with the statement might suggest a reluctance to share fully that responsibility.

Q49. Explanation: The decent and correct thing to do would be to report the fact that you were late irrespective of the circumstances. This question investigates aspects of the trait integrity; consider, for example, questions 13, 14, 20, 29, 68, 74, 75 and 95 for consistency as they too investigate aspects of this trait.

Q50. Explanation: To be demonstrative is to be warm and open, while someone reserved is formal, reticent or quiet.

Q51. Explanation: Agreement with this statement suggests someone who is secure in their dealings with other people while disagreement might suggest someone distrusting of the motives of others.

Q52. Explanation: Agreement with this statement risks the impression that you find it difficult to share someone's feelings. Imagine yourself having a health problem and living in a community which speaks a language you cannot speak and imagine how difficult that situation might be. You would want the health professionals to assist you as much as is practical and to uphold the principle that they will provide you with the best possible care despite any language barrier.

Q53. Explanation: You should be happy to agree with this statement as there is always the option of telling the truth and a medical professional should never need to lie. Check your answer for consistency with your responses to questions 5, 12, 27, 37, 41, 76, 84 and 91.

Q54. Explanation: To be thin-skinned is to be emotional or to be easily upset. There is a risk that someone who is thin-skinned may find the pressures and daily experiences of a medical professional hard to deal with. This question investigates an aspect of how emotional you are; consider, for example, questions 31, 36, 42, 57, 59, 61 and 79 which also investigate aspects of this trait and check your responses for consistency.

Q55.   Explanation: We all make mistakes but to admit that you allow yourself to be distracted to the point where you make them is something different and something we should all work to avoid.

Q56.   Explanation: You should agree with this statement; after all, the message is described as urgent and to delay and, for example, wait for a suitable pause in the conversation before you deliver the message may lead to an unaffordable delay.

Q57.   Explanation: Enthusiasm is a good thing but like most good things you can have too much of it. The ideal answer might be one that suggests you are enthusiastic but not so enthusiastic as to suggest emotional immaturity. This question investigates an aspect of how emotional you are; consider, for example, questions 31, 36, 42, 54, 59, 61 and 79 which also investigate aspects of this trait and check your responses for consistency.

Q58.   Explanation: A councillor is an elected member of a local or city authority; a counsellor is someone qualified to provide support for people with, for example, social or psychological difficulties. The role of a counsellor is very much an aspect of the work of a medical professional and for this reason might be the preferred answer.

Q59.   Explanation: It is hard to imagine that agreement with this statement would be desirable in a health professional or would support an application to medical school.

Q60.   Explanation: To be spontaneous can mean you are unstructured, unplanned and impulsive. And these may not be great qualities for a medical professional to display. Remember to keep at the forefront of your mind the world of work. You might be spontaneous in your social life or when in the company of friends or family, but would you be in the role of a medical professional at work? I suspect you might be far less spontaneous then, and it is in this context that you should answer the question.

Q61.   Explanation: To wear your emotions on your sleeve means that you do not hide your emotions. It implies that you may allow your emotions to interfere with what you are doing and this may not be desirable in the role of a health professional.

Q62.   Explanation: The correct thing to do in this situation would be to report the incident.

Q63.   Explanation: Both teamwork and keeping abreast of developments are key to the role of a health professional and by not agreeing with the statement you avoid the trap of falsely ranking one above the other.

Q64. Explanation: To agree that you prefer the familiar and routine is fine, but beware the suggestion in this statement that you prefer such work because it helps with your confidence. To agree that you prefer the familiar and routine because otherwise you lack confidence may not support your application to a role in which you must be able to deal with the unexpected.

Q65. Explanation: In the medical profession you are providing a service to people and whether or not they conform to conventions associated with good manners should in no way affect the service you provide or how you feel towards them; see question 2 to check that your response is consistent.

Q66. Explanation: You should be able to readily agree with this statement. Medics and dentists work in a fast-moving environment and when priorities change they have to interrupt what they are doing to do something else. Consider your responses to, for example, questions 17, 34, 46, 88, 92 and 97 all of which to some extent investigate your attitude towards aspects of the trait robustness.

Q67. Explanation: We should all be able to agree with this statement. At some time or another we have all concluded after reflection that we have done or said something that we could have handled better, and to have no regrets suggests an unthinking or unprincipled approach.

Q68. Explanation: Morals, principles, ethical behaviour are not luxuries that we can abandon when things get difficult. Imagine this proposal in a medical context and you will quickly see what is disagreeable about it. For example, imagine a very overworked doctor who decides he will only treat people with minor ailments and not treat the more complex cases.

Q69. Explanation: A considered, reflective approach may be highly desirable amongst applicants to the medical profession, so if this is a quality you possess, have the confidence to disclose it. Check for consistency your answers to, for example, questions 1, 16, 19, 25 and 58.

Q70. Explanation: Shrewd means smart or perceptive and is a desirable quality in applicants to medical school.

Q71. Explanation: In some cultures it is a sign of respect not to make eye contact and it should not trouble you at all if someone does not conform to your expectations of how they should conduct themselves. To agree with this statement might suggest that you were able to put yourself in someone else's shoes. Consider your response to, for example, questions 10, 22, 38, 44, 52 and 65 all of which to some extent investigate your attitude towards aspects of the trait empathy.

Q72.   Explanation: Unemotional has a negative connotation of being dispassionate or undemonstrative, while unassuming, which means modest or humble, does not.

Q73.   Explanation: In the medical profession, dealing with others in a delicate, diplomatic way might be preferred to a bold, decisive stance. Check for consistency your answers to, for example, questions 1, 16, 19, 25, 58 and 69.

Q74 and Q75.   Explanation: You should have found both statements to be false. Bad language in work is simply not acceptable and you must rely on other, more appropriate ways of dealing with a stressful day.

Q76.   Explanation: Medical professionals are placed in positions of great trust and their employers expect the very highest levels of honesty from them. You should have no difficulty agreeing with this statement. Check your answer for consistency with your responses to questions 5, 12, 27, 37, 41, 53, 84 and 91.

Q77.   Explanation: At work it would be inappropriate to try to impress another member of the team because of their looks or because they belong to the opposite gender. To suggest that such behaviour is natural is incorrect because at work it is neither usual nor acceptable.

Q78.   Explanation: Agreement with this statement is unlikely to signify anything that might support or undermine your application but check this answer with those to questions 15 and 87.

Q79.   Explanation: To classify yourself as insensitive is unlikely to enhance your application to medical school. It is also true that someone who is emotional might also be the less than perfect applicant. However, of the two adjectives, being emotional might be regarded as preferable to insensitive.

Q80.   Explanation: To agree with this statement suggests that you hold the view that you should only help those to whom you are related or with whom you share some common heritage. This implies that you do not sympathize or empathize with people who are not related to you in some way. Consider your response to, for example, questions 10, 22 38, 44, 52 and 65 all of which to some extent investigate your attitude towards aspects of the trait empathy.

Q81.   Explanation: To be approachable is to be easy to talk to, which must be a great quality in a medical professional. To be polite is also a desirable quality and means that you are, for example, respectful, but on balance perhaps approachable is the more valuable attribute. Check questions 11 and 45 for consistency of your responses.

Q82. Explanation: Someone who is wary is someone suspicious and distrustful in nature while someone naïve is inexperienced or youthful. Applicants to medical school might be forgiven for being naïve but if they were wary by nature they might find it hard to show the necessary understanding and compassion for the wellbeing of others.

Q83. Explanation: Jokes and humour in the workplace have a value and can help build a team or defuse a stressful situation, but jokes about someone's sexuality would not be appropriate and for this reason an employer would expect you to help discourage such behaviour.

Q84. Explanation: It is really stealing and the fact that a lot of people might do it does not mean it is not still wrong. Check your answer for consistency with your responses to questions 5, 12, 27, 37, 41, 53, 76 and 91.

Q85. Explanation: To be cheeky is to be disrespectful and it would count as inappropriate behaviour at work. Check for consistency your answers to, for example, questions 1, 16, 19, 25, 58 and 69.

Q86. Explanation: To agree with this statement risks the suggestion that you prejudge people according to stereotypes and this is not a desirable personal trait in someone applying to work in healthcare.

Q87. Explanation: Planning is an important part of the work of every medical professional and we would all rather work in a situation where things go to plan. However, dealing well with the unexpected is equally important and someone who finds it an effort to deal with the unexpected might not cope well in the role. Check the consistency of your answers with your responses to questions 15 and 78.

Q88. Explanation: In many practical situations we have to intervene before all the facts are known and this includes situations when painful choices have to be made. While it is more difficult to decide on the best course of action in these circumstances, it is sometimes necessary to do so and for this reason you should be willing to disagree with this statement.

Q89. Explanation: To disagree with this statement does not rule out the possibility that you are equally honest and trustworthy as you are non-judgemental. To agree with the statement might suggest that while you possess the necessary integrity you may lack the necessary tolerance required for the role. Check your response to question 43 for consistency.

Q90.   Explanation: Health professionals work collaboratively and often deal with complex matters that include compromises of one type or another. It is mostly wrong, therefore, to say that a compromise is rarely the right decision in healthcare.

Q91.   Explanation: There are no circumstances under which it is right to steal. Check your answer for consistency with your responses to questions 5, 12, 27, 37, 41, 53, 76 and 84.

Q92.   Explanation: It is normal for people to be affected by the circumstances of their work but the training they receive helps ensure that they are able to demonstrate professionalism and to cope. For this reason it is reasonable to expect you to have agreed with the statement.

Q93.   Explanation: To be impulsive is to be reckless, rash or hasty and these are not the best qualities for an applicant to medical school. You might be rash when you are with your friends and you might regret it afterwards, but would you be reckless and rash if you were working as a medical professional?

Q94.   Explanation: Matter-of-fact means unemotional or straightforward while down-to-earth means unpretentious, realistic or unassuming. Both are positive attributes but on balance it might be preferable that a medical professional was described as down-to-earth, as being matter-of-fact might mean you lack compassion.

Q95.   Explanation: The world of medicine places high expectations of honesty and morality on its professionals and responses that suggest you support or would indulge in dishonest behaviour (even if such behaviour might be widespread) would not enhance your application. This question investigates aspects of the trait integrity; consider, for example, questions 13, 14, 20, 29, 49, 68, 74 and 75 for consistency as they too investigate aspects of this trait.

Q96.   Explanation: Agreement with this statement suggests that what people say cannot usually be taken at face value and that you must establish their motive before you can realize what they really mean. Such a view suggests an untrusting, suspicious nature.

Q97.   Explanation: Agreement with this statement risks the impression that you might struggle to maintain consistently high standards when involved in the delivery of therapies or treatments for common ailments.

Q98.   Explanation: All applicants to medical school should be able to agree with this statement; after all, there will be many occasions when you will have to do just this.

Q99. Explanation: Agreement with this statement would suggest someone self-assured and a team player and such an impression would support most applications to medical school.

Q100. Explanation: To say one thing and do another can be insincere and in some cases deceitful. It is therefore something we should all avoid doing whatever the circumstances.